RETHINKING FAMILY MEDIATION

Perspectives on Law and Access to Justice

Series Editors: **Jess Mant**, Monash University and **Daniel Newman**, Cardiff University

---

This series forges a coherent field of access to justice scholarship, drawing connections between research from different disciplines such as civil and criminal law, family law, housing law, immigration law and social welfare law. It facilitates a multifaceted critique of the key issues and incorporates a diverse range of perspectives that will shape the future directions of this emerging field.

Find out more at:

bristoluniversitypress.co.uk/
perspectives-on-law-and-access-to-justice

RETHINKING FAMILY MEDIATION

The Role of the Family Mediator in Contemporary Times

Rachael Blakey

BRISTOL
UNIVERSITY
PRESS

First published in Great Britain in 2025 by

Bristol University Press
University of Bristol
1–9 Old Park Hill
Bristol
BS2 8BB
UK
t: +44 (0)117 374 6645
e: bup-info@bristol.ac.uk

Details of international sales and distribution partners are available at bristoluniversitypress.co.uk

British Library Cataloguing in Publication Data
A catalogue record for this book is available from the British Library

ISBN 978-1-5292-3296-7 hardcover
ISBN 978-1-5292-3297-4 ePub
ISBN 978-1-5292-3298-1 ePdf

Cover design: Nicky Borowiec
Front cover image: Stocksy/Yaroslav Danylchenko
Bristol University Press uses environmentally responsible print partners.
Printed and bound in Great Britain by CPI Group (UK) Ltd, Croydon, CR0 4YY

FSC
www.fsc.org
MIX
Paper | Supporting responsible forestry
FSC® C013604

Contents

Series Editors' Preface

Jess Mant (Monash University) and
Daniel Newman (Cardiff University)

In recent years, there has been increasing global interest in issues of access to justice and how these issues relate to our increasingly unequal societies. The concept of 'access to justice' – the protection of the law that enables citizens to enforce their rights – is far from new, but has often been approached from a range of different perspectives, methodologies and disciplines. This series provides a home for socio-legal scholarship which explores issues of access to justice. It will draw important connections between research undertaken across different sub-disciplines which intrinsically involve issues of access to justice but are not routinely in conversation with one another, such as civil and criminal law, family law, housing law, immigration law and social welfare law. The series will forge a coherent field of access to justice scholarship; incorporating a diverse range of perspectives to facilitate a multifaceted critique of the key issues, debates and challenges that underpin access to justice, and shape the future directions of this emerging field.

Table of Cases

Miller; McFarlane [2006] UKHL 24
R (Rights of Women) v Secretary of State for Justice [2016] EWCA Civ 91
R (Witham v Lord Chancellor) [1998] QB 575 (QB) 585
Re F (A Child) [2009] EWCA Civ 313

Table of Statutes

Children Act 1989
Children and Families Act 2014
Civil Partnership Act 2004
Divorce, Dissolution and Separation Act 2020
Divorce Reform Act 1969
Family Law Act 1996
Family Law Amendment (Shared Parental Responsibility) Act 2006 (Cth)
Family Procedure Rules, SI 2010/2955
Human Rights Act 1998
Legal Aid Act 1988
Legal Aid, Sentencing and Punishment of Offenders Act 2012
Legal Services Act 2007
Matrimonial Causes Act 1857
Matrimonial Causes Act 1973
Summary Procedure (Domestic Proceedings) Act 1937

Table of Instruments

Civil Legal Aid (Financial Resources and Payment for Services) Regulations 2013, SI 2013/480

Civil Legal Aid (Procedure) (Amendment) (No. 2) Regulations 2017, SI 2017/1237

Civil Legal Aid (Procedure) (Amendment) Regulations 2016, SI 2016/516

Matrimonial Causes (Amendment) Rules 1975, SI 1975/1359

Matrimonial Causes Rules 1973, SI 1973/2016

Matrimonial Causes Rules 1977, SI 1977/344

List of Figures and Tables

Figures

Tables

List of Abbreviations

FHDRA	First Hearing Dispute Resolution Appointment
FMA	Family Mediators Association
FMC	Family Mediation Council
FMSB	Family Mediation Standards Board
H	hybrid
L	lawyer
LASPO	Legal Aid, Sentencing and Punishment of Offenders Act 2012
LIP	Litigant in Person
MIAM	Mediation, Information and Assessment Meeting
NFCC	National Family Conciliation Council
NFM	National Family Mediation
T	therapeutic
UKCFM	UK College of Family Mediators

About the Author

Rachael Blakey is an Associate Professor at the University of Warwick, School of Law. She was previously a lecturer at the University of Exeter and a PhD student at Cardiff University. Her primary research focuses on family mediation. She is interested in dispute resolution, access to justice and the professionalism of legal service providers.

Acknowledgements

With this book being published over seven years since I first began my doctoral studies, there are a lot of people to thank!

This project would never have been possible without funding from the Economic and Social Research Council. I am also indebted to the socio-legal community at Cardiff University's School of Law and Politics, who I was lucky enough to spend eight years of my academic life learning from. My research, my teaching practices and even my approach to life have also been deeply shaped by my colleagues at the University of Warwick's School of Law.

Scholarship and research are nothing without learning from others. I have been taught this lesson by many individuals, but none other than my PhD supervisors, Dr Leanne Smith and Professor Sharon Thompson. I can still see their influence throughout many sections of this book, and will always be grateful for the time and love they have shown me over the years.

There are endless people outside the academic community who I would also like to thank. Of course, I owe a massive thanks to the 17 family mediators who agreed to participate in this project. I would also like to thank the wider family mediation community, who have spoken to me countless times about their experiences.

I have been blessed to be surrounded by such compassionate and kind people throughout my adult life. To friends old and new (school friends, housemates, hikers) – thank you. Needless to say, a big thank you goes to my family: Mum, Dad and Mike.

Finally, thank you to my partner, Dave, who met me when I was in the chaos of the final PhD edits and has stayed ever since. You make every day so much brighter.

1

Introduction

This monograph examines family mediation in the contemporary English and Welsh family justice system. It traces the development of family mediation from the late 20th century, arguing that significant changes to mediation's functioning and purpose have not been properly recognized. Family mediation, like many other procedures, is in a transitionary period. Several traditional concepts – neutrality, facilitation and non-legal support – continue to dominate the discussions around the role of family mediation and the family mediator. These notions remain fundamental to family mediator practice, though their hold has weakened over time. Following decades of reform to the family justice landscape, the work of family mediators is now underpinned by a number of other concepts: flexibility, evaluation and, sometimes, quasi-legal oversight. Family mediators continue to perform their traditional functions, but balance them alongside a rising demand to adapt. They follow a flexible conceptualization in order to provide more comprehensive support to their clients, many of whom have limited access to legal or other advice in the early 21st century.

This all has significant implications for family justice. The more controversial view advanced in this monograph is that family justice has developed to comprise a variety of dispute resolution procedures, as well as different meanings of 'justice' itself. This contemporary conceptualization is not always recognized because court and lawyer-based understandings of justice continue to command debate. The author does not seek to argue that family justice is always achieved through mediation, nor that mediation is the ideal option for private family matters. In fact, the findings underpinning later parts of this monograph demonstrate that the ability of mediators to ensure justice hinges on a number of elements that are not always followed through. However, similar criticisms can also be made of court – a process long associated, if not synonymous, with family justice. This monograph, therefore, is part of a growing body of literature that seeks to better understand how to support private family law disputants in achieving justice.

Rethinking Family Mediation adopts a new theoretical framework, corroborated by original empirical evidence, through which to understand the family mediator. It first tracks a shift in policy, research and practice from the *limited* mediator to the *flexible* mediator, symbolic of mediation's traditional and modern ideals. Earlier chapters argue that the latter conceptualization of family mediator practice could support a broader vision of family justice. A dual-methods study confirms the flexible mediator archetype, who is revealed to take on a number of functions, as well as a quasi-legal role, in the contemporary landscape. It is confirmed that if family mediators are more interventionist and adaptive than originally conceptualized, family mediation is better placed as a family justice apparatus (notwithstanding the introduction of further regulation and training).

This monograph is neither a complete endorsement nor a scathing disapproval of contemporary mediator practice. While its author ultimately believes that the flexible mediator archetype is a welcome development, she has reservations about viewing mediation as a family justice apparatus if there is the possibility that the profession incorrectly understands and applies various norms. Nonetheless, the primary goal of this monograph is to uncover the expansion of family mediator practice, and also family justice, in order to inform debate. On the one hand, the forthcoming chapters show that mediators do more to support individuals with little access to legal support than they did in the traditional family justice landscape. At the same time, they reveal a need to regulate mediation more effectively, particularly if the process is to play an increasingly important part in the family justice system. It is only by recognizing the validity of both arguments that the discourse around family mediation, and family justice more widely, can begin to find pragmatic solutions to the justice gap that many families now face.

Much of this monograph was written amidst government proposals to make family mediation a mandatory prerequisite to private family law proceedings (Ministry of Justice 2023b; 2023c). Early drafts of chapters were inundated with highlighted text and reminders to readjust content once the results of the consultation were published. The government response to the consultation, which decided to indefinitely postpone the mandatory mediation proposals, was released in late January 2024, at which point a draft manuscript of the monograph had already been submitted (Ministry of Justice 2024a). Some readers may be concerned that the arguments made in this monograph are already outdated, particularly as its empirical data was collected several years before publication. However, it is advanced that the monograph remains a relevant and important insight into family mediation in the 2020s and beyond, particularly if the mandatory proposals are revisited at a later stage.[1] If mediation's clientele is to become even

[1] Batagol and Brown (2011: x) make the same point about their research on family mediation in Australia prior to the Family Law Amendment (Shared Parental Responsibility) Act 2006 (Cth).

more diverse and complex than that seen in the 2010s and early 2020s, the demand for mediators to take on a contemporary understanding of their role will intensify. *Rethinking Family Mediation* provides a strong basis from which to explore whether those parties can obtain justice through out-of-court dispute resolution.

1.1 A study on family mediation

At its core, *Rethinking Family Mediation* investigates a simple question: what is family mediation? This question, while appearing somewhat elementary, necessitates an answer both nuanced and substantial. Furthermore, contemporary family mediation (and the flexible mediator archetype) can only be properly understood when compared to its original conceptualization. Finding the answer, therefore, requires an investigation into family mediation's development over the last five decades, rather than a static examination of the process at a single point in time.

Family mediation, previously known as conciliation, was introduced in England and Wales during the late 1970s and early 1980s. Parkinson was a pioneer of family mediation and wrote the following definition in 1986:

> Conciliation may be defined as a structured process in which both parties to a dispute meet voluntarily with one or more impartial third parties (conciliators) who help them to explore possibilities of reaching agreement, without having the power to impose a settlement on them or the responsibility to advise either party individually. (Parkinson 1986: 5)

Parkinson quoted the first definition of conciliation (as we understand it today) in policy, drafted by the Committee on One-Parent Families:

> [Conciliation is] assisting the parties to deal with the consequences of the established breakdown of their marriage, whether resulting in a divorce or a separation, by reaching agreements or giving consents or reducing the area of conflict … arising from the breakdown which calls for a decision on future arrangements. (Committee on One-Parent Families 1974: para 4.288)[2]

The similarities between these quotes suggest that family mediation was originally conceptualized as a process where a mediator with limited powers helped couples improve the dynamic between themselves and resolve their

[2] This quote is revisited in Chapter 2.

family disputes, particularly during divorce or separation. Legal norms and expectations were not part of the mediation process. Instead, mediation was focused on achieving an agreement that worked for everyone involved.

Family mediation continues to be understood in the same way five decades later. The Family Mediation Council (FMC), which is the umbrella regulatory body for registered family mediators in England and Wales, defines family mediation on its website:

> Family mediation is a process in which an independent, professionally trained mediator helps you work out arrangements. … Mediation helps you stay in control. No-one will make you do anything against your wishes. The mediator will help you find a solution which works for you both and will explain what needs to happen to make an agreement between you legally binding. (FMC 2024a)

According to the FMC, family mediation is solution-focused. The mediator supports disputants to make decisions on and maintain control over their family disputes. Party autonomy heavily underpins the mediation process as a result. In comparison to earlier descriptions, the FMC makes some reference to the law, though its wording implies that family mediation alone is not legally binding.

While these definitions do not reflect the intricacies of mediator practice, their many parallels lead to two opposing propositions. The first proposition is that the dominant understanding of family mediation has not changed because the process largely operates in the same way as when it was piloted in the late 1970s. The family mediator continues to have a restricted and facilitative role, sitting in stark contrast to the overriding judge or evaluative lawyer. She follows, in effect, a *limited* archetype. Family mediation is subsequently understood as a non-justiciable alternative to court, designed for a particular type of client who can settle their dispute with little assistance.

However, the contemporary family justice landscape is vastly different from that of the late 20th century. Over several decades, public funding and support for those navigating the family justice system has become inaccessible, causing a rise in unmet legal need. This development was particularly noticeable after the Legal Aid, Sentencing and Punishment of Offenders Act 2012 (LASPO). LASPO removed legal aid in a number of areas, including advice and representation for most private family disputes in court. Legal aid for family mediation was retained in an attempt to move disputes into the process, though intake immediately declined after LASPO's enactment and has remained low ever since. At the same time, evidence suggests that mediation's clientele has become more varied and often lacks access to a lawyer. The LASPO reforms subsequently prompt growing concern that (limited) family mediators are a poor fit for most family law matters, unable to adapt to their new and varied client base with little to no legal support.

Calls to reform the role of the family mediator have arisen as a result. Hitchings and Miles (2016: 176) discuss the decline in publicly funded family mediation and legal support after LASPO, asking if these developments 'prompt an evolution of – or, some might say, compromise – the mediator's orthodox facilitator role'. In the same vein, Barlow et al (2017: 211) refer to the 'unintended consequences' of LASPO which 'mak[e] mediation more difficult', calling for immediate reform if mediation is to have a central place in contemporary family justice. These critiques reflect a rising demand in the post-LASPO family justice literature for a re-envisioned family mediation process, or, more specifically, reform to the role of the family mediator. Family mediation is presented as the primary option for disputants, yet the family mediator is – by her very nature – limited.

Rethinking Family Mediation builds upon these discussions to reveal a flexible archetype of family mediators, enabling such re-envisioning to occur. It is premised on the second proposition: that a contemporary and flexible understanding of family mediation has developed in response to changes in the English and Welsh family justice system, but has yet to be openly acknowledged. To say that the role of the family mediator has stayed the same in the past 40 to 50 years, despite numerous developments, is certainly a bold claim to make. While informal mediation has existed for thousands of years, the real value of formal family mediation, a process still in its infancy, is yet to be uncovered. Since its introduction in the family law system, mediation has been surrounded by what Murch and Hooper (1992: 82) label as 'general ambiguity and uncertainty'. Girdner (1988: 55) similarly highlights a lack of 'a cohesive set of shared norms and values' for mediators. She echoes Roberts (1983: 539), who describes mediation as 'more an approach, a way of life, than the embodiment of a specific programme or reform'. Much of the literature on mediation up until the 1990s focused on how to establish mediation services across England and Wales, leaving little room to scrutinize the family mediation process (Maclean and Eekelaar 2016: 70). Despite increasing calls for mediation reform, academic critique since the 2010s has largely concentrated on the impact of LASPO on court. This emphasis is recognized by Moore and Newbury (2017: 6), who write: '[c]onsideration of the impact of LASPO has tended instead to focus on what's happening in the courtroom'. Of course, such research is incredibly valuable in understanding the consequences of LASPO on family justice, particularly where many disputants continue to use court to resolve their family problems. However, this focus means less attention has been paid to family dispute resolution.

It will take many more years, if not decades, to realize family mediation's full potential. Yet during this period, flexible family mediators may inadvertently encourage poor outcomes, or perhaps even injustice, due to the lack of recognition, regulation and thus guidance around their contemporary practices. Fortunately, interest in uncovering family mediation's real value has increased over time. As McEldowney (2012: para 76) summarizes: 'The time is ripe for major reform of the regulatory aspects of mediation.'

There is thus a growing need for family mediation reform that, first, adapts to the needs of its users in the post-LASPO landscape and, second, further regulates the (flexible) family mediator profession to ensure that the process is properly conducted. However, discussions appear to be at a standstill, halted by a lack of consideration as to what mediation could achieve if such reform were permitted. This state of stagnancy warrants a much-needed investigation into the purpose and role of *contemporary* family mediation in furthering *contemporary* family justice. *Rethinking Family Mediation* does not make specific recommendations for reform, though it does refer to potential directions for change and regulation in later chapters. Instead, the book is focused on uncovering the flexible mediator archetype and considering how this development could, and perhaps already does, assist those with reduced legal support in the post-LASPO era.

1.2 Implications for family justice

While the main purpose behind *Rethinking Family Mediation* is to discover the contemporary conceptualization of family mediation, its findings also allude to a shift in the delivery of family justice. Before outlining the methodology of the study discussed in this monograph, it is worth setting out what is meant by 'family justice'. How does someone obtain justice, and what does that justice involve?

The following section considers two particular strands of family justice. The first, procedural justice, relates to the use and availability of fair procedures. The second, substantive justice, is instead concerned with the fairness of the law and its legal norms. Under both elements, justice is clearly associated with the use of court, lawyers and legal aid. However, court (as well as traditional legal support) is no longer an accessible forum for family justice. Various avenues to obtaining family justice have emerged as a result. It is on this basis that family mediation materializes as a *potential*, but unconfirmed, apparatus for family justice.

1.2.1 (Access to) justice as (access to) court

Beginning with procedural justice, a system of laws is not enough for family law to have any effect. Rather, individuals must be able to enforce their rights through established legal structures and procedures. As Baroness Hale (2011: 3) argues: 'the law – and the content of it – needs to be accessible'.

Procedural justice, therefore, pertains to 'the ways in which decisions are made and their fairness' (King et al 2014: 13). This utilitarian or outcome-based reading of procedural justice emphasizes the need for 'accurate' legal outcomes (Meyerson and Mackenzie 2018: 4). Meanwhile, process-based or dignitarian accounts of procedural justice emphasize the need for a forum where disputants are equally heard and treated by a neutral practitioner, ensuring that their 'dignity' and 'agency' are respected throughout (Meyerson and Mackenzie 2018: 6). The ultimate goal of procedural justice, regardless of the reading taken, is to 'ensure that participants feel the dispute process has been fair and open' (King et al 2014: 14).

Whether someone can receive justice in the first place is determined by its accessibility. Consequently, (access to) justice has primarily centred on those 'with limited financial resources' (Hunter et al 2022: 303), and much of the broader literature on procedural justice has examined the legal aid scheme (Hughes 2008: 778). Through this emphasis on legal aid, an association between justice and court, as well as lawyers, becomes apparent.

Legal aid facilitates access to certain legal services, typically legal advice and representation. To provide a brief history of legal aid in England and Wales, the scheme was part of the post-Second World War welfare state. There was a particular demand for legal support in family matters following the 1940s 'divorce crisis' where more couples separated because of the additional pressures of post-wartime life (Goriely 1994: 550–555). In 1944, the Rushcliffe Committee was established to advise Parliament on legal welfare. The following year, the group proposed legislation 'to provide legal advice for those of slender means and resources, so that no one would be financially unable to prosecute a just and reasonable claim or defend a legal right' (Rushcliffe Committee 1945; Lord Chancellor 1948: para 4). The legal aid system was introduced through the Legal Aid and Advice Act 1949, characterized by Sommerlad (2004: 348) as 'the beginning of a new stage in the relationship between law and society'. In Elson's (1946: 134) words, the legal aid scheme created 'a right' to legal support – one which the state was obliged to protect. At the time of its introduction, around 70–80 per cent of the population was eligible for legal aid.[3]

Originally, legal aid was only available to people in court who sought legal representation. As Marshall (1950: 48) argues, legal aid was a 'social service designed to strengthen the civil right of the citizen to settle his disputes in a court of law'. This right to court was further supported by access to a qualified legal professional who minimized the barriers to participation (Davis 1988: 85; Mant 2017: 249). Legal aid for oral advice outside the

[3] This statistic includes legal aid recipients who made contributions to the scheme (Sommerlad 2004: 354; Webley 2015: 2352).

courtroom was introduced in the 1960s, though recipients were still required to be involved in court proceedings and solicitors were only reimbursed for communications with their clients or other lawyers (Moore and Newbury 2017: 18). In the 1970s, legal aid funding became available for written or oral advice on any legal matter, including those resolved outside of court by the parties themselves.[4] Nonetheless, the primary focus of the original legal aid scheme was to provide access to court. The courtroom, supported by lawyers, was seen as the optimum, and perhaps only, route to obtaining procedural justice.

Substantive justice, by comparison, is ensured through 'aspects of the process and the outcomes that result from such participation' (Noone and Ojelabi 2020: 111). Sandefur (2019: 50) contends that access to a legally trained professional or a dispute resolution forum does not guarantee a 'just, fair or successful' resolution. According to Roberts (2013: 8–9), the 'sole function' of courts is to apply the law to a particular dispute. A judge dispenses the law to promote justness and fairness, subsequently providing the best outcome. This approach follows that of a legal centralist, recognized by Galanter (1981: 1), whereby justice is 'produced' or 'distributed' by the state. To ensure the correct application of various statutes and precedents, an external forum – court – is required to resolve these disputes. Various checks and balances are then put in place to monitor the use of that forum, such as the right to a fair trial.[5]

Private family law problems (typically upon relationship breakdown) tend to be divided into child arrangements and financial (or property) matters, though both elements are present in many disputes. For these cases, substantive justice is said to depend on the correct application of legal rules. Many of these legal rules derive from legislation. For instance, child-related matters are heavily regulated by the welfare principle under section 1(1) of the Children Act 1989. This principle mandates that the child's welfare is the court's 'paramount consideration' when determining any question in relation to their upbringing or the administration of their property. A judge must 'have regard in particular' to various factors, including 'the ascertainable wishes and feelings of the child concerned', when considering a child arrangements or special guardianship order.[6] For financial disputes, the Matrimonial Causes Act 1973 gives the courts the power to make various orders in divorce proceedings.[7] Section 25 outlines a number of matters for

[4] The Legal Advice and Assistance Act 1972. See also Maclean and Eekelaar (2019: 9).

[5] Human Rights Act 1998, s 6.

[6] Children Act 1989, s 1(3).

[7] Analogous powers are available for civil partnerships under the Civil Partnership Act 2004, s 72 and sch 5.

the courts to consider when exercising these powers, such as the standard of living enjoyed by the family prior to separation.

Substantive justice is determined not by legislation alone, but also by the application of those rules in court. Thus, judges must be able to understand and apply an ever-growing list of case law that interprets legislation. For instance, case law shows that the courts will not usually make a child arrangements order that unjustifiably disrupts a child's living situation.[8] *Miller; McFarlane*[9] establishes criteria to determine the 'fair' outcome in ancillary relief cases, with subsequent precedent interpreting the concept even further.

The court system is often deemed the most, if not only, route to securing substantive justice for cases involving severe power imbalances or domestic abuse. This is because the application of legal rules, set out in both statute and precedent, 'provide a measure of protection to the powerless' (Freeman 1984: 16). The court provides an important safety net for weaker parties, although it is not the sole function of court to protect one group of disputants. In particular, Main (2005: 401) contends that reserving court for a certain type of case overlooks 'the important role of the courts in the tasks of applying the law and vindicating rights'. From this perspective, the court is a fundamental component in ensuring substantive justice for *all*, not just *some*, disputes. Baroness Hale (2011: 7) similarly describes access to the court system as 'one of the most precious' constitutional rights in England and Wales. She quotes Lord Laws, who famously declared: 'the right to a fair trial, which of necessity imports the right of access to the court, is as near to an absolute right as any which I can envisage'.[10] It is thus assumed that the court system provides a level of fairness that cannot be ensured in any other way, specifically because the process protects parties' rights through the accurate application of legal norms.

However, it would be incorrect – perhaps even *unjust* – to say that substantive justice solely relies on the use of legal norms. As Barlow et al (2017: 8) posit in the seminal *Mapping Paths to Family Justice*, 'legal rules are not always just'. The commentators argue that, while concepts like child welfare and fairness are 'indeterminate standards' to enable family law to adapt to the case at hand, they create 'wide parameters of possibility'. They subsequently adopt a feminist lens to substantive justice, one which 'pay[s] attention to the social and economic context of decision-making' (Barlow et al 2017: 9).

Under the traditional readings of both procedural and substantive justice, access to court alone is not enough. Rather, disputants must have the support

---

8 *Re F (A Child)* [2009] EWCA Civ 313.

9 [2006] UKHL 24.

10 *R (Witham v Lord Chancellor)* [1998] QB 575 (QB) 585.

of a qualified professional – a lawyer – in order to properly navigate and use the court system. Trinder et al (2014: 53) identify a 'full representation model', whereby all parties attend court with their respective lawyers. The parties take on the role of the 'audience', whereas the lawyers become the 'actors' who present to the judge. Family matters are streamlined because legal professionals, with the knowledge and ability to apply the law, have an active role in ensuring fair outcomes. Trinder et al's framework alludes to a family justice supported by access to legal representation (and legal aid) in court, through which the law is correctly and fairly applied. This is the 'default position' in private family law matters, albeit based on the assumption that the parties have legal support throughout their dispute (Trinder et al 2014: 35). Whether this form of family justice remains accessible, however, is heavily disputed.

1.2.2 Shifting ideas around access to court

While justice has been traditionally associated with 'access to courts and lawyers', there is some evidence that the concept has expanded over time (Partington 2005: 376). Of course, there will never be a complete consensus on the meaning of (family) justice, particularly as one's understanding of the concept is shaped by their experiences both within and outside the family unit (Okin 2016). Furthermore, it should not be forgotten that people involved in family disputes are more likely than those experiencing other legal problems to seek a traditional route to justice through court.[11] After LASPO, there has been a sharp rise in the number of individuals, known as Litigants in Person (LiPs), who attend court without legal representation: their prevalence is strong evidence of a lingering appetite for traditional justice (Mant 2022). Nonetheless, several developments suggest that access to justice has been in a 'renaissance' era for some time (Albiston and Sandefur 2013: 101).[12] *Rethinking Family Mediation* is subsequently premised on the idea that, in the early 21st century, a contemporary understanding of justice has developed, supported by different family justice procedures and professionals.

A large proportion of individuals involved in private family matters now settle their disputes outside of court. Genn's (1999) *Paths to Justice* survey, conducted from 1997 to 1998, sought to understand how individuals managed different justiciable problems. It found that 62 per cent of cases concerning divorce or separation went to court or tribunal (Genn 1999: 150).

[11] In a 2014–2015 survey on justiciable problems, those with a family problem were most likely out of all respondents to attend court or a tribunal (Franklyn et al 2017: 38).

[12] These developments, while discussed further in this chapter, will be fully examined in Chapter 2.

Fifty-six per cent of divorce or separation problems also ended with a court decision or order (Genn 1999: 158). In stark contrast, a 2014–2015 justiciable problems survey revealed that only 16 per cent of respondents with a family problem[13] attended court (Franklyn et al 2017: 44). Twenty-eight per cent had used a form of dispute resolution, such as mediation. Court statistics, therefore, now represent a small fraction of family matters in England and Wales. Despite perceptions of a litigation culture where excessive claims overload the court, people are '*under*-litigious' when it comes to family matters (Albiston and Sandefur 2013: 104, emphasis in original).

Individuals may not attend court for a variety of reasons. For example, it may be a personal choice. Alternatively, they may feel that traditional family justice does not provide the best solution to their dispute. Substantive norms, such as fairness, differ from what Felstiner et al (1980: 647) describe as 'ordinary morality'. In some instances, disputants may prefer an individualized form of justice that is not determined by a judge. Individualized justice, in essence, enables 'a resolution tailored to meet the needs of the parties' (Diduck 2016: 135).

It is important to note, however, that many families do not go to court because the process is widely inaccessible. Burnett and Sandefur (2022: 108) identify an 'access to justice crisis' on a global scale. In England and Wales, access to court (and thus access to a traditional reading of family justice) has drastically declined since the late 20th century. Policy documents from the 1960s and 1970s claimed that court increased hostility between the parties. By comparison, the same documents portrayed out-of-court dispute resolution as having a positive effect on post-separation relationships.[14] In the 1980s, policy also began to present legal aid as having gone well beyond its means (Hynes 2012: 28). This led to a cap on the scheme's budget towards the start of the 21st century (Kirwan et al 2017: 6; Moore and Newbury 2017: 23–24). The reduction of legal aid continued into the 2010s with the enactment of LASPO, rendering the full-representation model unavailable to most disputants. In the 2020s, family matters are resolved through a number of different avenues and supported by a variety of family justice professionals. Our understanding of family justice – and how to provide it – must develop as a result.

This argument may be taken as a far-reaching basis for *Rethinking Family Mediation*, but reform cannot move forward without new ideas. As Albiston and Sandefur (2013: 103) summarize, the literature on justice needs to consider 'how current definitions and understandings of access to justice

---

13 The researchers defined 'family legal problems' as 'problems arising from relationship breakdown' (Franklyn et al 2017: 6).

14 See sections 2.1.1 and 2.3.1.

may blind policymakers to more radical, but potentially more effective, solutions'. A number of family justice commentators have begun to propose such solutions, including Smith and Hitchings (2023: 673). They posit that the increasing use of non-lawyer services and extra-legal services to resolve family matters is appropriate, so long as those services are 'informed by justice norms'. And so, there is clearly room for a richer, multifaceted and nuanced understanding of justice that takes into account the contemporary family law landscape. Revealing this new justice is a key driving force behind *Rethinking Family Mediation*.

In particular, the discourse around family justice needs to acknowledge family mediation's potential value. During the late 20th century, family mediation was introduced as the answer to concerns around the adjudication process and legal aid budget. The process supposedly alleviated stress and also reduced costs (for both the disputants and the state). Following decades of promotion and statutory reform, the primacy of court weakened. Post-LASPO, most private family law disputants can only access legal aid through family mediation. The state's message is unmistakable: family mediation is now the primary route for resolving private family matters, and at the very least merits consideration. This stance is clear evidence of a neoliberal agenda that largely (if not solely) evaluates the family unit and the family law system in economic terms (Mant 2022: 17–22). Notwithstanding the negative consequences of this neoliberal trend, particularly in terms of how family matters are removed 'from their public meaning, public consequences and from public concern' (Diduck 2016: 136), it cannot be forgotten that mediation is now a leading player in the contemporary English and Welsh family law system.

Of course, this point alone is not a new revelation. Rather, this book makes a further claim: that mediation has the potential to become a family justice apparatus. To return to the meaning of justice, Trebilcock et al (2012: 3) define access to justice as 'the effective right of an individual to advance in appropriate *fora* legitimate legal claims or defences against claims by others' (emphasis in original). At present, family mediation is not viewed as a legal forum (or fora). In terms of traditional procedural justice, family mediation is not said to be based on legal outcomes since the parties can reach a tailored outcome that does not reflect any legal norms. While procedural justice requires equal participation and equal treatment, there are concerns that family mediation is, put simply, an unfair process. The prevalence of power imbalances and domestic abuse in private family matters, coupled with the limited mediator archetype's inability to address these issues, massively impacts the possibility of effective participation on both sides (Ojelabi and Gutman 2020: 205). Furthermore, if procedural justice is heavily correlated with access to court, then the mediation process, particularly if it is mandated, creates a visible barrier to justice. For these reasons, Genn (2010: 116–117), in considering non-family civil mediation, argues that the process does not 'contribute to access to the courts' and, subsequently, does not contribute to access to justice. Genn additionally submits that civil mediation neither 'contribute[s] to' nor is 'concerned about' substantive justice. She notes that, whereas court (supported by the use of lawyers and legal aid) ensures that the parties receive an outcome that upholds their legal rights, norms and obligations, mediation is more concerned with 'searching for a solution'. Diduck (2016: 134–135) similarly warns that alternative dispute resolution, including family mediation, 'seeks not the substantive justice of the law', but an individualized notion of justice that, by moving disputes into the private sphere, poses particular risks for women and victims of domestic abuse.

If the essence of procedural and substantive justice lies in access to a set of legal rules that are correctly applied in an appropriate forum, limited family mediators will struggle to achieve this goal. Entire Law School modules and endless textbooks are dedicated to dissecting and understanding the complex and unpredictable rules that underpin family law. As Dewar (1998: 468) famously declared, family law is 'chaotic, contradictory [and] incoherent'. The finding of a case is said to turn on its facts, making it difficult to determine the predictability of private family law rules and norms. Family lawyers spend years, if not decades, deciphering these principles. By comparison, family mediators historically originate from a non-legal background (Blakey 2023a: 142). At the time of writing this monograph, family mediators seeking accreditation were required to attend an FMC-approved training course, part of which was designed to cover the main principles of family law. However, these courses had a minimum of 60 hours contact time (spread over eight or more days), and knowledge about family law was only one small part of the competency standards (FMC 2022a: 28). There is, therefore, a valid concern that many family mediators lack the knowledge and skillset to correctly apply the complex rules of family law. Even if a family mediator originates from a legal background, they are prohibited from acting in a way that influences the outcome under their original (limited) conceptualization. Consequently, family mediation is said not to be concerned with family justice.

However, what if family mediation has developed in such a way that it has become a legal forum? Mediation does not and cannot provide the same form of justice as that acquired in court. Nevertheless, it may provide a form of 'non-adversarial justice', centred on the use of out-of-court dispute resolution (King et al 2014: 5). *Rethinking Family Mediation* explores this line of thinking in the context of the English and Welsh private family law system. In particular, it traces the transition from the limited to flexible mediator archetype, one which enables mediators to adapt the mediation procedure, and possibly even the mediated outcome, to improve the quality of settlement.

Genn (2010) is correct that out-of-court mediation (whether it is non-family mediation, as she discusses, or family mediation, as investigated in this monograph) does not 'contribute to access to the courts'. However, it should be recognized that family mediation has been embedded into the court system for several decades and, in the 21st century, continues to be provided in court by Cafcass officers.[15] In-court mediation undoubtedly does not provide access to traditional adversarialism, whereby a judge decides the outcome of a case in light of the evidence presented and the arguments made. Nonetheless, its existence alone illustrates how family mediation is part of the court process.

The majority of this monograph is focused on out-of-court family mediation – evidently, independent of court. In theory, this format can still ensure a contemporary procedural justice. Mediation is, like court, a 'dispute-resolving forum' which seeks to uphold procedural norms (such as the parties being equally heard by a neutral third party) (Sandefur 2019: 50–51). The empirical study underpinning Part II of this book demonstrates a growing recognition among family mediators that they are responsible for ensuring that the parties can effectively participate in mediation, in particular by redressing various power imbalances. If a practitioner is determining whether the parties can freely participate, they are seeking to create a 'fair' process, and are thus 'responsible for procedural justice' (Ojelabi and Gutman 2020: 210).

The research project underpinning *Rethinking Family Mediation* suggests that family mediators who adopt a flexible archetype also seek to ensure contemporary substantive justice. The data demonstrates a growing quasi-legal role for flexible family mediators, as well as an ever-increasing space for legal norms in the family mediation setting. As argued by Sandefur (2019: 50), access to justice can be obtained outside of court if a dispute is resolved 'with results that satisfy legal norms'. Ojelabi and Gutman (2020: 199) similarly recognize that dispute resolution can secure substantive justice if it enables the 'just resolution of disputes'. From this perspective, family mediation can transform into an apparatus that supports a contemporary and broader view of (substantive) family justice.

The court and its formal application of law must continue to sit at the heart of contemporary family justice. Genn (2012: 398) advocates for an accessible adjudication process, arguing that a 'flow' of court cases is needed to provide direction for other disputes and make 'new leaps' in precedent. Diduck (2016: 135) also voices a concern that the balance between official justice and individualized justice has wrongfully swayed

[15] FPR PD 12B, r 14. Reference will be made to in-court mediation throughout Chapters 2 to 4.

in favour of the latter. The author behind *Rethinking Family Mediation* does not seek to dis-embed court from the contemporary family justice system. Rather, she recognizes, much like King et al (2014: 13), that the court is not the only instrument through which to justly resolve family matters. The court process remains fundamental to a contemporary vision of family justice, but does not 'represent its totality'. Thus, a pragmatic response to the current access to justice crisis is to expand how justice is delivered. To return to Sandefur (2019: 51): 'When the relevant substantive and procedural norms govern resolution, that resolution is lawful and we have access to justice, whether or not lawyers are involved in the resolution.' Family mediation has been misappropriated by successive governments in an attempt to reduce expenditure, undoubtedly rendering the process a procedural barrier to court. However, the process should not be automatically cast aside from debates about how to ensure justice in today's family law system.

The empirical project behind *Rethinking Family Mediation* shows that dispute resolution procedures have the potential to become contemporary family justice apparatuses. Nevertheless, questions remain as to whether these processes actually secure justice for disputants. Ojelabi and Gutman (2020: 209) recognize this possibility, arguing that whether justice is delivered 'depends largely on how the process is conducted and managed'. Diduck (2016: 136) is particularly clear that family mediators must ensure that the norms they use and apply not only *seek to*, but actually *do*, protect victims of domestic abuse. The empirical study behind this monograph reveals that there is much more progress to be made in regulating and improving flexible mediator practice. Furthermore, its findings are based on empirical data from pre-existing regulatory documents and interviews with family mediators. The project can therefore only indicate what mediator practice *may* look like in contemporary times. Where the present findings show that family mediators (taking on a flexible archetype) believe they are both responding to power imbalances and using legal norms to create high-quality settlements, a fundamental question for forthcoming research is whether these tasks are correctly performed.

In summary, a contemporary conceptualization of family justice should reflect developments in the private family law system. This may not be the vision of justice that anyone forecast, or possibly even wanted. However, the neoliberal era is far from over. Focus must be placed on improving the situation for those navigating today's family justice system, many of whom have limited or no access to lawyers. While LASPO has caused significant damage to the family law system, it provides an opportunity to reconsider how family justice is protected and ensured. *Rethinking Family Mediation* adopts a pragmatic approach, considering a potential way forward in the post-LASPO landscape.

1.3 Methods

This work is *socio-legal* in its nature. It recognizes that the law and family mediation are both legal and social phenomena, influenced by numerous actors, and thus must be studied in their broader context.

Socio-legal studies are often supported through empirical research.[16] This approach tends to use social science methods to collect data, rather than consider the law from a sociological angle (Banakar and Travers 2005a: x; 2005b: 279). The same can be said for this study, as data was collected in order to uncover the contemporary conceptualization of family mediation. It was 'policy-driven socio-legal research', which sought to 'improv[e] the effectiveness and fairness of legal services' (Travers 2005: 343). The present study was also undertaken alongside a wider theoretical critique of family mediation and the family justice system at large. Mant (2022: 41) adopts a similar approach in her study on LiPs, acknowledging that the impact of policy-driven research is limited unless coupled with an analysis of the relevant legal structure. The current project, therefore, generated data on the development of family mediation, which in turn alluded to a contemporary vision of family justice.

Meaning cannot be determined through only one stance or perspective. Sarat and Felstiner (1995: 11) acknowledge that 'meaning is found and invented in the variety of locations and practices that comprise the legal world … those locations and practices do not exist outside the sites of signification that, in turn, make them meaningful'. Similarly, there is no single meaning for 'family mediation'. Regulatory bodies, mediators and disputants may come to mediation with different goals and expectations, resulting in numerous interpretations of the process. Each of these meanings contribute to the dominant understanding of family mediation. The empirical project behind this book (covered in Part II) subsequently adopted a dual methods approach. It considered the role of family mediation from the perspective of, first, family mediation's regulatory bodies and, second, family mediators themselves. These stages will now be considered separately.[17]

1.3.1 Stage one: regulatory bodies and Codes of Practice

The first stage involved a qualitative content analysis of family mediation Codes of Practice in England and Wales. As Webley (2010) points out in

[16] The meaning and reach of socio-legal studies has come into question in recent years. For further information, see Cowan and Wincott (2016) and Feenan (2013).

[17] Ethical approval for the project was obtained in June 2018 at Cardiff University, School of Law and Politics.

relation to legal practice, regulatory bodies instil certain values and principles in their members. Furthermore, regulatory guidance can shape a profession's identity and practices. Codes of Practice, in particular, symbolize a 'larger professional community' and can act as a 'source of both identity and esteem' for practitioners (Mather et al 2001: 46).

Nevertheless, the family law literature has rarely used regulatory documents as a source of data. Barlow et al (2017: 102) briefly considered family mediators' Codes of Practice in relation to domestic abuse. They commented that allowing domestic abuse cases to be resolved through mediation overlooked the impact of severe power imbalances on 'voluntary participation, fairness and safety'. Maclean and Eekelaar (2016: 79–81) also acknowledged that mediators struggled to uphold the distinction between information and advice found within Codes of Practice. Both publications draw useful insights from published guidance, but do not analyse the documents in further detail nor consider how they can be studied to uncover regulatory bodies' understanding of family mediator practice. This investigation was a key focus of the current research project, which also sought to uncover any changes in Codes of Practice over time. The study built upon the work of Webley (2010), who assessed solicitors' and mediators' approaches to divorce disputes in light of their professional training, accreditation requirements and regulatory guidance. Webley analysed two Codes of Practice on family mediation, one published by the UK College of Family Mediators (UKCFM) and another by the Law Society. Her findings revealed that the UKCFM, the main regulatory body for family mediation in England and Wales (as well as Scotland) at the time, emphasized facilitation in its Code of Practice (Webley 2010: 178). By comparison, the Law Society adopted a 'halfway approach' that occasionally enabled mediators to be flexible. Webley's work was a valuable backdrop to the current study, though her analysis of Codes of Practice made up a small part of a broader empirical project.

The Codes of Practice selected for the current study were first analysed via qualitative content analysis in 2018 and 2019, with additional analysis carried out in 2023. All data was coded through the computer program NVivo, with the author coding different words, phrases and sections into 'nodes' (categories or themes).

There may be some backlash to the use of the term 'content analysis' to describe this part of the study. A commonly adopted distinction is that content analysis is objective and quantitative, whereas thematic analysis is subjective and qualitative. By this definition, the study falls into the latter. However, content analysis is largely accepted as both a qualitative and quantitative research method in the social sciences. While the method traditionally involved the counting of specific words and phrases, it has evolved to include a qualitative design whereby 'inferences' are made from a text (Krippendorff 2003: 18; Prior 2003: 21). This development was even alluded to in the 1950s, with George (1959: 7) positing that a 'qualitative analysis of a limited number of crucial communications may often yield better clues' to the meaning of a text. Qualitative content analysis continues a 'rule-based step-by-step approach', as seen in its quantitative counterpart, that distinguishes the method from more thematic approaches. The data can be coded deductively and inductively, allowing for a thematic comparison later on (Puppis 2019: 379). For these reasons, the term 'content analysis' was adopted.

In total, six Codes of Practice were analysed. These documents are separated into two groups. The first group comprised Codes of Practice from 1985 to 1998, none of which were enforced after LASPO. This purposive sample of three regulatory documents provided insight into the introduction of family mediation in England and Wales, as well as an orthodox understanding of the process. The second group of documents comprised another three Codes of Practice enforced at the time of the original study. This representative sample was generated to assess regulatory bodies' conceptualization of family mediation after LASPO.

1.3.1.1 Historical regulatory documents from 1985 to 1998

Three historical Codes of Practice were sourced through the existing literature on family mediation. Unsurprisingly, most of the material on family mediation's regulatory bodies from this period was unavailable online. Locating physical copies of these sources was difficult, at times impossible. The selection and sampling stages for these regulatory documents were therefore blurred: the three Codes of Practice were analysed because they were possible to identify, not necessarily because they were preferred over other sources. The following outline sheds some light on the development of family mediation in late 20th-century England and Wales.[18]

The earliest Code of Practice was published in 1984 by the National Family Conciliation Council (NFCC), the first body for family mediation in England and Wales (NFCC 1984). Its 1985 Extended Code of Practice was selected for the study as it provided more detail on the expectations of regulatory bodies when family mediation was first introduced (NFCC 1985).[19] The NFCC was not an official regulatory body for accredited mediators, though the organization was later regarded as the representative for not-for-profit family mediation services. It was later renamed National Family Mediation (NFM).

[18] Further information is provided in Chapters 2 and 3.

[19] The 1984 Code of Practice was the only historical document in this project that was located but not studied. It largely replicates the 1985 version, albeit with less detail.

Table 1.1: The three historical Codes of Practice selected for content analysis

No.	Organization	Title	Year	Source
1	National Family Conciliation Council	*Extended Code of Practice for Family Conciliation Services*	1985	Family Law Journal
2	National Family Mediation and Family Mediators' Association	*Joint Code of Practice*	1994	UK College of Family Mediators Directory & Handbook 1997/98
3	UK College of Family Mediators	*Code of Practice*	1998	UK College of Family Mediators Directory & Handbook 1998/99

Family mediation services began to be established in the private sector, leading to the creation of the Family Mediators' Association (FMA) in 1989 (Roberts 2014a: 54). In 1994, NFM and FMA released a Joint Code of Practice to promote consistency across mediator practice (UKCFM 1997: A7). This was the second document analysed in the study.

A demand for a unifying set of standards was heightened following the introduction of public funding for family mediation under the Family Law Act 1996. Interestingly, the legislation stipulated that any mediator conducting mediation through legal aid must adhere to a Code of Practice (Roberts 2014a: 280).[20] In response, the NFM and FMA, alongside Family Mediation Scotland,[21] founded the UKCFM. The UKCFM is widely seen as the first formalized regulatory body for family mediators in the country. Its Code of Practice, published in 1998, was the third historical document studied for this project (UKCFM 1998: A169).

Table 1.1 summarizes the three Codes of Practice. It also lists the sources of these documents: for example, the NFCC's Extended Code of Practice was located in the Family Law Journal. To reiterate, these documents are no longer enforced or used by regulatory bodies. However, they remain crucial to understanding the orthodox conceptualization of family mediation and the role of the family mediator.

1.3.1.2 Contemporary documents from 2018 to 2019

Turning to the contemporary documents from the late 2010s, three Codes of Practice were selected for analysis. This material was chosen according to

20 Family Law Act 1996, s 27.

21 Family Mediation Scotland is now part of Relationships Scotland (Dick 2020).

Table 1.2: The three contemporary Codes of Practice selected for content analysis

No.	Organization	Title	Year	Source
4	Family Mediation Council	*Code of Practice for Family Mediators*	2018	www.familymediationcouncil.org.uk
5	Resolution	*Guide to Good Practice on Mediation*	2018	www.resolution.org.uk
6	College of Mediators	*Code of Practice for Mediators*	2019	www.collegeofmediators.co.uk

straightforward eligibility criteria: the Code of Practice was in force at the time of the initial study, applied to family mediators in England and Wales, and was published by a family mediation regulatory body. Unlike the first group of documents, these sources were relatively easy to locate. All material was available online and accessible to the public. Following selection, a representative sample of three documents was analysed.

The FMC was established in late 2007 as a 'unified body for family mediation to negotiate with government and other parties' (Resolution 2007). This organization replaced the UKCFM, which later became the College of Mediators (Bramwell 2008). The fourth Code of Practice in the study was the FMC's (2018a) Code of Practice for Family Mediators.[22] This Code must be followed by all registered family mediators in England and Wales, including those seeking accreditation.

There are currently five Member Organizations under the FMC: FMA, NFM, the College of Mediators, the Law Society, and Resolution.[23] Two Member Organizations had published their own regulatory guidance at the time of the original study. The fifth document studied was Resolution's (2018) Guide to Good Practice, although the removal of a direct hyperlink to this document on their website in early 2019 suggests that this guidance is no longer enforced. The College of Mediators last updated its Code of Practice for Mediators in 2019, and was the final regulatory document selected for this study. Table 1.2 outlines the three contemporary Codes of Practice.

[22] The FMC's (2024b) Code of Practice was updated in September 2024. However, there were only three modifications to the 2018 edition, two of which were unrelated to the content in this monograph. The third modification concerned the conduct of MIAMs, as explained in section 6.1.

[23] The ADR Group was another Member Organization. It was removed from the FMC's list of affiliated institutions in 2019.

1.3.2 Stage two: interviews with family mediators

The second stage involved semi-structured qualitative interviews with family mediators. Unlike content analysis, interviews are a regularly used method in socio-legal studies. They are a common source of data for family law researchers studying a variety of procedures and concepts (Sarat and Felstiner 1995; Trinder et al 2014; Smith et al 2017; Mant 2022), including mediation (Davis 1980; Hitchings and Miles 2016); Barlow et al 2017). Interviews generate data on a participants' viewpoint, rather than what they practice in reality (Eekelaar et al 2000: 200). It was subsequently decided that interviews were the most appropriate research method to study family mediators' perceptions of their role and the family mediation process.

A list of potential participants was collated via the FMC's (2024c) 'Find Your Local Mediator' webpage. This tool provides information about a mediator's service, legal aid provision and length of experience. Invitations to interview were sent to 28 mediators. In total, 17 family mediators were interviewed, three of whom were recruited through snowballing.[24]

Participants were sent an information sheet and consent form prior to their interview.[25] The interviews were conducted from July to September 2019, and analysed that same year. Further analysis was then undertaken in 2023. The interviews ranged from 34 minutes to 1 hour 49 minutes, with an average length of 59 minutes. Conversations were recorded on an electronic device and subsequently transcribed.[26] The data was then analysed through NVivo.

1.3.2.1 Sample characteristics

Potential interviewees were selected in order to create a purposive sample of family mediators with a range of backgrounds and experiences. While the sample did not account for the views of every single family mediator, saturation point was reached in relation to the sample's dominant conceptualizations of their role and the family mediation process.

Participants were selected across three regions to identify any geographical differences in mediators' understanding. Six mediators primarily worked in South Wales, another six in Southwest England, and five in London. However, there was no significant difference in the sample's responses based on their geographical location. The participants' gender also had no

[24] All data concerning actual and potential interviewees was password-protected and stored on an encrypted database. This information was deleted upon the completion of all interviews.

[25] All participants signed the consent form before the interview took place.

[26] The audio files were deleted upon transcription.

Table 1.3: Mediators interviewed by experience

Length of experience	Number of mediators
0–4 years	1
5–9 years	4
10–14 years	1
15–19 years	1
20–24 years	5
25–29 years	4
30+ years	1
Total	**17**

impact on the research findings, though this may be because only three interviewees identified as male. Most mediators – 14 in total – identified as female.

The study was also designed to investigate whether participants' views changed depending on their length of experience as a mediator. However, the number of trainee mediators obtaining accreditation has declined in recent years. This decline is attributed to the closure of mediation services after LASPO, as well as increasing procedural barriers to achieving accreditation (Bramwell 2020). These factors appear to have impacted the sample. As listed in Table 1.3, most of the sample had practised as a family mediator for over 20 years. Newly qualified mediators were contacted to participate in the study, but only one interviewee had under five years of experience. Another four participants had worked as family mediators for 5–9 years. Thus, it was no surprise that the lack of newly accredited mediators became a noticeable trend in the data analysis.[27]

This sample is not representative of all family mediators in England and Wales according to length of experience. In a 2019 survey by the FMC (2020: 10), 41 per cent of 115 respondents had practised as a mediator for under ten years. Twenty-five per cent had practised for 11–20 years, and 35 per cent had practised for over 20 years. By comparison, the profile of the mediators in this study was switched: 29 per cent had under 10 years' experience as a mediator, 12 per cent between 10 and 19 years' experience, and 59 per cent over 20 years' experience. While the sample in the current study was not designed to be representative, the lack of engagement from

[27] See section 7.2.2.

Table 1.4: Mediators interviewed by professional background

Professional background	Number of mediators	Number practising as original profession
Lawyer	5	4
Therapeutic	7	1
Hybrid	5	3
Total	**17**	**17**

newly accredited mediators was concerning and should be taken into account when interpreting the research findings.

Family mediators were also sampled according to professional background. Mediators are often separated into two professional sub-groups: *lawyer* mediators and *therapeutic* mediators. Lawyer mediators are typically qualified solicitors or barristers who also train as mediators. Therapeutic mediators originate from a range of backgrounds. For instance, two mediators in the sample previously worked in the education system. Sufficient samples of both groups were reflected in the sample: ten lawyer mediators and seven therapeutic mediators.

Five lawyer mediators had also undertaken some therapeutic training in their career or had further experience in a therapeutic or other background. One solicitor had trained as a psychotherapist, and another as a counsellor. Another provided training to therapists and counsellors. Two other solicitors had previous experience in education. While the range of backgrounds of these five participants was broad, they each brought additional experience to their work as lawyer mediators. For this reason, the lawyer mediator sub-group was separated into participants from a purely legal background, and those who had taken additional therapeutic training, named *hybrid* mediators. Interestingly, the majority of mediators with a legal background continued to practice as solicitors, whereas most therapeutic mediators no longer worked in their original profession at the time of the study. Listed in Table 1.4, the sample comprised five lawyer mediators, seven therapeutic mediators and five hybrid mediators.[28]

[28] The author has written about the hybrid mediator in published work (Blakey 2023a). Note that hybrid mediators include therapeutic mediators who went on to practice or undertake training in a legal field, though no hybrid mediators of this kind were identified in the present sample.

Table 1.5: Mediators interviewed by legal aid provision

Legal aid provision	Number of mediators	Number by professional background
Provided legal aid	9	1 Lawyer 6 Therapeutic 2 Hybrid
Stopped providing legal aid after LASPO	5	3 Lawyer 1 Hybrid 1 Therapeutic
Never provided legal aid	3	1 Lawyer 0 Therapeutic 2 Hybrid
Total	**17**	**17**

Participants were additionally selected on the basis of legal aid funding (Table 1.5). Nine mediators provided family mediation through legal aid at the time of the study. Interestingly, only three mediators in the sample never had a legal aid contract for family mediation, suggesting that publicly funded mediation was more accessible before LASPO. The sample was thus divided into: participants who provided legal aid mediation (n = 9); participants who stopped providing legal aid mediation after LASPO (n = 5); and participants who had only conducted privately funded mediation (n = 3). Six out of seven therapeutic mediators still provided legal aid at the time of interview, compared to one out of five lawyer mediators and two out of five hybrid mediators.

1.3.3 Subjectivity and the dual-methods approach

When first designing the project, the author was aware that her subjectivity would impact the research findings. It was felt that this was an inevitable consequence of qualitative research. Like any written document, Codes of Practice are open to interpretation. In practice, the meaning drawn by an academic could massively differ from what a mediator would take from the very same document. Acknowledging this reality was particularly important where interviewees had attended different training courses, practised mediation for different lengths of time, and mediated different types of private family disputes. These factors, and numerous others, all contributed to a mediator's professional identity, as well as the author's subconscious perceptions of them. While similarities (and differences) could be identified among the interviewees, analysis remained subjective because the interview data was collected one year after the content analysis. The findings from stage two were subsequently analysed in light of a particular hypothesis, rather than a wholly objective standpoint.[29] These limitations do not negate findings, but rather demonstrate the effect of one's lived experiences upon the interpretation of data.

The dual-methods approach adopted for this study goes some way to resolve the limitations of content analysis. Content analysis alone cannot provide findings on what Webley (2010: 9) describes as 'the subtleties of individual practice' – the method only generates findings on what is expected of a practitioner, often in very generic or limited terms. Stage two of the empirical work was therefore designed to produce findings on mediators' conceptualization of family mediation. Combined, the content analysis and qualitative interviews uncovered a plethora of data on the flexible mediator archetype. The findings were not constrained to one perspective, widening the project's scope. Eekelaar et al (2000: 36) adopted a similar approach in their study on the daily work of divorce lawyers, conducting both observations and interviews. The researchers praised the 'combination of the two techniques' for creating 'an accurate picture of the daily workings of a family law practice', strengthening the validity of their findings. Ultimately, the dual methods adopted in the current study provide a much-needed and currently unavailable insight into the conceptualization of family mediation after LASPO.

Nonetheless, interview data is unreliable to the extent that an interviewee may say something that does not reflect reality. Della Noce (2009: 193) argues that research into mediator practice should include 'empirical evidence of what mediators actually *do*, not just what they *say* they do' (original emphasis).[30] The risk of relying too heavily on interview data was apparent in Mulcahy's (2001: 517) study on community mediation: the mediators claimed loyalty to a traditional model of family mediation and absolute neutrality during their interviews, yet acted very differently in practice. This possibility must be taken into account when considering the interview data from the present study. Even so, a variety of readings are to be welcomed, rather than considered as a limitation of this research. The hope is that this project will be followed by further research into family mediation, including observations of mediator practice.

[29] Interestingly, this point reflects the issues surrounding mediator neutrality that are discussed in Chapter 3. It is incredibly difficult for a mediator to maintain absolute neutrality, particularly where they are required to intervene in light of a power imbalance. The mediator may also hold subconscious beliefs and assumptions about the two parties. Similarly, it is difficult for a researcher to remain completely objective as they become acquainted with their research participants. A researcher will have subconscious views about a participant, the purpose of the data, as well as the participant's responses.

[30] Hitchings and Miles (2016: 179) similarly argue that it is 'important to acknowledge the limitations of data based on professionals' reports of what they do'.

1.4 Chapter outlines

Rethinking Family Mediation comprises two parts, both of which contribute to the overarching investigation into contemporary family mediation and family justice after LASPO.

In Part I, the author sets out the background to the inquiry and argues that the role of the family mediator has evolved over several decades. Chapter 2 tracks the development of family mediation in policy from the late 20th century to the LASPO reforms. It identifies three policy concerns that were used by successive governments to justify the promotion of family mediation: the effectiveness of court; the demand for settlement; and the cost of legal aid. After setting out the intentions behind the LASPO reforms, the discussion connects these reforms to a long-standing neoliberal agenda. However, it is argued that the value of family mediation as a potential family justice apparatus has been overlooked. There is a place for both court and mediation within the contemporary family justice system, justifying the remainder of the monograph.

The family law context is then dissected in Chapters 3 and 4, with a specific focus on the family mediator. Chapter 3 considers the original conceptualization of family mediation. Through examining various pilots on family mediation in late 20th-century England and Wales, the discussion identifies the *limited mediator* archetype: a professional bound by a facilitative framework and an absolution vision of her neutrality. It is acknowledged that the limited mediator was an effective third party in the late 20th century because legal advice and representation were generally accessible, though some warning signs had become apparent by the 1980s. Chapter 4 subsequently shifts attention to the contemporary family justice system and recognizes the issues with the limited mediator type after LASPO. It identifies a demand for the second archetype – the *flexible mediator* – who can adapt to the contemporary landscape by taking on both facilitative and evaluative practices. Nonetheless, it is discovered that the flexible mediator type remains hidden by their traditional, limited conceptualization. This concealment persists despite evidence that mediators already adopt flexible practices. It is consequently concluded that more must be done to recognize and regulate the flexible mediator archetype.

Part II uses findings from the empirical project to advance this investigation. Chapter 5 uncovers a new theoretical framework based on four mediator functions. Through analysing data from both the content analysis and interviews, it is revealed that flexible mediators act as helpers, referrers, assessors and intervenors. Mediators continue to align their work with the helper function, which could be taken as evidence that the profession continues to reflect a limited archetype. However, the remaining three functions reveal a plethora of hidden, evaluative practices. The tacit or subconscious acceptance of mediator evaluation – and therefore the flexible mediator type – by both regulatory bodies and their mediators suggests that more must be done to openly recognize and regulate contemporary mediator practice. In Chapter 6, it is proposed that many mediators adopting a flexible archetype take on a quasi-legal role. The findings show that mediators see access to justice as connected to court, yet simultaneously believe a major part of their role is to determine the *quality* of agreement. This quality is often determined in accordance with legal norms, alluding to a more active role for flexible mediators in the post-LASPO landscape. The chapter ends by critiquing this development, though it is concluded that the rise of the flexible mediator archetype is a welcome development so long as more is done to ensure that the profession understands (and correctly applies) family law's norms, rights and obligations.

Chapter 7 takes the book in a different direction. It recognizes that, even if the flexible mediator type is acknowledged, reform to the structures surrounding mediation is also necessary. The chapter subsequently considers some extrinsic and structural barriers to family mediation reform. This discussion is based on data from the mediator interviews and provides a fresh insight into the impact of LASPO on mediation services. Chapter 7 then ends by considering whether and how family mediation should be considered a legal service. The concluding chapter summarizes the study's key findings, before outlining various implications for future research and debate.

Altogether, *Rethinking Family Mediation* establishes a valuable foundation upon which to revitalize the discussions around the contemporary family justice system. It shows that the status of the family mediation profession must be carefully articulated – for without this clarification, reform will remain unresponsive to the issues within contemporary family justice. Rather than viewing these findings as a sign of how family justice has declined over time, it is hoped that this monograph is a source of optimism, providing insight into the type of pragmatic change that could be enacted in the near future.

PART I

Tracking Family Mediator Practice

2

The Rise of Family Mediation in Law and Policy

Family mediation plays a significant part in the contemporary family justice system. Its use is not only encouraged, but often expected. However, it is widely accepted throughout the family justice literature that mediation is only effective in certain cases and that its promotion hinders access to court for many individuals. This leaves the process in an unusual position: while family mediation has garnered increasing government support every decade since the late 20th century, it has failed to grasp the attention of both the public and academic scholars. How exactly did this contradiction occur, and what does this uncertainty mean for family mediation in the 2020s and beyond? Chapter 2 investigates this development by situating family mediation in its broader policy context. This background is vital to the remainder of Part I, which uncovers the transition from the limited to the flexible mediator archetype.

The chapter first sets the scene by considering the main concerns within family justice policy from the late 20th century. It shows that policy portrayed court as an adversarial and harmful process in comparison to private settlement, whereas legal aid was criticized for extending well beyond its economic means. Section 2 covers the launch of family mediation in the late 1970s and early 1980s as a solution to these policy concerns, though the discussion acknowledges that court remained the primary option for private family matters. Attention then shifts to a number of developments in the 1990s, notably the Family Law Act 1996, which envisioned a wider role for mediation in the family law system. Section 3 reveals how family mediation took centre stage in early 21st-century policy with a particular focus on the Legal Aid, Sentencing and Punishment of Offenders Act 2012 (LASPO) reforms. A subsequent investigation into LASPO's impact reveals a sharp decline in mediation numbers and a simultaneous rise of self-representing litigants in court. The final section of Chapter 2 reflects on the widespread criticism of mediation as a neoliberal tool. Notwithstanding the validity of these concerns, it is submitted that it is the state's appropriation of mediation, not mediation itself, that is neoliberal. This discussion refers to the 2023 proposals to introduce mandatory family mediation, as well as their subsequent postponement. Chapter 2 concludes by reiterating the need to fully investigate the value of family mediation and, consequently, the contemporary understanding of family justice after LASPO. This lens paves the way for the remainder of the monograph, which offers a pragmatic and evidence-based investigation into mediation's position in the contemporary family law system.

2.1 The three policy concerns in late 20th-century family justice

The 20th century saw increased public interest in divorce (Goriely 1994: 550). Under the Matrimonial Causes Act 1857, a petitioner could only obtain a divorce decree if their spouse had committed a matrimonial offence on the grounds of adultery. Women additionally had to show that their husbands had committed an aggravating factor, such as cruelty or incest, up until 1923. These rules, unsurprisingly, made divorce inaccessible to most. In the *Field of Choice* report, the Law Commission (1966: para 15) established two objectives of a 'good divorce law'. The first objective of the system was to support, rather than weaken, the institution of marriage. If the marriage was irreparable, the second objective materialized: to permit divorce 'with the maximum fairness, and the minimum bitterness, distress and humiliation'.

Subsequent reforms were concerned with how to make divorce more accessible, as well as how to promote a positive post-separation relationship when divorce did occur. Under the Divorce Reform Act 1969, effective from January 1971,[1] the element of matrimonial offence was replaced with the sole ground of irretrievable breakdown. This ground was proven by one of five facts: unreasonable behaviour,[2] adultery, desertion, two years' separation with the respondent's consent or five years' separation without the respondent's consent.[3] The legislation coincided with a number of 'demographic, socio-economic and attitudinal changes' (Law Commission 1988: para 2.14; Smith 1997: 541), including an increased acceptance of divorce within society (Freeman 1996: 32). Improved access to divorce, coupled with social developments, meant more people than ever before

---

1 Changes were later consolidated under the Matrimonial Causes Act 1973.

2 This ground was listed as: 'the respondent has behaved in such a way that the petitioner cannot reasonably be expected to live with the respondent'. See Matrimonial Causes Act 1973 s 1(2)(b).

3 The five facts for irretrievable breakdown were abolished in April 2022 under the Divorce, Dissolution and Separation Act 2020.

began to use the divorce system. In the year after the Divorce Reform Act 1969 was enforced, the number of divorces in England and Wales rose by 60 percentage points from 74,437 to 119,025, reaching a peak of 165,018 in 1993 (Office for National Statistics 2024).

Soon after the Divorce Reform Act 1969, family justice policy shifted attention to three broad concerns which sought to reduce state responsibility for, and the economic burden of, the family law system. The first concern was whether the court process (premised on adjudication and adversarialism) was the most effective system for family problems. The second related to the value of settlement and private resolution. The third and final concern was the unjustified extension of legal aid. These policy interests will be examined separately.

2.1.1 The efficiency and suitability of court

Following the Divorce Reform Act 1969, family law became 'a victim of its own success' (Maclean and Eekelaar 2019: 9). The increase in divorce applications had a colossal impact on the court system; judges were faced with a high caseload, and criticized for resulting delays (Eekelaar and Dingwall 1988: 10). The introduction of the special procedure in 1974 meant that divorcing parties with no dependent children were no longer required to attend court if the application was uncontested.[4] Childless couples could go on to use the special procedure for all divorce petitions from 1975, as well as all couples from 1977.[5] Despite the extension of the special procedure, the sheer number of applications alone continued to burden the court system.

Policy raised concern around the use of court for divorce-related disputes in the 1980s. In 1981, the Law Commission (1981: para 13) advised that more should be done to ensure that the only contested cases coming to court were those that 'require' adjudication, warning that the adversarial process created 'inevitable unhappiness' for many individuals. A report by the Matrimonial Causes Procedure Committee (1985: para 2.28) later acknowledged the growing perception that court 'enhances bitterness and hostility'. However, the Committee felt that this animosity was not attributable to court itself, but rather the element of fault required in most divorce cases. The Law Commission (1988: para 3.22) backtracked from its original stance some years later, framing the antagonism in court as 'unfortunate'.

4 Matrimonial Causes Rules 1973, SI 1973/2016, r 48.

5 Matrimonial Causes (Amendment) Rules 1975/1359, r 3 and Matrimonial Causes Rules 1977/344, r 48. See Jeffs (1996: 24) and Matrimonial Causes Procedure Committee (1985: paras 2.14–2.18).

In the years following these reports, government confidence in the court process declined. Late 20th-century reform was influenced by the growing perception that judges and lawyers had an 'adversarial mindset' that 'exacerbate[d] rather than resolve[d] interpersonal and social conflict', leading to poor outcomes for all parties involved (Hunter 2003: 156). The Lord Chancellor's Department (1993: para 7.3) openly criticized the 'adversarial model' in court: 'This [adversarial model] can undoubtedly add to the stress and pain of the divorce for all those involved. It can also affect the cost of the divorce to the couple concerned and, where one or both are legally aided, to the state.' A follow-up paper subsequently recommended that the divorce process should be reformed to enable spouses to consider their relationship 'in an environment that allows them to address together what went wrong' (Lord Chancellor's Department 1995a: para 2.17). The adversarial model was deemed ineffective, and it was believed that conflict between separating couples would be reduced if they avoided court. Families were encouraged to seek a different forum, linked to the second concern in late 20th-century policy.

2.1.2 Promoting settlement

Semple (2012: 234) identifies a 'settlement mission' in family law, which he defines as 'the informal and unregulated encouragement or pressure to settle'. Since the late 20th century, the settlement mission has played a prominent role in private family law. Mnookin and Kornhauser (1979) submit that the main function of contemporary divorce law is not to impose the decisions made by a judge, but to provide a framework for the resolution of disputes. Most academic commentators accept this view, with Hitchings (2017: 359–360) describing settlement as a 'practice norm' laden with a rhetoric of 'agreement, conformity and harmony'. Barlow et al (2017: 22–23) similarly comment that a 'conciliatory, settlement-oriented approach' dominates contemporary family law.

The alleged issue advanced in late 20th-century policy was that lawyers and judges could 'impose their own construction' of a dispute which often caused a party's preferred outcome to be completely overlooked (Roberts 2013: 10).[6] Even if a judge's determination was legally sound, their decision could be unviable or unrealistic for the parties involved. And so, the rising demand for settlement was heavily premised on the idea that decision-making power should rest with the parties themselves. The *Marriage Matters* report was one of the earliest examples of government policy that advocated for the self-resolution of private family matters, with the Home Office

[6] Eisenberg (1976: 658) makes a similar remark, acknowledging that the judge is a 'stranger … coupled with the binary character of traditional adjudication'.

(1979: para 1.10) identifying an increased demand for alternative services that 'help[ed] couples resolve their problems'. The drive for settlement became more prominent in the 1980s, with the Matrimonial Causes Procedure Committee (1985: para 3.2) writing: 'We are firmly of the view that the primary decision-making responsibility should rest with the spouses themselves and that they should be given all necessary help in deciding for themselves what should happen to their children, their property and their marriage.' In the Committee's own words, disputes arising from relationship breakdown were not simply 'matter[s] just to be left to lawyers' (Matrimonial Causes Procedure Committee 1985: para 3.11). This approach marked the beginning of a concerted effort among successive governments to promote individual responsibility for family disputes, an objective that is still heavily pursued in the post-LASPO landscape.

The idea of personal responsibility was – and continues to be – hidden behind the notion that settlement reduces conflict. The Law Commission (1988: para 3.2) advocated for out-of-court settlement, writing: 'if solutions can be agreed between the parties rather than imposed by the court, the traumatic effect of marital breakdown … may be reduced'. Building on their 1966 *Field of Choice* report, the organization added two further objectives to a good divorce law:

> [T]hose basic objectives of a 'good' divorce law, as set out by our predecessors in 1966, still command widespread support … however, any summary would include two further objectives : *to encourage so far as possible the amicable resolution of practical issues* … and, for many people the paramount objective, to minimise the harm that the children may suffer. (Law Commission 1990: para 1.6; emphasis added)

The wording of the first objective was a tactical choice to drive settlement. The Law Commission did not explicitly place responsibility for settlement on the parties. Instead, they encouraged 'amicable resolution'. Yet it is harder to argue against the idea of amicable resolution than the notion that the parties are personally responsible for settlement, similar to how it is easier to defend the promotion of autonomy than the suggestion that parties are completely accountable for their disputes (Diduck 2016: 145). Thus, the phrasing of various policy documents advanced the notion of individual responsibility under the friendly guise of settlement, obscuring the withdrawal of state responsibility in the process.

2.1.3 Legal aid and the taxpayer

Hynes (2012: 26–28) describes 1973 to 1986 as a 'golden period' of legal aid. Public funding for legal advice outside court proceedings was available to a significant proportion of the population, and lawyers could receive remuneration for various services. However, Hynes comments that this era 'came to an abrupt end' in the late 1980s. After the Divorce Reform Act 1969, the state witnessed what was described by the Law Commission (1988: para 2.6) as a 'rapid escalation in legal aid expenditure'. An obvious solution to this problem was to restrict the legal aid budget. The government claimed it was 'committed' to providing legal aid, but various reforms meant that funding would only be provided to those with 'the greatest need' (Lord Chancellor's Department 1995b: para 1.11). The idea of 'need' continued well into the 21st century, becoming a particular focus of the LASPO reforms (Kaganas 2017: 176–180).

As Rickman et al (1999: 262) argue, state expenditure was limited through adjustments to 'the demand for, and supply of, legal aid'. From the late 1980s, Conservative governments narrowed the eligibility tests for legal aid and increased the level of contributions that recipients would be expected to pay towards their dispute. Legislative reform was enacted through the Legal Aid Act 1988, which aimed 'to bring legal aid spending under control' (Moore and Newbury 2017: 21–22). The statute led to the creation of the Legal Aid Board, which took responsibility for the administration of legal aid from the Law Society.[7] With legal aid spending still on the rise, the Board continued to restrict the rules on eligibility in terms of parties' income and capital (Hynes 2012: 29). The legal aid scheme became increasingly focused on families from lower socio-economic households, again connecting the justification for such funding to a demand to support those in need.

Successive governments also justified the narrowing of legal aid by reference to the 'abused' taxpayer (Wiggan 2012: 390), a notion that first became evident in 1990s family law policy. In one report, the Lord Chancellor's Department (1993: para 1.4) claimed that the legal aid scheme must 'keep to the minimum the cost to the parties and the taxpayer'. Subsequent proposals to cap legal aid were similarly justified by the need to protect the 'interests of the client and the taxpayer' (Lord Chancellor's Department 1995b: para 4.2). While the Lord Chancellor's Department (1996: para 5) later admitted that the proposed cap on legal aid was 'radical', it reasserted that the reforms were warranted on the grounds of public spending. The government frequently referred to the 'interests of the taxpayer' throughout its *Striking the Balance* paper, again arguing that legal aid was only warranted in cases of 'genuine

[7] The Legal Aid Board was replaced 11 years later through the Access to Justice Act 1999, enacted under the New Labour government. In addition to creating the Legal Services Commission, the 1999 legislation restructured the legal aid scheme and placed a cap on civil legal aid (Hynes and Robins 2009: 39; Hynes 2012: 49–50).

need' (Lord Chancellor's Department 1996: para 1.1). As a result, the focal point of policy shifted from supporting legal aid recipients, to protecting the taxpayers who funded the scheme.

Unsurprisingly, this cost-saving analysis was not framed as an affront to access to justice. In fact, the development was portrayed as quite the opposite. Upon announcing the proposed cuts to legal aid, one policy paper began with the sentence: 'The aim of the Government is to improve access to justice' (Lord Chancellor's Department 1995b: para 1.1). Despite presenting themselves as supporters of a 'social democratic discourse', ministerial departments sought to introduce 'a meaner and more conditional form of legal aid' (Sommerlad 2008: 180). It was on this basis that legal aid continued to be limited in the early 21st century.

2.2 The solution: family mediation

The three policy concerns reveal an increased interest in family justice reform from the 1970s. Changes to divorce law rendered the process more accessible, but also put a noticeable strain on the court system. Numerous policy papers and reforms subsequently sought to reduce state responsibility for family matters. However, it is important to acknowledge that these concerns reflect an additional objective: to alter the meaning of (access to) family justice. As Chapter 1 explained, access to justice was historically associated with access to court. Yet successive governments sought to reconceptualize access to justice in a way that was not necessarily dependent on court and lawyers. Instead, they envisioned a justice negotiated and funded by the parties themselves. State funding and legal oversight would consequently only be deemed necessary when parties were found to be in need, reserving traditional notions of justice for a select few. The primary task for policy, then, was to find a way to move disputes outside the court process.

Family mediation was the answer. For centuries, the informal process was used to resolve conflicts within different communities. This is recognized by Folberg (1983: 3), who describes the formal mediation process as 'an adaption of something that has existed in other cultures or in other times'.[8] The idea of mediation is effectively second nature to humans, whether it is something witnessed in schools, social circles, work environments or the family unit. Nonetheless, the late 20th century was the period in which *family mediation* became formalized and gradually implemented into the English and Welsh family justice system.

---

8 Mediation has origins in a number of countries, including India (Bhatt 2009), China (Xianyi 2009) and Japan (Folberg 1983).

2.2.1 Family mediation's humble beginnings

While this monograph is focused on the purpose of out-of-court family mediation, it is worth noting that the formalized procedure originates from the early to mid-20th-century court system. The Summary Procedure (Domestic Proceedings) Act 1937 originally allowed probation officers to 'attempt to effect a conciliation' between the parties. Conciliation was understood 'in the marriage-saving sense', akin to what is now widely described as *reconciliation* (Cretney 1998: 132).[9] There was a slight shift towards viewing conciliation as a means of settling disputes, rather than saving marriages, in the mid-20th century.[10] Yet this notion did not come 'into clear focus' until the 1974 Finer Report, written by the Committee on One-Parent Families (James and Hay 1993: 24). The publication is widely regarded as the 'catalyst' for contemporary conciliation in England and Wales (Parkinson 2020: 7), and marks a 'watershed' for the contemporary discourse around marital breakdown (James and Hay 1993: 24).

The Committee on One-Parent Families (1974) highlighted the disjointed application of the law relating to family breakdown, acknowledging that the options were limited for those who did not want to attend court but felt unable to resolve their dispute alone. It was submitted that many parties had no choice but to unwillingly engage in direct negotiation or issue proceedings, even if this resulted in poor outcomes. The Committee recommended several reforms, including reorganizing the family law courts 'to provide the best possible facilities for conciliation' (Committee on One-Parent Families 1974: para 4.283). Conciliation was defined as 'assisting the parties to deal with the consequences of the established breakdown of their marriage, whether resulting in a divorce or a separation, by reaching agreements or giving consents or reducing the area of conflict ... arising from the breakdown which calls for a decision on future arrangements' (Committee on One-Parent Families 1974: para 4.288).

Even in the early stages of conciliation's development, the process was presented as the solution to the adverse effects of the traditional adjudication system.[11] Conciliation was said to avoid bitterness and hostility, instead

[9] While the statute did not provide any further information on what conciliation included, published guidance for magistrates clarified that a conciliator would help parties to decide if they could 'remedy' the issues within their marriage 'and rebuild from the start' (Cretney 1998: 132).

[10] For instance, conciliation was referenced in a 1971 Practice Direction by the President of the Family Division. See James and Hay (1993: 24) and Ogus et al (1989: para 2.23).

[11] Federal governments within the United States adopted the same view towards the start of the 20th century. Mediation was said to situate disputes within their social context (the family) and support a 'marginal clientele' that regularly faced significant court delays. See Auerbach (1983: 97, 120).

'engendering common sense, reasonableness and agreement' (Committee on One-Parent Families 1974: para 4.305). The Home Office (1979: para 7.11) was positive about conciliation in the *Marriage Matters* report, and argued that conciliators (who were usually probation officers or welfare officers within the court system) helped parties to manage the difficult emotions triggered by relationship breakdown. The organization envisioned a role for conciliation next to 'the legal structure', comparing it to the adversarial court process:

> Whereas the function of the courts is judicial, the main purpose of the conciliation service would be to help individuals and couples to sort out their views, attitudes and feelings, make decisions which are most beneficial to the mental and emotional health of themselves, their spouses and their children, and begin to adapt themselves to the implications of those decisions. (Home Office 1979: para 7.10)

Policy additionally commended conciliation for its strong alignment with settlement. The process supposedly gave parties the space to reach their own outcome, with the conciliator prohibited from making any determinations. Several years after the *Marriage Matters* report, the Matrimonial Causes Procedure Committee (1985: para 3.2) argued: 'We are firmly of the view that the primary decision-making responsibility should rest with the spouses themselves and that they should be given all necessary help in deciding for themselves what should happen to their children, their property and their marriage.'

In proposing procedural reform, the Matrimonial Causes Procedure Committee (1985: paras 3.10–3.3.13) praised conciliation as a process that meant 'responsibility remain[ed] at all times with the parties themselves to identify and seek agreement'. It recommended that conciliation should be 'a recognised part of the legal procedure' and become available to parties at their initial hearing.[12] The Committee claimed that conciliation would place the responsibility for settlement on the parties before and during the initial hearing, with a court determination only becoming necessary if negotiations were unsuccessful (Matrimonial Causes Procedure Committee 1985: para 4.61).

Later policy also celebrated the process in relation to its costs. In the 1993 *Looking to the Future* consultation paper, the Lord Chancellor's

[12] At this point, conciliation was primarily used for child arrangement matters, previously known as custody or access matters. The Committee, while not making an explicit recommendation on this point, also argued that conciliation could be used to help resolve financial disputes. See section 3.2.1 for a discussion on the introduction of all-issues mediation.

Department (1993: para 7.20) claimed that mediation (opting for this term over conciliation) 'reduce[d] costs' between the parties. The same report claimed that the costs of family disputes 'should be borne by the couple themselves', an objective which would be supported by moving family disputes into the private sphere (Lord Chancellor's Department 1993: para 9.7). Two years later, a follow-up report called for the increased promotion of mediation within a simplified divorce system (Lord Chancellor's Department 1995a: para 9.8).

And so, family mediation (or conciliation, as it was known until the early 1990s) was a perfect fit for the three concerns in late 20th-century family justice policy. First, mediation was said to avoid the bitterness and hostility caused in court. Second, the process was premised on the self-resolution of disputes. Third, it was alleged that both the government and its families would make financial savings if cases were resolved without recourse to a judge. Combined, these factors meant that mediation was highly appealing to the government. However, policy did not instantly place mediation at the heart of family justice. This transition was gradual, with early policy continuing to emphasize the importance of access to court.

2.2.2 Mediation as an alternative to court

Family mediation was originally described as a form of alternative dispute resolution. It was portrayed not as a replacement to court, but rather as an alternative for families seeking something different from adversarialism or adjudication. The court was the conventional route for legal matters, particularly when families were involved in a financial (or property) dispute that required additional legal oversight. Access to court, therefore, continued.

The Law Commission's (1988: para 5.32) *Facing the Future* consultation was one of the first policy papers to support a move to no-fault divorce. The Law Commission considered whether parties should be required to attend counselling before their divorce could be granted, concluding that this would rarely lead to reconciliation or resolution. Most respondents agreed that compulsory mediation would also be 'counter-productive' and potentially compel settlement when it was damaging to one or both disputants (Law Commission 1990: para 5.34). The Law Commission subsequently warned of the 'dangers in relying too heavily upon conciliation', adopting a court-centric approach: 'It is important that, whatever encouragement is given by the system to alternative methods of dispute resolution, the courts are not deterred from performing their function of determining issues which require to be determined' (Law Commission 1990: para 5.34).

Policy throughout this period continued to associate family justice with court, even though the same documents were often critical of the adversarial process. This was because limiting access to court significantly impeded the court's key function: 'determining issues that need to be determined'. A judge applied the law to determine the outcome, whereas a mediator could only encourage settlement. Procedural and substantive family justice was best achieved, if not only achieved, through the court system.

From this position, a hierarchy of dispute resolution procedures comes to light. In the early 1990s, Murch and Hooper (1992: 60–62) described the family justice system as comprising two 'zones'. The inner zone reflected 'the traditional "heart work" of the system', specifically litigation within court. The outer zone was much wider, comprising solicitor advice, support from advice agencies and alternative dispute resolution. As the term suggests, the inner zone remained central to the private family law system and was understood as the primary route to justice for most of the late 20th century. The inner zone was funded, and the outer zone was generally regarded as an alternative group of systems. Nevertheless, successive governments slowly began to encourage the use of the outer zone, leading to drastic shifts in the operation of the family law system by the early 2010s.

2.2.3 Mediation as a replacement for court: a creeping rhetoric

A change in government thinking became apparent from the mid to late 1990s. During this period, family mediation was not strictly conceptualized as an alternative to court. Rather, mediation was sometimes understood as the optimum process for separating couples and their disputes. In the *Looking to the Future* consultation paper, the Lord Chancellor's Department (1993: para 7.11) envisioned a new role for family mediation. The Department continued to recognize mediation as an 'alternative' to court, but claimed: 'The aim would be for mediation to become the norm rather than the exception.' The consultation resulted in the Family Law Act 1996, a wide-reaching piece of legislation intended to reshape the family law system. Part Two of the Family Law Act 1996 would introduce no-fault divorce, with a judge only approving a divorce application (notwithstanding certain exceptions) if the parties first attended an information meeting to discuss the possibility of family mediation.[13] These reforms were considered too radical, with little evidence that they actually improved the divorce process (Barlow et al 2017: 11). Part Two of the legislation was subsequently scrapped, though it nevertheless demonstrated the intention of John Major's Conservative government to move more disputes into family mediation. This push was further underscored by Part Three of the Family Law Act 1996, which still received Royal Assent. Enforced in March 1997, Part Three introduced legal aid funding for family mediation. To encourage the use of publicly

[13] Family Law Act 1996, s 8.

funded mediation, section 29 stipulated that a party could not receive legal aid for private family law proceedings unless they first attended an intake meeting. This meeting was similar to the information meeting envisioned in Part Two, though intake meetings could only be conducted by mediators.[14] These reforms were driven by the expectation that parties would, at the very least, consider using mediation – an expectation that would only become more onerous over time.

The Family Law Act 1996 was a blatant example of legislation that sought to regulate parties' behaviour upon relationship breakdown. In *Divorcing Responsibly*, Reece (2003) identified a change in late 20th-century divorce law. She argued that earlier legislation sought to prevent divorce and emphasized the importance of reconciliation. This approach meant divorcing couples were criticized, whereas couples who reconciled were commended for saving their marriage. By comparison, this distinction could no longer be used to regulate parties' behaviour once society became more accepting of divorce. And so, successive governments shifted their attention to 'those who divorce well and those who divorce badly' (Reece 2003: 127). The 1996 Act gave parties the power to manage their relationships, but hidden underneath this notion of autonomy was the opportunity for the state to 'educate' the family on how to behave responsibly. As Reece (2003: 156–157) summarized, divorce became 'a golden opportunity for intervention'.[15] The promotion of mediation furthered this goal of behaviour modification, teaching parties that a good divorce was only possible through out-of-court settlement (Reece 2003: 149).

Similar prompts for good behaviour were found in the civil justice sphere. The Civil Justice Review (1988: 1–2) proposed reform 'to reduce delay, cost and complexity' in court, though the impact of such changes was somewhat limited (Sorabji 2014). In 1994, the government commissioned Lord Woolf to undertake a comprehensive review of civil justice (Genn 2012: 399). An interim report was published the following year, in which Woolf (1995) criticized the adversarial nature of most civil proceedings. Woolf (1996: 4) continued his disapproval of the formal court system in his final report, arguing that adjudication should become a 'last resort' that is reserved for the select few instances where intervention is deemed necessary. In a bid to encourage settlement, Woolf advocated for the use of alternative dispute resolution before parties went to court. His proposals culminated in the Civil Procedure Rules 1998, which gave judges the power to compel parties to

[14] For further information on these intake meetings, see section 3.3.2.

[15] Piper (1993: 5) made the same argument several years prior, stating that legislative reform used the idea of responsibility 'to delineate socially acceptable behaviour in a situation of rapid change'.

attempt alternative dispute resolution.[16] Genn (2012: 401–402) argues that the Woolf reforms intended to move alternative dispute resolution to the centre of civil justice, with policy from the late 1990s placing an even greater emphasis on mediation. The state was not concerned with preventing civil disputes, but rather how to encourage (or effectively force) parties to take responsibility for their civil matters and resolve them outside court. These reforms were said to 'bring about a significant increase in access to justice', albeit a justice that secured 'the best value for the taxpayers' money' (Lord Chancellor's Department 1998: para 1.9). Attempts to promote mediation beyond its image as an alternative procedure were thus evident across the family and civil justice systems.

What was the impact of these developments on the meaning of family (or civil) justice? As advanced in Chapter 1, fewer individuals now use the courts or lawyers to resolve their disputes, whether that is by their own choice or due to the unavailability of these mechanisms. Theoretically, individuals are still able to access court. Yet various governments in the late 20th century clearly intended to make family mediation the starting point for many disputes. This move would significantly alter the function of court from 'determining issues that need to be determined', as posited by the Law Commission, to determining issues that had not been resolved through mediation. The inner zone of family justice, comprising court proceedings and adversarialism, would be decentred as a result. This change in rhetoric was, unsurprisingly, heavily criticized for limiting access to court and obstructing judges' ability to apply the law (Main 2005: 401). Procedures like mediation did not provide the same justice ensured in the inner zone: if it did, there would be no point to the family justice system's two-tiered structure. And so, by moving more disputes into mediation, successive governments actively sought to reduce the accessibility of family justice in the traditional sense.

However, rather than view this development as the destruction of family justice, perhaps it could be seen as providing a different type of (contemporary) justice altogether. Hitchings (2017) advances a 'paradigm of justice' comprising three conceptualizations, each corresponding to a different route to settlement for family matters. The first form, official justice, signifies formal justice through the courts whereby 'defined legal principles' govern agreement (Hitchings 2017: 363). Although official justice can include negotiations outside the courtroom, this conception reflects the centrality of legal norms in the discourse around access to justice. Hitchings' (2017: 367) second form of justice, operative justice, begins to afford parties more power over the outcomes of their dispute.

[16] The same power for judges dealing with family matters is now found under Part Three of the Family Procedure Rules: FPR, SI 2010/2955, r 3.4.

Legal oversight is reduced, meaning the outcome may not be determined by a judge or heavily influenced by a lawyer. As decision-making power moves from a legal professional to a disputant, personal responsibility for settlement increases (Hitchings 2017: 370). This form of justice is typically available through the outer zone of the family justice system. Hitchings herself notes that mediation is underpinned by operative justice because the process is premised on party autonomy and individualized outcomes. Therefore, mediation provides a form of family justice, even though that justice is different to that available in court. This difference is not inherently problematic, so long as certain notions of justice and fairness are upheld. If this is the case, the promotion of family mediation throughout late 20th-century policy and subsequent legislation sought to erode not family justice, but the operation of formal justice. Family justice has consequently evolved into a category, comprising a variety of forms and different services. The pivotal question, of course, is whether this ongoing development is appropriate.

A noticeable problem occurs when legal oversight is so reduced that the outcome of a dispute can be unfair, unjust or even undecided. Hitchings' (2017: 372) third conception, outsider justice, involves a significant departure from the traditional and official approach. Under this form of justice, the parties resolve family breakdown matters with limited (or no) assistance. Hitchings explains that these parties occupy a delegalized space in which there is effectively no state or legal oversight, providing them with very few opportunities to understand their legal rights and obligations. Unsurprisingly, outsider justice can be damaging for various reasons. For example, there is the risk that the parties apply an incorrect interpretation of the law or rely on social notions of justice without any support. Furthermore, outsider justice is highly inappropriate in cases involving severe power imbalances or vulnerabilities that require a high level of oversight. Outsider justice provides flexibility in relation to both process and outcome, though it may not lead to an objectively correct outcome.

While mediation is said to provide an operative form of justice, it is questioned whether the procedure is plagued with the same issues as its outsider counterpart. The ability of family mediators to adequately perform a number of tasks that would ensure oversight has been doubted for some time. Family mediators were, after all, designed to be limited third parties. If a mediator does not have adequate legal training, mediation may result in a legally incorrect outcome. If a mediator's role is to assist rather than direct the parties, she may be unable to respond to instances of severe power imbalances or abuse. Operative justice, in this sense, could be damaging and harmful to the family justice system at large. Nevertheless, a contemporary understanding of the family mediator enables the profession to be more active. If most mediators take a more adaptable approach to their role, the likelihood of proper and legally correct operative justice may increase. Chapter 4 outlines this type of mediator – the flexible mediator – whose archetype is then confirmed in Part II.

Regardless of whether a mediator adopts a limited or flexible understanding of her role, it is clear that the promotion of family mediation in the late 20th century symbolized a wider trend towards operative (or, worryingly, outsider) justice. This development could become a particular problem if people were steered into mediation when justice could only be obtained in their case through formal forums. As a result, mediation became widely regarded as a process that *could* help disputants, but only when less direct support was required. Concern about the ability of family mediators to support those more complex cases has intensified in recent decades, most notably following LASPO.

2.3 The Legal Aid, Sentencing and Punishment of Offenders Act 2012

In November 2010, the Conservative-Liberal Democrat Coalition published the *Proposals for the Reform of Legal Aid in England and Wales*. LASPO was not the first attack on legal aid, but undoubtedly one of the broadest in both scope and impact. If introduced, the proposals would remove legal aid funding in various areas, including private family matters in court. The consultation's Executive Summary acknowledged the breadth of the proposals:

> The Government strongly believes that access to justice is a hallmark of a civil society. The proposals set out in this consultation paper represent a radical, wide-ranging and ambitious programme of reform which aims to ensure that legal aid is targeted to those who need it most, for the most serious cases in which legal advice or representation is justified. (Ministry of Justice 2010: para 1.2)

Most of the 5,000 responses to the consultation were against the reforms (Ministry of Justice 2011a: paras 5–6). Nevertheless, the Ministry of Justice went ahead with the proposals, citing four key objectives:

> [T]he legal aid scheme needs fundamental reform to:

- discourage unnecessary and adversarial litigation at public expense;
- target legal aid to those who need it most;
- make significant savings in the cost of the scheme; and
- deliver better overall value for money for the taxpayer. (Ministry of Justice 2011a: para 10)

These objectives, all echoing earlier concerns in policy, will now be analysed in relation to the family justice system. Aims three and four are discussed together as a cost-saving objective.

2.3.1 Discouraging unnecessary and adversarial litigation

The first objective of LASPO was to reduce unnecessary and adversarial litigation. Kenneth Clarke, the Secretary of State for Justice from 2010 to 2012, explained the problem in a ministerial foreword to the consultation:

> The current scheme bears very little resemblance to the one that was introduced in 1949. It has expanded, so much so that it is now one of the most expensive in the world, available for a very wide range of issues, including some which should not require any legal expertise to resolve. I believe that this has encouraged people to bring their problems before the courts too readily, even sometimes when the courts are not well placed to provide the best solutions. This has led to the availability of taxpayer funding for unnecessary litigation. (Ministry of Justice 2010: 3)

The same stance was adopted by Jonathan Djanogly, the Under-Secretary of State for Justice at the time, who criticized the legal aid scheme for becoming 'too lawyer-based and too court-based' (House of Commons Justice Committee 2011a: 69). In a similar move to earlier policy, the Ministry of Justice portrayed court as a process that increased bitterness and tension between the parties. Later parts of the LASPO consultation directly connected these views to the resolution of child-related matters:

> The vast majority of children had the contact arrangements with their non-resident parent arranged informally without the assistance of the Courts, lawyers or mediators (85% of children whose resident parent was surveyed and 75% of children whose non-resident parent was surveyed). We are concerned that the provision of legal aid in this area is creating unnecessary litigation and encouraging long, drawn-out and acrimonious cases which can have a significant impact on the long-term well-being of any children involved.
>
> We do not consider that it will generally be in the best interest of the children involved for these essentially personal matters to be resolved in the adversarial forum of a court. The Government's view is that people should take responsibility for resolving such issues themselves, and that this is best for both the parents and the children involved. We therefore consider that scarce resources should be targeted to areas where publicly funded legal assistance is more likely to be justified

> and of practical benefit to the parties involved. (Ministry of Justice 2010: paras 4.209–4.210)

The preference for out-of-court settlement was apparent, with the Ministry of Justice arguing that separating parents should make their child arrangements themselves. Whereas earlier policy attempted to conceal this idea with a language of autonomy, the push for individual responsibility had become far more explicit. The Ministry of Justice (2010: para 4.157) similarly acknowledged that the majority of ancillary relief orders were uncontested, and praised those who were 'able and willing to take responsibility for organising their own financial affairs'.

The Family Justice Review, published between 2010 and 2011, expressed a similar stance. Headed by David Norgrove, the interim report concluded that the family justice system was neither 'coherent' nor properly 'managed' (Family Justice Review 2011a: para 2.61). Reasons included long delays to proceedings, confusion among parents and their children, and a lack of trust between the different organizations involved (Family Justice Review 2011a: paras 2.27–2.60). While the Family Justice Review (2011a: para 5.62) did not adopt the exact same rhetoric as the Ministry of Justice in terms of personal responsibility, the panel stated that the private family law system should be organized to give families the information they needed 'to resolve any issues independently'. State funding for private family law proceedings was consequently framed as unnecessary and unjustified throughout both the LASPO proposals and the Family Justice Review. This similarity, furthermore, highlights a long-standing consensus among policy makers that more disputes should be moved outside the court process.

The objective to reduce unnecessary litigation also involved downplaying the seriousness of private family disputes, particularly financial matters upon divorce. In the LASPO consultation, the Ministry of Justice (2010: para 4.155) argued that disputes relating to ancillary relief were not 'of sufficiently high priority routinely to receive legal aid support'. It further claimed that separating couples did not 'face the same issues as clients who are at immediate risk of being made homeless', giving little weight to the consequences of relationship breakdown. This stance was reiterated in a later part of the consultation paper:

> While we understand that those going through relationship breakdown may be dealing with a difficult situation, both emotionally and often practically too, *we do not consider that this means that the parents bringing these cases are always likely to be particularly vulnerable* (compared with detained mental health patients, or elderly care home residents, for example), or that their emotional involvement in the case will necessarily mean that they are unable to present it themselves. *There is*

> *no reason to believe that such cases will be routinely legally complex*. As noted in paragraph 4.156, there are also other sources of advice available to help couples following the breakdown of their relationship. (Ministry of Justice 2010: para 4.207; emphasis added)

The trivialization of private family matters was two-fold. First, people involved in family disputes were not recognized as 'vulnerable'. The Ministry of Justice used extreme examples of vulnerability to support this point, overlooking the high levels of stress and ill-health that were experienced by people involved in family disputes (YouGov 2020: 18). The Ministry of Justice in this excerpt also disregarded the extremely vulnerable disputant who faces the risk of homelessness upon relationship breakdown. Second, family disputes were considered straightforward in terms of legal content. If a matter was not 'legally complex', there was supposedly little justification for funding legal advice or representation. The Ministry of Justice argued that parties could still access 'other sources of advice', though only cited online material to support this point.[17] While the Ministry of Justice (2011a: para 47) later admitted that some private family law matters could 'raise particularly complex issues', it maintained that these cases were not 'routinely complex'.

Unsurprisingly, the government did not present these proposals as an affront to family justice. In written evidence to the House of Commons Justice Committee's review of LASPO, the Ministry of Justice (2014: 2) advanced: 'Access to justice should not simply be equated to access to government funded legal advice. Courts should be seen as the last resort, not the first. The Government is satisfied that LASPO does not undermine access to justice.' Traditionally, legal support was regarded as vital to navigating the family law system. By comparison, the Ministry of Justice was now claiming that few family matters merited legal advice. Yet nowhere in the proposals did the government explain how family law disputants could still achieve justice without legal aid. If 'government funded legal advice' was no longer a prerequisite to family justice, how exactly was justice to be achieved?

The solution, once again, was to move more disputes outside court. Under the LASPO proposals, legal aid would remain available for cases heard in family mediation. Whereas the court was depicted as a damaging environment, Jonathan Djanogly described mediation as 'less contentious, less adversarial and actually where the parties buy into the results' (House of Commons Justice Committee 2011a: 73). The Ministry of Justice claimed:

[17] 'In addition, there is advice available online to help couples to navigate the divorce process. The presence of these alternatives is not determinative, but makes the provision of legal aid in these cases less likely to be justified' (Ministry of Justice 2010: para 4.156).

> Legal aid funding can be used to support lengthy and intractable family cases which may be resolved out of court if funding were not available. In such cases, we would like to move to a position where parties are encouraged to settle using mediation, rather than protracting disputes unnecessarily by having a lawyer paid for by legal aid. (Ministry of Justice 2010: para 4.211)

The cuts to legal aid were thus justified on the basis that funding would be redirected from legal assistance and representation to family mediation. In the words of the Ministry of Justice (2010: para 4.212), the legal aid scheme would 'provid[e] access to mediation'. This stance marked a significant departure from the long-standing idea that access to justice was achieved through access to court and lawyers. Simply put, the government no longer saw traditional justice as pivotal to the resolution of family matters. Instead, the intention was to move parties out of court, regardless of whether that new process provided a different type of justice or something different altogether. The Family Justice Review (2011b: para 115) summarized this objective in its final report, writing: 'It should become the norm that where parents need additional support to resolve disputes they would first attempt mediation or another dispute resolution service.' This stance is strong evidence of a shift in policy from an official to an operative form of family justice: family mediation was to become the primary option for family matters, resulting in reduced funding for court.

2.3.2 Targeting legal aid

The second aim of LASPO was to target and reduce legal aid. The Ministry of Justice wrote:

> [W]e also believe in light of the way the [legal aid] scheme has expanded since its establishment, that it is right in principle to reduce its scope. We have concluded that it is no longer affordable to provide legal aid for the extensive range of issues for which it is currently available. (Ministry of Justice 2010: para 4.3)

According to the government, the legal aid scheme had gone way beyond its means. Reinstating the previous and supposedly limited system was therefore justified. However, the Ministry of Justice failed to acknowledge that legal aid had 'never been a universal service available to all who needed it' (Hynes and Robins 2009: 131). It also did not consider how, as mentioned in section 2.1.3, various reforms had already reduced the demand and supply of civil legal aid. These developments included a tightening of eligibility criteria, as well as some adjustments to the mean-tested thresholds in line with inflation

(Richardson and Speed 2019: 137). An increasing number of families fell outside the scope of the legal aid scheme as a result. While 70–80 per cent of the population was originally eligible for legal aid (Sommerlad 2004: 354), this proportion declined to 40 per cent by 1973 (Hynes 2012: 21) and 29 per cent by 2009 (Brooke 2017: 23). The Ministry of Justice, as expected, did not cite these figures in the consultation paper or government response. The Rushcliffe Committee understood the problems within the legal system to be 'inequality in access to justice' (Kaganas 2017: 172), yet the LASPO reforms appeared to place all fault – and thus responsibility – on disputants themselves.

By reducing the scope of legal aid, funding would again be targeted to those in *need*. In opening the consultation, the Ministry of Justice (2010: para 2.2) claimed LASPO would 'ensure that legal aid is targeted to those who need it most, for the most serious cases in which legal advice or representation is justified'. This objective was to take priority over all the other aims of the family justice system:

> Although we recognise that the issues which arise in these cases [private family law matters] will sometimes be of high importance, it is necessary, in order to reduce spending on legal aid, to target scarce resources in a fair and balanced way at those cases for which legal aid is most justified. (Ministry of Justice 2010: para 4.158)

Throughout the LASPO proposals, the Ministry of Justice adopted a narrow interpretation of need. In particular, need was strictly associated with vulnerability (Ministry of Justice 2010: para 4.12). The government did not perceive people in private family law cases as particularly vulnerable, nor view their issues as legally complex. Fewer family law disputants were thus understood to need financial support.

Academic commentary is particularly critical of LASPO on this point. Kaganas (2017: 177) submits that the use of the term 'vulnerable' portrays legal aid recipients as incapable of resolving their disputes without support. This depiction creates a harsh distinction between legal aid recipients and privately funded disputants. While the former is regarded as lacking the autonomy to take responsibility for their legal disputes, the latter is praised for funding their dispute. Diduck (2013: 97) similarly describes vulnerability as 'the friendly face of dependency'. She argues that vulnerability implies 'a state for which the individual is not so obviously to blame', warranting state support. Legal aid recipients were thus construed as vulnerable and dependent, whereas those who paid for their disputes were applauded for being resilient and autonomous. Diduck (2013: 97) adds that this position was so narrowly construed in the LASPO consultation that the only people considered vulnerable were 'the incompetent' and victims of abuse. To illustrate Diduck's point, it is worth returning to an earlier excerpt from the LASPO proposals. In one part of the consultation document, the Ministry of Justice (2010: para 4.207) stated that those involved in relationship breakdown were not 'particularly vulnerable (compared with detained mental health patients, or elderly care home residents, for example)'. The Ministry of Justice adopted a high threshold of vulnerability, meaning very few individuals involved in family matters would be considered in need of support.

Even when the Ministry of Justice identified a specific group as vulnerable, the definitions employed were often so narrow that many members of that group were still unable to receive legal aid. A key population affected by this issue were victims of domestic abuse. Under the LASPO proposals, victims would continue to receive legal aid for private family law proceedings (Ministry of Justice 2010: para 4.67).[18] Implicit within this exception was an understanding that adjudication was preferable in certain disputes, notably where the victim 'may be unable to assert their rights and may face intimidation because of risk of harm'. However, the level of evidence required to obtain legal aid became a noticeable source of contention as LASPO progressed through Parliament. According to the consultation document, legal aid would be available if there were ongoing domestic abuse proceedings, if a non-molestation order (or other relevant order) had been issued against the other party, or if the other party had been convicted of a criminal offence relating to family abuse. Critics of the proposals described this criterion as a 'high hurdle' that excluded the majority of domestic abuse cases where victims did not come forward or initiate formal proceedings against their ex-partner (Legal Aid, Sentencing and Punishment of Offenders Bill Deb, 6 September 2011: col 358). By comparison, LASPO's advocates prioritized a cost-saving analysis. For instance, Jonathan Djanogly argued that the state must 'prioritis[e] our resources so that legal aid will be available for the cases in which the most serious issues are at stake' (Legal Aid, Sentencing and Punishment of Offenders Bill Deb, 6 September 2011: col 232). Kenneth Clarke similarly acknowledged the tension between protecting domestic abuse victims and reducing unnecessary litigation:

> We have a clear, wide definition trying to catch the variety of circumstances that will evidence recent domestic violence so that the argument that the victim should not have to face her abuser without having legal representation can be countered. But we do not want to shift the vast majority of private family law cases away from mediation

[18] This category includes potential victims of domestic abuse: Legal Aid, Sentencing and Punishment of Offenders Act 2012, sch 1, para 12(1).

> into publicly funded adversarial litigation. (Hansard HC Deb, 17 April 2012, vol 543: cols 220–221)

Despite Clarke's claim that a 'wide' interpretation would be adopted, the domestic abuse exemption was limited to a tiny pool of cases upon LASPO's enactment (House of Commons Justice Committee 2015: paras 66 and 69). Originally, the alleged abuse (and its subsequent evidence) had to have occurred no more than 24 months before the legal aid application. This time limit was extended to 60 months in 2016 following a legal challenge by Rights of Women and completely removed in 2018.[19] Regardless, the domestic abuse exception remains heavily criticized. Choudhry and Herring (2017: 160), for instance, submit that the restrictions on legal aid infringe on victims' human rights. The types of evidence required to demonstrate domestic abuse have also been extended, yet the exemption remains inaccessible to victims of coercive control who often struggle to prove that this abuse has taken place (Ministry of Justice 2019: para 652). Many victims without the funds to pay for legal support subsequently cannot receive legal aid. They must choose between self-representation in court (considered in section 2.3.5) or family mediation, two options that are widely regarded as inappropriate in this context.

2.3.3 Saving costs and delivering value to the taxpayer

The LASPO proposals were part of a broader austerity programme following the 2007–2008 financial crisis and subsequent recession. In a bid to reduce the country's deficit, the government proposed to cut the Ministry of Justice budget by 23 per cent (HM Treasury 2010: para 2.68). In one section of the 2010 Spending Review, headed under the word 'Fairness', the Coalition government proposed: 'The Government will consult on major reforms to the legal aid system to deliver access to justice at lower cost to the taxpayer. This will involve taking tough choices about the types of case that should receive public funding, and focusing support on those who need it most' (HM Treasury 2010: para 2.73).

To the Coalition government, an effective legal aid scheme balanced the rights of legal aid recipients with their funders – the taxpayers. Yet the LASPO proposals, released just one month after the Spending Review, were anything but fair to the disputants who would lose all access to public funding in court. Moore and Newbury (2017: 35) recognize this disparity,

[19] *R (Rights of Women) v Secretary of State for Justice* [2016] EWCA Civ 91; Civil Legal Aid (Procedure) (Amendment) Regulations 2016, SI 2016/516, reg 2(2); Civil Legal Aid (Procedure) (Amendment) (No. 2) Regulations 2017, SI 2017/1237, reg 2(2)(a).

warning that 'the arguments about the social benefit of legal aid have been sidelined'. Mant (2017: 254) similarly comments that the LASPO proposals were based on an assessment of legal aid 'in terms of its expense, rather than the non-economic role it has' in ensuring access to justice. The cost-saving rhetoric was not employed fairly, but rather used in a way that completely disregarded the social utility of legal aid.

Under the LASPO proposals, the taxpayer received preferential treatment. This is demonstrated in an excerpt from the consultation paper in which the Ministry of Justice (2010: para 2.8) claimed that the high number of court cases 'led to the availability of taxpayer funding for unnecessary litigation'. The Ministry of Justice (2010: para 4.3) also wrote that individuals should 'work to resolve their own problems, rather than resorting to litigation at a significant cost to the taxpayer'. Jonathan Djanogly expressed the same view in a foreword to a 2011 paper:

> Instead of ensuring that the use of law is generally a matter of last resort, today's legal aid system too often encourages people to bring their problems before courts, even when they are not the right place to provide good solutions, and sometimes for litigation that people paying from their own pocket would not have pursued. (Ministry of Justice 2011b: 3)

Djanogly constructs a negative, almost criminal, picture of legal aid recipients who take money from the taxpayer to fund an egocentric legal venture they would not pay for themselves. He overlooks the possibility that individuals do not finance their disputes because they cannot afford representation, or seek legal aid for genuine reasons beyond the limited interpretation of need. This stance is symbolic of a common trend in New Right politics which separates the 'citizen' into three identities: the taxpayer, the scrounger and the consumer (Clarke 2004: 39). The taxpayer is pitted against the other two groups, leading their interests to be prioritized above all other concerns.

If the taxpayer was to take priority in all instances, why was it acceptable for legal aid to be used in family mediation? Nowhere in the LASPO consultation does the Ministry of Justice describe legal aid for family mediation as unnecessary or unjustified. Nor does the organization explain how legal aid recipients for mediation are different to those wanting to attend court. The likely reason is the perceived cost of mediation to the state. In one part of the consultation document, the Ministry of Justice (2010: para 4.72) posited that 'the wider benefits' of mediation included those 'to the taxpayer' as it 'reduc[ed] the volume of business that ends up in court'. Mediation, like all other procedures, was assessed in terms of its cost to the public purse. The need for a comprehensive investigation into the value of mediation – as well as its limitations – was subsequently disregarded.

A simultaneous consultation on civil county court reform further demonstrates the exploitation of mediation by the Coalition government. In *Solving Disputes in the County Courts*, Kenneth Clarke claimed that civil cases were 'resolved too late, too expensively, with business in particular exposed to high and disproportionate costs' (Ministry of Justice 2011c: 4). Clarke's statement was not unique. However, it was his 'rejection of the language of justice', as Genn (2012: 415) explains, that is particularly shocking. Clarke advanced: 'The result is a system that needs to focus more on dispute resolution and debt recovery for the majority of its users, rather than the loftier ideals of "justice", that cause many to pursue their cases beyond the point that it is economic for them to do so' (Ministry of Justice 2011c: 7).

In just one sentence, Clarke associated the government's cost-saving objective with a workable idea of justice. By comparison, he described traditional images of justice as aloof and unnecessarily expensive. Clarke was not concerned with ensuring the optimum process or outcome, but rather how to run the most cost-effective system for both the state and the taxpayer. While it will be argued throughout *Rethinking Family Mediation* that the value of mediation in both the family and civil justice systems has often been overlooked, it cannot be forgotten that successive governments have misappropriated the process in an attempt to save costs. This neoliberalist trend (discussed in section 2.4) was a key driving force behind mediation's development within England and Wales.

2.3.4 LASPO's implementation

LASPO was given Royal Assent on 1 May 2012. Part One, covering the changes to legal aid, was implemented on 1 April 2013. Legal aid funding remained for those attending family mediation. Meanwhile, legal aid for private family law court proceedings was limited to a small number of cases, notably where there was evidence of domestic abuse (including child abuse) or the dispute came under exceptional case funding.[20] The regulations published under LASPO also tightened the eligibility criteria for legal aid in terms of income and capital.[21] From April 2013, legal aid was only available to civil and family law disputants if their gross income was under £2,657 a month. Recipients must also have had a disposable income and disposable capital under £733 a month and £8,000 respectively. These thresholds have not been increased over ten years since LASPO's enactment.[22]

20 Legal Aid, Sentencing and Punishment of Offenders Act 2012, ss 8–11.

21 Civil Legal Aid (Financial Resources and Payment for Services) Regulations 2013, SI 2013/480, regs 7–8.

22 The same thresholds are cited by the Legal Aid Agency (2023) in their guidance on determining financial eligibility for legal aid.

Turning to LASPO's impact on family mediation, the Ministry of Justice and Legal Aid Agency (2014: para 10) predicted that the reforms would lead to an extra 10,000 mediations a year. In reality, family mediation intake declined drastically. From 2013–2014 to 2014–2015, the number of legal aid family mediation starts dropped by 38 percentage points from 13,609 to 8,438 (Ministry of Justice 2024b : table 7.2). Mediation intake failed to recover, reaching a low of 6,321 in 2017–2018. More recent figures suggest some improvement, with 7,353 mediation cases being funded through legal aid in 2022–2023 and 7,166 in 2023–2024. Nonetheless, these numbers are nowhere close to pre-LASPO levels.

A key reason for the decline in family mediation numbers was the withdrawal of legal advice from the legal aid scheme.[23] Concerns were raised during the LASPO proposals that removing funding for early legal advice would lead to fewer settlements (Ministry of Justice 2011a: para 44). This was because most parties only became aware of mediation after meeting with a lawyer (House of Commons Justice Committee 2015: para 142). If fewer parties saw a solicitor, fewer people would learn about mediation and subsequently attempt the process. The withdrawal of legal aid would also remove the financial incentive for lawyers to refer their clients to mediation, as they would receive more money by encouraging the parties to try solicitor negotiation (Bloch et al 2014: 13). Combined with the poor quality of public information on alternative procedures to court, family mediation services took the hit (House of Commons Justice Committee 2015: para 144).

In a bid to increase mediation numbers before LASPO, a 2011 Pre-Application Protocol stipulated that all parties to private family law matters were *expected* to attend a Mediation, Information and Assessment Meeting (MIAM).[24] A MIAM is analogous to the intake meetings introduced under the Family Law Act 1996. Its objectives are to, first, educate potential users about mediation, and, second, screen their dispute for suitability. The Pre-Application Protocol, however, had little impact on the number of people attending both MIAMs and mediation. This is because judges were reluctant to delay court proceedings if a party had not attended a MIAM (Hunter 2017: 191). After LASPO's enactment, the number of publicly funded MIAMs decreased by 56 percentage points from 30,665 to 13,390 (Ministry of Justice 2024b: table 7.1). The government quickly enacted the Children and Families Act 2014 in response. Under section 10, most applicants to court for private family law matters (including child arrangements orders) were, and still are, *required* to attend a MIAM.[25] Respondents were *expected*

[23] For the withdrawal of lawyers within family justice more generally, see section 4.1.1.

[24] FPR, SI 2010/2955, PD 3A.

[25] Also see FPR, SI 2010/2955, PD 3A para 2.

Figure 2.1: Number of family mediation starts and Mediation, Information and Assessment Meetings through legal aid, by financial year

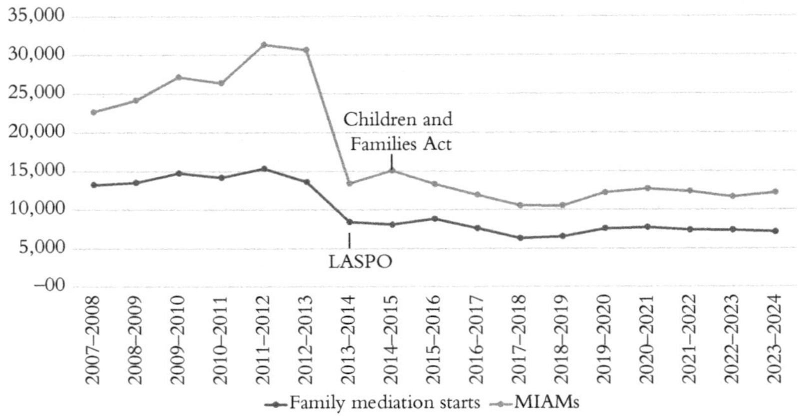

Source: Ministry of Justice 2024b

to attend. Similar to the rules under LASPO, some parties were exempt from the MIAM requirement.[26] While the Ministry of Justice did not propose to mandate family mediation until 2023, parliamentary debates at the time of the 2014 Act reveal a clear intention 'to reduce unnecessary litigation' and move disputes out of court (Children and Families Bill Deb 14 March 2013: col 261).

Nonetheless, the Children and Families Act 2014 had limited effect (Figure 2.1). The number of legal aid MIAMs slightly increased to 15,076 in 2014–2015, but reached a low of 10,506 in 2018–2019 (Ministry of Justice 2024b: table 7.1). MIAM numbers have remained poor in the early 2020s, sitting at 11,629 in 2022–2023 and 12,159 in 2023–2024. Anecdotal evidence further suggests that many disputants still go to court despite attending a MIAM (Cameron 2015). Notwithstanding decades of attempts to decentre court, it is clear that most families do not view mediation as an attractive option. Many individuals continue to opt for court even though they have little to no access to legal support, drastically changing the profile of the family justice disputant.

2.3.5 The growing number of Litigants in Person

Since LASPO, there has been a sharp rise in the number of individuals attending court without legal representation, known as Litigants in Person (LiPs). Between January and March 2013, two-fifths of private family cases

---

26 This included victims of domestic abuse.

had legal representation on both sides (Ministry of Justice 2024c : table 10). In 14 per cent of cases, both parties were LiPs. Yet by January to March 2014, the number of cases involving two LiPs had doubled to 28 per cent. Only a minority of cases after LASPO involve full legal representation, with over four-fifths of private family law cases in both 2022 and 2023 involving at least one LiP. Put simply, LiPs now dominate the family court.

Similar to the drop in mediation intake, the sharp rise of LiPs was a foreseeable consequence of the LASPO reforms. The Ministry of Justice (2010: para 4.267) acknowledged the possible increase, but reiterated that many of these cases could be resolved outside of court.[27] It conceded: 'litigants are entitled to bring their cases to court, and to represent themselves, if they wish'. From this statement alone, it appears that the government did not have an issue with the actual use of court. Instead, their problem was with these cases being funded by the legal aid scheme and its taxpayers. While the Ministry of Justice (2019: para 609) later admitted that LASPO did not lead to a reduction in litigation for family matters, very little change has since been enacted to support LiPs. This is because, in the contemporary family justice system, the parties have the autonomy – or responsibility – to resolve their disputes how they wish. The main difference to the traditional system, then, is that disputants are now expected to foot the bill.

LiPs pose a noticeable problem for the family court system. This is because the court process is premised on the 'full representation model', whereby both parties have legal representation (Trinder et al 2014: 53).[28] Under this format, private family law proceedings are highly standardized and rehearsed. However, Trinder et al's (2014) research on LiPs in private family law cases pre-LASPO shows that most self-representing litigants struggle to navigate court proceedings. LiPs regularly file the wrong form, incorrectly complete documentation and present matters that are irrelevant to the dispute (Trinder et al 2014: 23–30). These problems are exacerbated by the complexity of family law disputes, many of which involve serious welfare concerns, substance abuse and instances of poor mental health (Trinder et al 2014: 29). Similar findings are identified by Mant (2020; 2022) post-LASPO, who confirms that disputes involving LiPs do not follow a consistent format. In her interview sample of 23 LiPs, some individuals understood advocacy as part of a broader 'fight' (Mant 2020: 434). These participants spoke in court as if presenting was the only opportunity to make their case. Meanwhile, other LiPs adopted a 'flight' response to advocacy and focused on written

[27] The Family Justice Review (2011a: para 5.55) also predicted the development in their interim report, noting that LASPO 'may result in greater numbers of people representing themselves'.

[28] Trinder et al's model was previously discussed in section 1.2.1.

communication. These different approaches had a significant impact on the direction of a case, as well as the type of support required from a judge. Mant (2020: 437–439) concludes that the court system has not adapted to the needs of LiPs, and can only begin to do so if the various experiences of LiPs are placed at the centre of reform.

Beyond the courtroom, the amount of legal need not met by lawyers has increased over time.[29] In an early 2000s survey, 96 per cent of respondents with a justiciable problem sought advice for divorce, followed by 97 per cent for relationship breakdown (Pleasence 2004: 58). Yet in a similar survey conducted in 2014, only 45 per cent of respondents with a family problem obtained legal advice (Franklyn et al 2017: 57). A more recent legal needs survey, conducted by YouGov (2020: 46–47) in 2019, found that only one-third of individuals with a family law issue used a solicitor. Many individuals sought advice and support through other means, including the not-for-profit advice sector (YouGov 2020: 47). The Ministry of Justice has regularly used the availability of these services, such as Citizens Advice Bureaux and Law Centres, to justify the cuts to legal aid. However, evidence submitted to the House of Commons Justice Committee (2015: paras 73–80) suggests that the availability of advice (in both the for-profit and not-for-profit sectors) has declined after LASPO. The number of organizations providing free or affordable legal support has drastically reduced in certain areas, creating what are widely known as 'advice deserts' (Byrom 2017: 223). With lawyers primarily removed from family justice, traditional legal support has become an optional add-on for a small population who can afford the costs involved.

How can family justice be secured after LASPO with limited access to lawyers? The reintroduction of the full representation model is unlikely as the format costs money that the Ministry of Justice simply will not spend. To continue to understand family justice in the traditional and official sense will therefore provide little support for the rising number of LiPs. This problem is recognized by Mant (2022: 8), who writes that LASPO has 'torn up the rulebook on how the various institutions of family justice are supposed to respond'. She argues that LASPO is not the 'end of family justice', but rather a 'turning point' from which to develop a contemporary family law system. Engler (2012: 159–160) likewise envisions a 'coordinated access to justice strategy' that involves adjusting the roles of legal professionals to provide further support to those without any representation.[30] The alternative, then, is to accept that the purposes of different family law apparatuses have changed and adjust our dominant understanding of family justice accordingly.

[29] Further detail is provided in section 4.1.1.

[30] This adjustment is one of 'three prongs' to Engler's vision, alongside the use of assistance programmes and the introduction of a civil right to counsel.

Rethinking Family Mediation takes a similar approach by considering whether justice is, or can be, achieved for families through mediation. Rather than viewing mediation as separate from the justice system and thus incapable of ensuring justice, it suggests that the purpose behind family mediation (and the role of the mediator) has adapted to the post-LASPO contemporary climate. Mediation has become more about justice, though whether this type of justice is desirable or can even be secured by its mediators remains to be confirmed.

2.4 Reclaiming mediation from a neoliberal agenda

LASPO was not a one-off event. Rather, LASPO embodied a long-standing agenda by successive governments to reduce state support in family matters and only provide public funding in exceptional circumstances. The inner zone of family justice, specifically court, has lost its primacy as a result of these developments. While mediation cannot provide justice in the traditional sense, it is submitted that the process has developed in such a way to become one of many potential family justice apparatuses.

Some readers will view this argument as controversial because of the way in which family mediation has been misappropriated by successive neoliberal governments. Without further explanation, there is a risk that *Rethinking Family Mediation* could be read as a commendation of neoliberal thought. There is also a risk that its findings could be used to justify future reform that furthers the attack on traditional and official family justice. However, the real purpose behind this monograph is to encourage a full investigation into the potential of family mediation in supporting a contemporary family justice system. Mediation's value in sustaining this notion of family justice has been overlooked, particularly where the process is regularly associated with neoliberal thought.

A neoliberalist approach promotes the unregulated free market, viewing 'human action' in economic terms (Harvey 2005: 2–3). This cost-based analysis is felt across society and is applied to numerous policies, including the non-economic (Brown 2015; Mant 2017: 247–248). Legal concepts fundamental to the welfare state, notably legal aid and access to justice, are similarly 'clothed in marketspeak' (Giddings and Robertson 2002: 438). Harvey (2005: 33) summarizes the current position: 'neoliberalism has meant, in short, the financialization of everything'. The LASPO reforms are an obvious example of a neoliberal agenda, with the Ministry of Justice evaluating justice in terms of its economic costs throughout the proposal documents. This neoliberalist approach has, unfortunately, continued long after LASPO's introduction. In the post-implementation review of LASPO, the Ministry of Justice (2019: para 676) acknowledged that the reforms made significant savings to the legal aid scheme. They noted, however, that the reforms only partially delivered better value for money for the taxpayer (Ministry of Justice 2019: para 684). Their agenda remained focused on saving costs, overlooking LASPO's detrimental impact across the family law system.

This emphasis on costs was, of course, anticipated. LASPO was, as previously mentioned, the amalgamation of several decades of (neoliberal) disdain for legal support and access to court. Throughout the mid to late 20th century, the divorce rate rose at an alarming rate which placed a noticeable strain on public spending. The subsequent reduction of legal aid and upsurge of mediation occurred alongside various economic and social policies under late 1970s to 1990s Thatcherism that limited the power of trade unions, reduced taxes and furthered the privatization of previously public institutions (Harvey 2005: 22). Family mediation was the perfect match for a neoliberalist state; the process was cheaper than court and also promoted individual responsibility for family matters. In the words of Barlow et al (2017: 16), family mediation was never a 'neoliberal Trojan horse', but quickly became 'co-opted' into its agenda.

2.4.1 2020s policy on family mediation

During the early stages of writing this monograph, the Ministry of Justice published proposals that would solidify family mediation's position in the contemporary justice system. These proposals were part of a broader policy agenda that sought to alleviate the knock-on effects of LASPO, albeit within the confines of affordability and low costs.[31] *Rethinking Family Mediation* would be outdated before its release if these developments were not taken into account.

In March 2021, the Ministry of Justice announced the Family Mediation Voucher Scheme, providing parties with up to £500 towards the cost of mediation (Ministry of Justice 2021a).[32] Parties were not means-tested to obtain this funding, and could even use the voucher scheme if they received legal aid. The scheme was initially funded with £1 million, receiving an additional £800,000 in funding in August 2021 (Ministry of Justice 2021b). The scheme was extended with a further £1.27 million in January 2022 (Ministry of Justice 2022b) and another £5.4 million in June 2022 (Ministry of Justice 2022c). At this point in time, the Family Mediation Voucher

[31] Other developments included the potential introduction of a new means test for civil legal aid, following a review by the Ministry of Justice (2023a). The proposed test had not been published as of July 2024.

[32] £500 was available for each mediation case that applied for the scheme. This money did not have to be equally split between the parties.

Scheme was funded until March 2023. The government heavily praised the scheme, finding that full or partial agreement was reached in roughly two-thirds of cases where a voucher was used (Ministry of Justice 2022c; Sixsmith 2023).

The same month that the Voucher Scheme was set to expire, Dominic Raab, Secretary of State for Justice from October 2022 to April 2023,[33] spoke to the Constitution Committee. His response suggested that upcoming reform would promote mediation even further:

> If the mediation is the carrot, I am also looking actively, and we will prepare legislation in due course, at what the – 'stick' is not quite the right word – check is. That is so you do not get people going into mediation, resolving the issue, or being on the cusp of resolution, but thinking that they will double dip and have another crack, just in case they could get something better in court. (House of Lords 2023: 16)

Raab did not specify what the potential reform could look like, though he acknowledged that 'we will need to invest in the mediation to make it work'. Several weeks later, the government announced the extension of the Voucher Scheme (until April 2025) alongside a consultation on the resolution of private family law arrangements (Ministry of Justice 2023b; 2023c).[34] The consultation included proposals to require all parties to child arrangements or financial disputes to demonstrate a 'reasonable attempt to mediate' before commencing court proceedings (Ministry of Justice 2023c: 27–29). The Ministry of Justice appeared to take a firm stance on the proposals, asking respondents for their views on the meaning of a 'reasonable attempt to mediate', not whether this requirement was desirable in the first place.[35] Parties would be exempt from this requirement if they were self-certified (for instance, on the grounds of domestic abuse) or deemed unsuitable for mediation by a mediator at an information meeting. To ensure that mediation was attempted where appropriate, the Ministry of Justice (2023c: 37–39) proposed to grant judges new powers to compel parties to mediate, in addition to the option to order court fees if an individual refused to engage in mediation with no genuine reason.

33 Raab was also Secretary of State for Justice from September 2021 to September 2022.

34 A similar consultation on the introduction of mandatory mediation for small claims cases in the county court was also released the previous year (Ministry of Justice 2022d).

35 Question 8 read: 'What should "a reasonable attempt to mediate" look like? Should this focus on the number of mediation sessions, time taken, a person's approach to mediation or other possibilities?' (Ministry of Justice 2023c: 41).

The Ministry of Justice gave the following justification for its proposals:

> The Government remains committed to ensuring effective access to the family courts. However, we also believe a balance can be found which supports families, where appropriate, to resolve child arrangements and financial matters out of court. This will allow the resources of the courts to be focused on families and children who are most in need of the court's involvement and protection. (Ministry of Justice 2023c: 6)

This consultation largely replicated the rhetoric underpinning the LASPO proposals. The Ministry of Justice emphasized the importance of access to court, yet simultaneously called for that right to be balanced with the push for settlement. The proposals for mandatory mediation, in fact, went further than LASPO by indicating that access to court itself, not only funded access, would be reserved for those in 'need'. While this perspective was not explicitly connected to a cost-saving objective, it was clearly underpinned by a neoliberal agenda.

Nonetheless, the Ministry of Justice backtracked from its proposals just ten months later. In the government response, the Ministry of Justice (2024a: 18) acknowledged respondents' concerns that the proposals would compel victims of abuse into mediation, as well as the need to consider the relative benefits of other dispute resolution procedures (including a 'one-lawyer-two-clients' model of legal advice).[36] It subsequently concluded:

> The Government remains committed to helping more families understand and benefit from dispute resolution. However, we are not proposing to change the law to introduce a requirement on parties to attend mediation before applying to court at this time. Instead, we will focus on delivering the package of measures that helps parents/carers resolve their issues at every stage of the process. (Ministry of Justice 2024a: 18)

The suggested package of measures – including the provision of 'earlier targeted information' for families and 'increased support for parties who need it' – appeared wide-ranging. The Ministry of Justice also announced plans to work with the Family Mediation Council to improve domestic abuse screening and training for mediators.[37] Nonetheless, the Ministry of Justice provided no further information on these provisions. To this extent, the package of measures appears weak in their impact and may, once again, do

36 See section 8.1 for further discussion on the 'one-lawyer-two-clients' model.

37 The use of mediation in cases involving domestic violence has become heavily debated since LASPO, as mentioned in sections 4.1.2 and 6.1.

little to provide further support to those impacted by the LASPO reforms. Forthcoming developments are instead likely to continue a neoliberal misappropriation of mediation, only improving access to the procedure if it leads to a reduction in state expenditure and responsibility for family matters.

2.4.2 Calls for a return to traditional family justice

An obvious response to the issues within the post-LASPO landscape is to call for the legislation to be repealed. Legal aid could be reinstated to provide funding for people who want to use court. Hurdles to court, such as mandatory MIAMs, could also be removed. This reinstatement would support traditional notions of both procedural and substantive justice, reversing some of the changes enacted by neoliberal governments.

It is understandable to view the late 20th century as a golden age where funding was prevalent and most legal needs were met. However, the family justice system during this period was far from perfect. In fact, court and solicitor-based negotiation have never been ideal forums for all family disputes. As Davis (1988: 86) recognizes, the service provided by solicitors can 'vary spectacularly in quality'. In support of this argument, Davis et al (1994: 139) find that financial and property matters are prolonged in court. Solicitors regularly put their clients under pressure to settle, even if a proposed agreement is unfair. The authors identify a number of problems with the legal divorce process, including overburdened lawyers and a lack of predictability in court proceedings (Davis et al 1994: 253–254). In a similar vein, Sarat and Felstiner (1995: 45–48, 57) discover that divorce lawyers tend to keep their clients at a distance, preferring to only engage with the legal aspect of the case. High levels of procrastination from lawyers and their clients mean that court hearings are regularly drawn out and delayed (Sarat and Felstiner 1995: 59).[38] Lawyers also provide very little emotional support to their clients, generating further frustration and upset.[39] Additional work by Eekelaar et al (2000: 86) shows that solicitors frequently minimize allegations of abuse as one-off events. More recent research, including Barlow et al's (2017: 114–115) Mapping Paths to Family Justice project, identifies similar issues with solicitor negotiation.

Even if the court was the optimum process for all family matters, it is highly unlikely that a future government would reinstate the pre-LASPO rules around legal aid. The fact the Ministry of Justice even proposed to introduce mandatory family mediation suggests that policy will continue to

[38] This view is supported by Davis (1988: 107).

[39] This finding should be contrasted with Davis (1988: 88), who finds that lawyers often act as counsellors and can be a 'sounding board' for clients. Nonetheless, Davis acknowledges that lawyers regularly devalue this line of work.

view the process as a solution to the primary issues within the contemporary family justice system. This stance is also evidenced by a 2022 consultation on the means test for legal aid eligibility, which set out proposals to increase the income threshold and capital threshold for potential recipients (Ministry of Justice 2022a). While the specific reforms are outside the scope of this monograph, the Ministry of Justice's interpretation of the history of legal aid is worth a brief investigation. Early in the consultation, the Ministry of Justice (2022a: para 11) referred to the 'scale of contributions' used to fund the original legal aid scheme, meaning most of the public was eligible for legal aid but made some financial contribution to the costs of their dispute. The Ministry of Justice (2022a: para 12) then claimed: 'Similarly, the [LASPO] consultation stated … "The Government's rationale for reform is to ensure that those who can afford it should pay for, or contribute towards, the costs of their case".'

In this excerpt, the Ministry of Justice submitted that the LASPO reforms adopted the same understanding of legal aid as found in the 1944 Rushcliffe report.[40] The Ministry of Justice is, to some extent, correct: the initial legal aid scheme was never designed to provide comprehensive support for all individuals. However, the scheme was certainly more expansive and readily available in the mid-20th century compared to the post-LASPO landscape. Over several decades, successive governments have shrunk the objectives of legal aid to provide funding on the basis of need. The Ministry of Justice (2022a: para 90) even reiterates this focus in the consultation paper by arguing that legal aid should not be provided to individuals with median incomes because they are not 'in need'. The responsibility for dispute resolution rests with the parties, again justifying the withdrawal of state expenditure.

Maintaining the status quo is not an option. The rising number of LiPs means that the orthodox court system is no longer fit for purpose. Even if justice is best supported through continuous legal support from a lawyer, that provision is no longer realistic. As Goriely (1994: 562) argues, there is a 'pressing need to rethink the way advice and legal services are provided', rather than solely advocating for the reinstatement of the traditional system. A contemporary understanding of family justice needs to be pragmatic, as well as comprehensive. An extract from the Family Solutions Group (2020: 133) supports this view: 'We need to move away from old assumptions that family breakdown is automatically a legal issue in which parents work against each other and towards an acceptance of "working together" as the norm where appropriate, with professional support alongside to resolve issues.'

Nonetheless, the suggestion that private family matters are not inherently legal problems is far from perfect. Mant (2022: 161) is cautious of this

[40] See section 1.2.1 for further information on the introduction of legal aid.

trajectory, recognizing that legal norms are present both in court and private negotiations. Removing the legal dimension of family problems may entrench power imbalances and limit the effectiveness of individualized settlements altogether. Furthermore, many of the non-lawyer services used by family law disputants in replacement of lawyers are still informed by justice norms (Smith and Hitchings 2023). And so, Mant (2022: 162–163) posits that contemporary family justice will remain just as complicated and multifaceted as its traditional counterpart. This argument (which *Rethinking Family Mediation* is also premised upon) is symbolic of a growing recognition that the post-LASPO family law system is untenable in its current state, and must be changed to better serve its disputants.

2.4.3 Revealing family mediation's contemporary purpose

If the traditional court system does not support a contemporary view of family justice, the same can be said of the traditional mediation process. The post-LASPO climate necessitates the rethinking and reshaping of all family law procedures, including family mediation, to provide better dispute resolution forums for disputants. A growing body of work investigates how to reform the court process to suit the needs of LiPs (Engler 2012; Trinder et al 2014; Mant 2022; McKeever et al 2022). Yet what about the equivalent of LiPs in mediation? If few people in court can afford a lawyer, it is plausible that only a minority can afford a lawyer in family dispute resolution. This possibility increases the risk of outsider justice within the family mediation process, particularly if mediators are prohibited from providing more explicit legal oversight. Consequently, only a select number of cases appear to receive the equivalent of the full representation model in family mediation after LASPO.[41] The process and its mediators must, therefore, adapt.

Yet what if significant reform to family mediator practice has already occurred? Originally, family mediation was reserved for children's matters. In the 1990s, the rules were changed to allow mediators to mediate financial and property disputes.[42] Legal aid funding for mediation was also introduced during this period. Family mediation has become increasingly professionalized over time, with the Family Mediation Council becoming the main regulatory body in 2007. MIAMs were then mandated for most private family law applicants in 2014. Fast-forward to the 2020s, additional funding became available through the Family Mediation Voucher Scheme and the Ministry of Justice even considered mandating the process. Given

[41] This reality is discussed in sections 4.1.1–4.1.2.

[42] See section 3.2.1.

all these advancements, surely family mediator practice has undergone *some* kind of change.

The remainder of *Rethinking Family Mediation* uncovers these developments. Throughout both Parts I and II, this monograph argues that family mediation has evolved since it was introduced in the late 20th century. These advancements are, in some sense, a natural part of mediation's evolution. At the same time, many of these changes have been instigated by reforms to the family justice system. Regardless of the reasons behind this expansion, it is clear that the days of the limited mediator are long over. Rather, mediators are increasingly taking on a flexible archetype.

This argument is particularly important where the contemporary understanding of family mediation has yet to be fully explored in policy or academic commentary. Starting with policy, the government commissioned a Call for Evidence on dispute resolution in late 2021. The Ministry of Justice (2021c: 8) wrote that it would 'consider the changes necessary to move towards a holistic system of dispute resolution, one in which users are supported and directed towards the dispute resolution option that is right for their circumstances'. The summary of responses, published in March 2022, outlined the main views from the consultation (Ministry of Justice 2022e). The Ministry of Justice (2022e: 23) mentioned that the respondents to the consultation 'saw the need for dispute resolution as an integrated pathway to justice', though it does not clarify how many of the 193 responses advanced this view. The consultation concluded with a brief paragraph:

> The Ministry of Justice would like to thank all respondents for their contribution to the Call for Evidence on Dispute Resolution in England and Wales. The information gathered from this consultation exercise will inform the government's developing work on how to utilise dispute resolution processes to deliver swifter, more cost-effective and more consensual access to justice. Any future policy proposals will be subject to further public consultation. (Ministry of Justice 2022e: 25)

The consultation presented an opportunity for both the Ministry of Justice and its respondents to investigate the potential of dispute resolution in the long-term post-LASPO landscape. Unfortunately, the subsequent report reads as if mediation's purpose has been taken for granted. There was no consideration as to whether mediators could provide more support to parties in the post-LASPO era, nor whether their practices have changed. Unless these discussions take place, the true value of mediation in securing justice remains obscured.

Much of the empirical research and academic commentary on the development of family mediation post-LASPO will be outlined in Chapter 4. For the purposes of the present discussion, attention is drawn to the House of Commons Justice Committee's review of LASPO. Moorhead submitted evidence about the rise of LiPs, explaining: 'I am assuming that the Committee will be receiving significant evidence from other sources on the administration's approach to mediation' (House of Commons Justice Committee 2011b: 51). In reality, only ten out of the 47 written submissions published in the report mentioned mediation, most of which only considered the process in passing. While this inquiry is not representative of all discussions surrounding LASPO, it alludes to a widespread misconception that mediation's development has been comprehensively scrutinized.[43]

Family mediation is likely to be increasingly promoted in the future. The LASPO reforms do not mark the end of a neoliberal agenda to reduce state responsibility: rather, the legislation demonstrates a sustained vision for a contemporary family justice system where disputes are primarily handled by the parties themselves. This development seems even more likely following the Ministry of Justice's 2023 proposals to mandate family mediation, despite their postponement the following year. In fact, the Ministry of Justice (2024a: 18) makes it clear in its response to the consultation that mandatory mediation will not be introduced 'at this time', implying that the proposal may be revisited at some point. Academic debate and commentary must, therefore, continue (and perhaps even begin) to consider the meaning and purpose of family mediation in the post-LASPO era.

It is in light of this research gap that the basis for *Rethinking Family Mediation* is justified. The monograph's starting argument is that the discussion around family mediation's conceptualization has remained stagnant since the late 20th century. Consequently, there is a pressing need to uncover the contemporary purpose behind mediation. The mediator is at the heart of this story: her role determines what can happen in mediation, and whether just settlement is achieved. This realization prompts a critical examination of whether family mediation is an apparatus of family justice, and if more can be done to refine (or constrain) the practices of family mediators. *Rethinking Family Mediation* consequently makes a pivotal contribution to both the literature and the debate on the future of family justice, laying the groundwork for further deliberations going forward.

2.5 Conclusion

The current family law landscape is the result of several decades of policy and legislation that withdrew state responsibility for family matters. This agenda

---

[43] A similar example in policy is the Joint Committee of Human Rights' (2018) Tenth Report. A large section of the report is dedicated to the impact of LiPs on access to justice, but there is no corresponding section on out-of-court family dispute resolution.

was first visible in the 1960s when government policy sought to minimize the alleged bitterness caused in court. Successive governments continued this discourse alongside a preference for party-led settlement and an aversion to an overly excessive legal aid scheme. Family mediation was an obvious solution to these three policy concerns: it was distinct from court, the parties themselves decided the outcome, and the process was supposedly cheaper for the state to fund. At this point in time, primacy remained with court. Post-LASPO, the outer zone of family justice is no longer in the periphery. This chapter has argued that the LASPO reforms are a continuation of the three concerns in earlier policy. As of April 2013, the majority of parties in private family law proceedings are no longer eligible for legal aid. Legal aid for family mediation, in comparison, remains. More recently, policy from the 2020s suggests that family mediation may be mandated in the future. Simply put, family mediation is now the primary option for private family matters.

The widespread criticism of these neoliberal reforms is justified. However, the problem is not necessarily with family mediation per se, but its misappropriation by successive neoliberalist governments with little to no appraisal of the process. Thus, a fundamental question for both scholars and practitioners is how to claim back family dispute resolution from the neoliberal state. This investigation necessitates a consideration of how to best utilize mediation, and various other procedures, in order to engender an effective approach to family justice in the post-LASPO era.

The remainder of Part I uncovers the transition to a contemporary understanding of family mediation that can support, not hinder, family justice. Chapter 3 considers the original conceptualization of family mediation, represented by the limited mediator. As Chapter 4 moves onto the contemporary purpose of family mediation, the flexible mediator archetype is revealed. This typology of family mediators serves as a crucial basis for the empirical work, covered in Part II.

3

The Limited Mediator

The primary argument behind *Rethinking Family Mediation* is that family mediator practice has evolved over time. This development is symbolized by the transition from the limited mediator to the flexible mediator. While the flexible mediator type is more common in the post-Legal Aid, Sentencing and Punishment of Offenders Act 2012 (LASPO) landscape, her evolution was not suddenly prompted by the 2013 reforms. Similar to how LASPO was not a one-off event, the transition to a flexible mediator practice has developed over several decades in response to various challenges with the mediation process (and the family justice system more widely). Nonetheless, the image of the limited mediator persists in the dominant understanding of, and discussions around, family mediation. In order to fully understand this development, both the limited and flexible archetypes must be discussed. The former is the focus of Chapter 3, whereas the latter is considered in Chapter 4.

As an archetype, the limited mediator underpins the traditional conceptualization of family mediation. The limited mediator is a professional bound to an absolute vision of her neutrality. She is facilitative and confined to a circumscribed set of practices, such as information provision. The limited mediator type thus ensures that decision-making power rests with the parties at all times. Consequently, the limited mediator cannot do anything to direct a particular outcome.

The first section of Chapter 3 sets the scene by outlining the theory behind family mediation. Primary attention is placed on the idea of mediator neutrality, which is then situated on a continuum of facilitative to evaluative mediator practices. While the combination of these two theories is supposed to provide mediators with an adaptable skillset, it is argued that family mediation's traditional conceptualization confines mediators to a strictly neutral and facilitative approach. It is this restriction that gives rise to the limited mediator archetype. Section 2 uncovers the emergence of the limited mediator in the late 20th-century family law system. It shows that there was little appraisal of family mediator practice in empirical research at the time because most parties had access to lawyers and, therefore, evaluative support. As a result, there was little need for mediators to go beyond their limited role, and little interest in investigating her practices. The final section of this chapter goes on to critique the limited mediator type, recognizing that the problems with her conceptualization were apparent long before LASPO. Specific reference is made to the neutrality dilemma regularly faced by mediators, as well as the naivety of her conceptualization. The rising demand for a more contemporary family mediator – a flexible mediator – subsequently comes to light, paving the way for the discussion in Chapter 4.

3.1 Uncovering the limited mediator: mediation theory

Before returning to the late 20th-century family justice system, it is important to set out the theory behind the limited mediator archetype. Of course, the literature on mediation theory is so expansive that only a few concepts can be comprehensively covered within this book. As Regina (2011: 12) recognizes, family mediation 'lacks a unifying theoretical foundation'. Some examples of relevant theory include chaos theory (Parkinson 2020: 49–50), conflict theory (Tjosvold and van de Vliert 1994) and transformative mediation (Bush and Folger 1994). The work behind *Rethinking Family Mediation* is premised on two theories that are central to the current debate: mediator neutrality, and the facilitative to evaluative continuum of mediator strategies.

3.1.1 Mediator neutrality

Neutrality is fundamental to Western ideas of fairness, as well as justice (Astor 2007: 221). Judicial neutrality, for instance, is vital to maintaining public confidence in the legal system. In the words of Lord Devlin (1979: 9): 'those whom change hurts should be able to count on even-handed justice calmly dispensed, not driven forward by the agents of change'. If the parties are treated equally and the judge has no personal interest in the outcome, it is assumed that the court applies the law in a fair and just manner. In this sense, judicial neutrality is said to promote both procedural and substantive justice in court.

Mediator neutrality, likewise, sits at the centre of the family mediation process. Mediation is premised on the idea that the parties reach their own settlement. To support this objective, no third party has the power to impose an outcome within negotiations. The family mediator is thus said to be a guide. This conceptualization was adopted throughout the late 20th-century policy, with the Matrimonial Causes Procedure Committee (1985:

para 3.10) writing that a mediator 'should be neutral not only in the sense that he does not take sides as between the parties, but also in the sense that he does not have a preconceived solution'.

Much of the academic literature on family mediation accepts neutrality as a dogma that shapes – and restricts – mediator practice. Rifkin et al (1991: 153) posit that mediator neutrality is a means to an end to the extent that the concept reduces the potential for a mediator to act inappropriately in any negotiations. They write that mediator neutrality is also an end in itself as neutrality is so central to the mediator role that it becomes a form of quality assurance. Mediator neutrality thus ensures that decision-making power rests with the parties which, in turn, 'legitimises the mediation process' (Izumi 2010: 76).

However, the precise meaning of neutrality is ambiguous. The concept is 'inconsistently defined', a problem exacerbated by its many interpretations (Astor 2007: 226). There is also a lack of distinct and precise vocabulary to explain mediator neutrality without reference to other concepts (Rifkin et al 1991: 152). Neutrality is regularly conflated with impartiality, despite some scholars viewing these ideas as distinct concepts.[1] Mediator neutrality should therefore be seen as an 'umbrella term' that comprises multiple characteristics (Cohen et al 1999: 341). While the following discussion is not a comprehensive outline of mediator neutrality, it identifies three broad understandings of the concept: neutrality as even-handedness; neutrality as to the outcome; and neutrality as non-bias.[2]

First, mediator neutrality is commonly associated with *even-handedness*. Field (2000: 16) posits that mediators must 'be fair and even-handed' throughout the mediation process. Under this interpretation, a mediator is neutral when they treat all parties equally. This understanding of mediator neutrality can be found in family justice policy. For example, the earlier extract from the Matrimonial Causes Procedure Committee (1985) signalled that a mediator must 'not take sides'. To provide another example, the Arbitration and Mediation Services (Equality) Bill, proposed by Baroness Cox in 2011, aimed to strengthen discrimination law within arbitration and mediation.[3] While the specifics of the Bill are outside the scope of this monograph,[4] Cox identified a connection between even-handedness and mediator neutrality. She argued: '[mediation] relied on the genuine consent of the parties, a clear knowledge of what they were entering into and an

1 Section 4.3.2 returns to the distinction between mediator neutrality and impartiality.

2 These interpretations of mediator neutrality are not fixed understandings. Neutrality as even-handedness, for example, could be seen as similar and connected to neutrality as non-bias.

3 Also see the Arbitration and Mediation Services (Equality) HL Bill (2016–2017), 18.

4 For an analysis of the Bill, see: Thompson and Sandberg (2017); Eekelaar (2011).

understanding that they were equal before the [mediator]' (Hansard HL Deb, 27 January 2017, vol 778: col 895). From this perspective, mediation is founded on voluntary participation. This voluntariness is followed by informed consent and, importantly, equal standing before the mediator. If these principles are upheld, mediator neutrality is assured. Mediators are subsequently unable to act as partisans, as doing so favours one party over the other (Astor 2007: 223).

The second interpretation, *neutrality as to the outcome*, rests on a distinction between process and outcome. A family mediator is typically allowed to alter the mediation process in order to advance negotiations (Astor 2007: 223). She can decide the sequence of talk between the parties, as well as the layout of the room. However, she must be neutral as to the outcome and cannot exert any influence over the proposed settlement. Essentially, a mediator cannot act in any way that would change the outcome, even if their inaction meant that a settlement was not reached. This interpretation of neutrality distinguishes mediators from judges who routinely decide the outcome of a dispute (Smoron 1998: 261). Similar to neutrality as to even-handedness, neutrality as to the outcome is said to promote autonomous decision-making because the parties have control over, and are consequently responsible for, settlement (Douglas 2009: 40).

Third, mediator neutrality is understood as *non-bias*. To return to judicial neutrality, adjudication is founded on 'the impartial application of legal rules to relevant facts' (Moorhead 2007: 418). Various rules and norms are put in place to limit the possibility of bias. For instance, a judge is bound to apply the law as it was written in statute and interpreted in case law. Judicial judgments are also publicly available to allow for scrutiny and transparency (Delgado et al 1985: 1367–1373). By contrast, anything said in family mediation cannot be referred to in any subsequent proceedings unless it discloses a safeguarding risk or the possibility of a criminal offence (FMC and Family Justice Council 2021: 4). While the confidential nature of family mediation is said to encourage openness and transparency, it could enable a mediator to prioritize one party's interests over the other. The first interpretation of mediator neutrality, as even-handedness, would be massively impacted as a result. Neutrality as non-bias is subsequently reinforced through the conflict-of-interest principle (Douglas 2009: 29). Under the Family Mediation Council's (FMC) Code of Practice, family mediators must not have any personal interest in a case (FMC 2018a: s 5.1). They also cannot mediate if they have any prior knowledge about the case or the parties involved. In general, neutrality as lack of bias requires the mediator to remain conscious of her assumptions, beliefs and opinions, taking active steps to ensure that these views do not influence her behaviour. She cannot act in any way that leads to one party being advantaged over the other, even if this consequence was unintended (Izumi 2010: 84–85). To this extent, neutrality as non-bias may be seen as a way through which to achieve neutrality as to even-handedness, as well as neutrality as to the outcome.

The significance of mediator neutrality cannot be understated. Regarded as an absolute rule by many commentators and regulatory bodies, its interpretation holds considerable sway over the mediation setting. For example, a strict understanding of neutrality means (limited) mediators are prevented from acting in light of a power imbalance between the parties, yet are simultaneously required to act when inaction would otherwise influence the outcome. By contrast, a relaxed interpretation of mediator neutrality may allow a (flexible) mediator to respond depending on the situation, though adequate checks and balances must be put in place to ensure that parties retain an acceptable level of autonomy. Uncovering the dominant meaning of mediator neutrality in the contemporary family justice system is thus crucial to understanding what family mediators are allowed and expected to do after LASPO. This investigation, in turn, reveals a variety of practices carried out by mediators, as represented by Riskin's continuum of facilitative to evaluative mediator strategies.

3.1.2 The continuum of facilitative to evaluative mediator strategies

In 1996, Leonard Riskin published 'Understanding mediators' orientations, strategies, and techniques: a grid for the perplexed'. The article outlined a continuum of 'strategies and techniques that the mediator employs to achieve her goal of helping the parties address and resolve the problems at issue' (Riskin 1996: 23). On one end of the continuum is *facilitation*. This strategy follows the presumption that the parties are best placed to understand their dispute. Through a facilitative approach, the mediator helps the parties to understand the strengths and weaknesses of their claims in order to reach an agreement (Riskin 1996: 24, 28). She can ask the parties to consider the consequences of settlement, whether a similar outcome would be reached in court, and encourage them to communicate. On the other end of the continuum is *evaluation*. Evaluative practices are 'intended to direct some or all of the outcomes', giving a mediator additional power in negotiations (Riskin 1996: 23–24). She can use these directions to support the parties, taking on a more active and visible role in the mediation setting. A mediator adopting an evaluative approach can also examine any relevant documents before the mediation begins and, in some instances, give her opinion on the proposed settlement (Riskin 1996: 27).[5]

[5] Riskin's work is premised on a grid of mediator practices, comprising the facilitative to evaluative continuum and the 'problem definition' continuum (Riskin 1996: 22). A mediator adopting the narrowest approach to problem definition only considers issues that would be decided in court. As her approach widens, she moves beyond the court's

Figure 3.1: The facilitative to evaluative continuum of mediator strategies

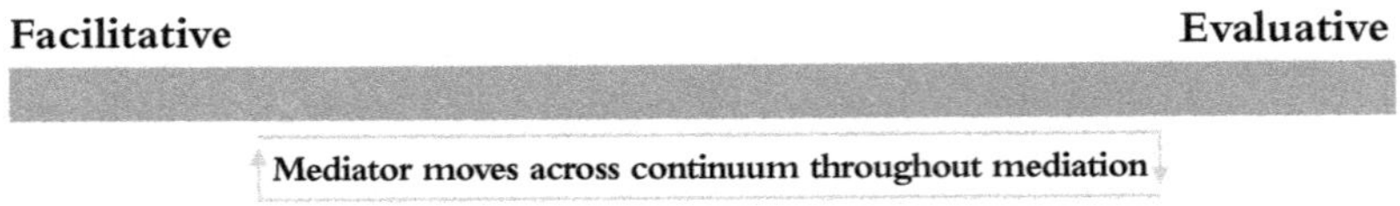

Riskin presented facilitation and evaluation as two interconnecting strategies. He argued that mediators freely move across the continuum, as depicted in Figure 3.1, to adapt to the parties' needs. For instance, a mediator may commence mediation as a facilitator. However, she can become more evaluative and provide 'guidance as to the appropriate grounds for settlement', possibly even notifying the parties that the proposals are not in their best interests (Riskin 1996: 24). Evaluation may subsequently prevent an unfair outcome, though it occurs at the expense of party control.

The terms 'facilitation' and 'evaluation' are widely adopted in the American mediation literature, with even Riskin (2003: 6) recognizing that they 'have become part of the language in the field'. His 2003 article cites a range of material that uses the continuum, including academic commentary, mediation training programmes and university courses. Some of the English and Welsh family justice literature also refers to Riskin's continuum. For instance, Webley (2010: 65) considers the facilitative and evaluative 'styles of mediation', citing Riskin. She scrutinizes the professional bodies for family solicitors and family mediators, describing the latter as facilitative. Hitchings and Miles (2016: 190–191) likewise engage with Riskin's continuum towards the end of their article when setting out the different types of legal information provided by family mediators, acknowledging that the 'temptation' to evaluate may have increased after LASPO. Maclean and Eekelaar (2016: 123) describe mediator approaches as facilitative and evaluative, though they do not cite Riskin as the source of this distinction. Barlow et al (2017: 3–4) also do not reference Riskin, but describe mediation as a 'facilitative' process at the start of their monograph. It appears that Riskin's thesis is deeply embedded into the family justice literature, though scholars rarely question the meaning of 'facilitation' and 'evaluation' in practice. This common oversight may reflect an enduring perception that family mediators are limited practitioners who, as will now be revealed, are prohibited from moving across the facilitative to evaluative continuum of practice.

---

jurisdiction and also assesses different business, personal and community issues. A mediator conducting a facilitative task may, therefore, adopt a narrow or broad view of the problems in a dispute. The same can be said of a mediator adopting more evaluative practices.

3.1.3 Theory mixed with reality: a 'bright-line distinction'

In theory, mediators have a wide variety of tools at their disposal. Yet in reality, the traditional understanding of family mediation is heavily premised on an absolute vision of mediator neutrality. This conceptualization leads to a binary interpretation of Riskin's facilitative to evaluative continuum. Facilitation is equated with mediator neutrality, party autonomy and, consequently, good mediation. By comparison, evaluation is regarded as an unneutral action that removes power from autonomous disputants. Mediator evaluation becomes synonymous with bad mediation as a result, forcing mediators to adopt a limited understanding of their role to avoid being labelled as second-rate practitioners. A mediator may employ evaluative techniques to provide flexibility, but her neutral image is eroded in the process.

Welsh (2001: 28–30) summarizes two broad critiques of mediator evaluation. First, mediator evaluation is said to be 'unfettered'. Without adequate checks and balances, the action could completely command the mediation outcome or even compel parties to settle. This criticism recognizes the impact of mediator evaluation on party autonomy, as well as the risk of poor practice if mediators are allowed to go beyond facilitation. Nonetheless, it acknowledges that mediators can evaluate so long as adequate safeguards are implemented. The second and more staunch criticism is that the evaluative framework contradicts the idea of mediation itself. Kovach and Love (1996: 31–32) allege that a mediator cannot evaluate because it undermines the 'primary goals' of family mediation, namely, to further understanding and reduce conflict between the parties. The writers subsequently label mediator evaluation an 'oxymoron'. They argue that the framework should be reserved for partisan practitioners, including lawyers, who are not bound by any notions of neutrality.

The orthodox conceptualization of family mediation is premised on the latter critique, meaning mediator evaluation is completely prohibited (Figure 3.2). Facilitation and evaluation are understood as opposing ideologies, rather than two strategies on the same continuum.[6] Described by Kovach and Love (1996: 32) as a 'bright-line distinction', this approach imposes significant restrictions on the mediator. The profession is consequently confined to the facilitative realm and unable to conduct any form of evaluation (Moberly 1997: 671).

[6] The firm dichotomy between mediator facilitation and evaluation may also be a natural consequence of Riskin's work. In a later article, Riskin (2003: 13–14) reiterated that mediators 'evaluate *and* facilitate' (original emphasis). However, he admitted that his choice of wording may have caused this flexibility to be overlooked in the mediation literature. By placing 'facilitation' and 'evaluation' at opposite ends of a spectrum and setting out their relative benefits separately, Riskin had unintentionally created a binary between the two frameworks.

Figure 3.2: The continuum of mediator strategies as a binary

This strict interpretation of Riskin's continuum underpins the limited mediator archetype. To summarize her position, a limited mediator is bound to an unfaltering vision of her neutrality. Her role is narrowly defined and confined to assistance, ensuring that decision-making power firmly remains with the parties. A limited mediator is, in effect, a facilitative mediator. Any hint of evaluation is seen as something well beyond her professional remit, and thus regarded as bad practice.

3.2 The limited mediator in the traditional family law system

The limited mediator archetype was prevalent throughout the late 20th century. The following discussion builds on the policy focus in Chapter 1 and considers family mediation's development through empirical research conducted in the 1970s to 1990s. By doing so, it reveals how the limited mediator archetype was largely justified in a family justice system where most disputants had access to legal support, and thus evaluation, through another practitioner.

3.2.1 Early empirical research on mediation

The rise of family mediation is attributed to a number of pilot studies. As recognized in Chapter 2, family conciliation originated in court. The first in-court conciliation scheme was trialled in 1977 at the Bristol County Court (Roberts 2014a: 45). Prior to a full hearing, the parties would meet with the registrar and a welfare officer to determine the issues in the dispute. If it was felt that settlement was possible, the parties attended a private conciliation with the welfare officer that usually lasted under an hour. The Bristol County Court conciliation scheme was initially limited to decree proceedings, but extended to contested custody and access applications in 1979 (Davis and Bader 1985a: 42).

However, academics quickly raised concerns about the effectiveness and impact of in-court conciliation. While Davis and Bader (1985a: 42) acknowledged the 'growing enthusiasm' around in-court conciliation both in terms of its settlement-seeking objectives and the potential to save costs, their study on the schemes at Bristol and Newport County

Courts revealed serious problems with the process. They found that most conciliations took place in overcrowded waiting areas with parties being made to remain in the same room as their ex-partner (Davis and Bader 1985a: 43). Solicitors dominated the actual negotiations, with 56 per cent of parties at Bristol County Court not taking an active part in any stage of the conciliation. Another major concern related to the fact that conciliation was conducted by a welfare officer who was responsible for writing a welfare report.[7] The welfare officer was thus expected to mediate disputes yet simultaneously act as 'adviser to the court' (Davis and Bader 1985a: 46–48). This role led to the misconception that welfare officers were there to determine the dispute, rather than assist the parties in reaching an agreement. Davis and Bader (1985b: 84) concluded that in-court conciliation had become so integrated into the court process that it was often conducted 'very badly', giving rise to the same criticisms that were often directed towards adversarialism.

Interest began to rise in a conciliation format that was conducted independently of the court process. Out-of-court family conciliation was also trialled for the first time in Bristol. Established in 1978 and funded by the Nuffield Foundation, the Bristol Courts Family Conciliation Service provided out-of-court conciliation for child-related matters (Davis 1988: 16; Parkinson 2020: 8).[8] In the first year of the pilot, Davis (1980: 6) found that 78 per cent of cases reached full or partial agreement through conciliation.[9] Factors associated with settlement included 'helpful solicitors' and 'personal maturity', though Davis did not expand on the latter term. In contrast, the likelihood of a settlement being reached through conciliation was reduced when parties resented their ex-partner, refused to accept the end of the marriage or were unwilling to engage. Davis also assessed the second out-of-court conciliation service, the Bromley Conciliation Bureau, which was established in 1979. This scheme attained lower levels of settlement with 63 per cent of cases reaching full or partial agreement (Davis and Roberts 1988: 51). Nevertheless, both pilots were regarded as highly successful, and family conciliation was rolled out through a number of local initiatives (Dingwall 1986: 7; Roberts 2014a: 51; Parkinson 2020: 8). By 1983, over 20 independent out-of-court conciliation services had been set up across England and

[7] The Matrimonial Causes Procedure Committee (1985: para 4.61) went on to recommend that the same welfare officer should not conduct in-court conciliation and prepare the welfare report.

[8] Roberts (2014a: 51) mentions that the service was initially designed as a 'pre-court service' to complement the in-court scheme.

[9] Thirty-five per cent of cases reached full agreement, and 43 per cent partial agreement.

Wales (Ogus et al 1989: para 2.35). Subsequent studies on these services continued to measure conciliation's success through settlement rates (Walker 1992: 156; Stylianou 2020: 286).

Research was then conducted to compare the effectiveness of in-court and out-of-court family conciliation.[10] The Conciliation Project Unit, led by Ogus et al (1989), was the most extensive study on family conciliation at the time (Walker 1992: 157). The project assessed several in-court and out-of-court conciliation services through questionnaires and interviews with legal professionals, conciliators and users, as well as an analysis of case files (Ogus et al 1989: paras 7.3–7.5, 7.71–7.75). Despite the breadth of research methods, the Conciliation Project Unit continued to focus on settlement. It reported that 71 per cent of parties reached full or partial agreement through conciliation (Ogus et al 1989: para 17.1). While this statistic was not broken down into the different conciliation services, a graph from the report shows that in-court conciliation resulted in fewer agreements (Ogus et al 1989: para 16.13).

The Conciliation Project Unit concluded that in-court conciliation was better received when the parties perceived it as 'totally separate from the judicial process' (Ogus et al 1989: para 20.22). In general, out-of-court services were said to provide the 'most effective form' of conciliation. Ogus et al (1989: para 20.19) specifically praised out-of-court conciliation for giving decision-making power to the parties: 'conciliation's distinguishing feature should be to enable couples to retain control of the decision-making process consequent on separation and divorce, encouraging them to reach their own agreements'.

During this period, conciliation was only available for child-related disputes. It was a 'social workers' movement', typically provided by welfare professionals or counsellors in not-for-profit services (Davis 1988: 53). A concordat between the National Family Conciliation Council and the Law Society later formalized a ban on finance-related conciliation (Dingwall 1986: 9; Roberts 2014b: 110–111). While this agreement alluded to a general consensus that conciliators should be limited practitioners, there was some demand for the profession to go beyond these confines. The Conciliation Project Unit concluded that financial and property matters should not necessarily be excluded from the conciliation, finding that parties often struggled to separate their child-related disputes from the other issues that arose upon family breakdown (Ogus et al 1989: para 20.34). The profession began to diversify in the 1980s, with an increasing number of therapists and

[10] The Matrimonial Causes Procedure Committee (1985: para 3.12) explicitly supported this project, recognizing that conciliation may be more effective if it was used before court proceedings.

lawyers becoming interested in conciliation (Roberts 2014b: 112; Blakey 2023a: 143).

All-issues (or comprehensive) mediation, allowing mediators to mediate both financial and child-related matters in the same case, was piloted in the early 1990s. From 1990 to 1993, Walker et al (1994: 14–25) examined five all-issues family mediation pilots. The research methods were again extensive, comprising a case record analysis, observations, surveys and interviews. The outcomes from all-issues mediation were then compared to mediation for child-related matters. Altogether, 80 per cent of cases heard by all-issues services reached an agreement, compared to 60 per cent of cases in the comparison group (Walker et al 1994: 71). The researchers emphasized that mediation simultaneously engendered settlement and improved the post-separation relationship between the parties:

> Family mediation is a process in which an impartial third person, the mediator, assists couples considering separation or divorce to make arrangements, to communicate better, to reduce conflict between them, and to reach their own agreed joint decisions. … The mediator has no stake in any disputes, is not identified with any of the competing interests, and has no power to impose a settlement on the participants, who retain the authority to make their own decisions. (Walker et al 1994: preface)

Family mediation was presented as a settlement-focused process, whereas court was an adversarial process that increased bitterness and hostility.[11] The limited family mediator – an impartial third party that assisted parties in obtaining settlement – was pivotal to this distinction.

An interesting feature of these pilots was their minimal scrutiny of the mediator. The limited mediator's behaviours and values, as well as those of the clients she mediated, received little to no attention in published work. While Davis' research on the Bristol Courts Family Conciliation Service included interviews with solicitors and case records, no formal conversations with conciliators or their clients took place. Six years after the findings from the pilot were released, Dingwall (1986: 19) argued that the Bristol pilot revealed nothing about 'what conciliators have done and how this has contributed to, or impeded, the resolution of the material dispute'. Davis

[11] The Lord Chancellor's Department (1995a: para 5.4) used a very similar definition of family mediation in a policy paper. It wrote: 'Family mediation is a process in which an impartial third person, the mediator, assists couples considering separation or divorce to meet together to deal with the arrangements which need to be made for the future'.

(2004: 60) himself went on to acknowledge the 'painfully wide' gap between the aims of the project and its findings.

What prevented the investigation into the family mediator? Originally, family mediation was provided for free or at a reduced cost. This structure caused a 'perennial search for funding' (Dingwall 1986: 9). Yet the government and its local authorities would only fund mediation if it could be shown that the process was deserving of such financial support. These institutions would not be swayed by academic commentary alone. Rather, mediation's potential had to be proven through quantitative and objective settlement rates. Empirical research consequently focused on the outcomes of family mediation. Kelly (2004: 3) described this body of work as 'first-generation research' that investigated 'basic questions', such as how many agreements were reached through mediation and what proportion of clients were satisfied with the process. While these studies played a crucial role in establishing family mediation across the country, they overlooked the intricacies and nuances of mediator practice, something which remains obscured in the contemporary landscape. This missing appraisal continued well into the late 1990s, despite legislative reform that aimed to encourage further use of family mediation.

Kelly (2004: 31) called for further work on the relative benefits of different mediation models, as well as whether mediation could be adapted to cases involving domestic abuse. She wrote: 'The field would be advanced considerably if analyses were conducted of mediator behaviours and interventions, participant characteristics and behaviours, and the relationship of these to outcomes.' Unfortunately, the limited mediator archetype was taken for granted, with little consideration as to whether a more flexible role was necessary or desirable.[12]

3.2.2 The reliance on lawyers for evaluation

It is important to emphasize that the limited mediator's conceptualization was not accidental (Blakey 2023a). In fact, the archetype was designed in light of the family justice landscape at the time. As explained in what follows, the majority of mediation users in the late 20th century had access to legal advice and support through a solicitor. Lawyers not only referred parties to mediation, but screened cases for suitability, provided legal advice and drafted consent orders to make any settlements legally binding. Strict confines were placed on the mediator – the limited mediator – as a result. This backdrop

[12] This oversight was first mentioned towards the end of Chapter 2 and will be revisited in Chapter 4.

also explains why the limited mediator role was largely accepted: there was, by and large, no need for her to evaluate.

Solicitors were originally the main gatekeepers into family mediation. In the Bromley Conciliation Bureau pilot, all but two of the 51 participants attending conciliation had consulted a solicitor about their divorce (Davis and Roberts 1988: 28). Over half of the solicitors interviewed in the Conciliation Project Unit also referred their parties to conciliation (Ogus et al 1989: para 19.2). In the all-issues mediation pilots, most parties appointed a solicitor before attempting dispute resolution (Walker et al 1994: 132). Family mediators were subsequently reliant on the legal profession for most of their caseload.

The prominence of solicitor referrals meant that most parties only attended mediation if a lawyer thought the process was appropriate for their dispute. Screening was an evaluative act, carried out to ensure that a case suited the family mediation process. Because lawyers were the primary gatekeepers into family mediation, they were originally responsible for screening parties out of the process. The number of self-referrals appeared to increase over time, with only a third of mediation users from the all-issues study being referred by a solicitor (Walker et al 1994: 30). However, this statistic is misleading when read alone, as most of the participants who referred themselves to mediation only did so after meeting with a solicitor. Lawyers were therefore crucial to family mediation's intake, as well as the traditional conceptualization of the limited mediator, throughout the late 20th century.

When mediation did take place, mediators were once again dependent on lawyers to provide support. A mediator could only *inform*, whereas a lawyer also *advised*. This distinction was a central justification for the limited mediator type. Policy papers define information as 'an abstract statement of legal principles and procedures', whereas advice involves 'an explanation of how the law applies' (Lord Chancellor's Department 1995a: para 7.9). Information is consequently presented as a 'neutral act' that can be carried out by the limited mediator (Maclean and Eekelaar 2016: 125–126). Meanwhile, advice is an evaluative action and reserved for the partisan lawyer. A solicitor is a prompter, advising her client on the best way forward in negotiations. Meanwhile, the mediator is the audience in an interactive theatre. She can break her silence to facilitate discussions and give information, but she cannot impose an outcome. Mediators and solicitors thus provide distinct, albeit complementary, services. Barlow et al (2017: 133) make a similar observation, describing legal advice alongside family mediation as the 'optimum process'.

Lawyers could provide additional legal oversight when mediation resulted in a full or partial agreement. At the end of mediation, the mediator usually prepares a Memorandum of Understanding.[13] This is a written document that

[13] This document is sometimes referred to as a Parenting Plan in child-related disputes.

Figure 3.3: The continuum of mediator strategies with lawyers providing evaluation

sets out the mediation outcome, the proposed settlement and potential areas where legal advice is desirable (Parkinson 2020: 308–310). The Memorandum of Understanding is not legally binding: for those who seek an enforceable agreement, particularly when dealing with financial or property matters, a consent order must be obtained. Traditionally, a consent order could only be written by a lawyer and then approved by a judge. Mediators were thus also dependent on lawyers to turn mediated agreements into enforceable outcomes. The drafting and issuing of a consent order is an extension of legal advice, solidifying the lawyer's role as an evaluative prompter.

To summarize, mediators were traditionally conceptualized as limited third parties and prohibited from any action considered even somewhat evaluative. Providing legal information was facilitative because the parties were responsible for applying this information to their dispute. Yet facilitative support only went so far, and disputants would often seek an evaluation of their dispute. This evaluation tended to be provided in the form of legal advice, geared towards the parties' circumstances. Through advice, a lawyer could freely give their preferred solution and direct their client towards that outcome. Lawyers could also screen parties for suitability and draft consent orders. Hence, the limited mediator archetype heavily relied on lawyers to provide evaluative support. A mediator *facilitated*, whereas a lawyer *evaluated*. Figure 3.3 depicts this separation of powers.

3.2.3 Deliberately restricting the limited mediator

Mediators' confinement to the facilitative realm was not purely by chance. When family conciliation was first piloted in England and Wales, it was a novel process. It posed a particular danger to solicitors who had monopolized the family justice system for decades, if not centuries. The conciliator was a 'major, if ill-defined, figure', and her impact on lawyers' work was unknown at the time (Roberts 2002: 18). And so, conciliation services not only had to gain approval from the state and local authorities to receive funding, but also from the legal profession to ensure that clients were actually referred into the process (Blakey 2023a: 142–143). If conciliation had been presented as a replacement for advice, the legal profession may have viewed the process as a threat to their monopoly over the family justice system. The best tactic, therefore, was to conceptualize family conciliation in a way that did not encroach upon the work of lawyers. Conciliators were subsequently only allowed to conciliate child-related disputes, enabling lawyers to concentrate on financial and property matters (Walker 1996: 55). The profession was also given a limited role, prohibited from straying into evaluation. While the introduction of all-issues mediation in the 1990s alluded to some extension of the limited mediator archetype, this development was only possible following a statement by the Law Society that lawyers were also allowed to work as mediators (Parkinson 2020: 9). By acting in a different professional capacity, lawyers could solidify their primary position in the family justice system.

The limited family mediator was also justified by mediation's clientele at the time. In the late 20th century, most people using family mediation were from a high socio-economic background. This was apparent in the 1970s, with Davis (1980: 5) suggesting that the Bristol Family Courts Conciliation Service was better suited to 'the values and social skills of middle-class clients'. Davis provided no detail for this reasoning other than a brief recognition that most fathers in the pilot were in intermediate managerial, administrative or professional occupations.[14] While the solicitors at the Bristol Family Courts Conciliation Service acknowledged the 'complexity of many cases', they associated several factors with agreement (Davis 1980: 3). These characteristics included a willingness to settle, a focus on children's needs and amicability among the parties. The population of those using family mediation became more varied over time, with Ogus et al (1989: paras 7.71–7.75, 20.6) describing the parties in the Conciliation Project Unit as a 'heterogeneous population in terms of both social and personal circumstances'.[15] The sample of clients was also more varied in the all-issues pilots, though it remained skewed towards the middle class: 56 per cent of mediation users were in high socio-economic occupations, compared to 9 per cent in semi-skilled or unskilled manual work (Walker et al 1994: 44). Despite some variation over time, mediation services consistently expressed a preference for a homogeneous and high socio-economic clientele. Walker et al (1994: 122) summarized the ideal mediation case as involving 'two well-educated, middle-class people, both in employment, jointly owning a house in which there was sufficient equity to provide a reasonable home for each of them … and who were both sufficiently sure that the marriage had ended'. Thus, families from high socio-economic backgrounds were thought to streamline the mediation process. 'Well-educated' individuals were

[14] These occupations are listed as Grade B, or middle class, under the NRS social grade.

[15] Dingwall (1986: 11) also comments that the matrimonial home is the only asset for many families using mediation in Britain, and that high rates of unemployment reduce the 'family's economic resources'.

ideal for mediation as they supposedly had the skills to negotiate effectively. Furthermore, if the parties in a financial dispute were 'middle-class', 'in employment' and had 'sufficient equity' to both purchase a home after separation, the pool of assets to divide between them was abundant. With fewer concerns around the needs of both parties, negotiations were simplified and the demand for mediators to respond to any power imbalances was low. If a party required additional support, this was available through their lawyer. The limited mediator consequently suited the needs of a standardized client base, and the restrictions surrounding her role were justified. In short, there was no need for mediators to evaluate.

3.3 The naivetes and shortcomings of the limited mediator archetype

To summarize the chapter thus far, the limited mediator archetype was relatively unproblematic in the late 20th century. This was because most parties could access a mediator and a lawyer, in other words both facilitative and evaluative support, to resolve their dispute. The role of the limited mediator as a neutral informer was also logical where the profession largely saw a homogeneous population with straightforward disputes. There was little demand and, therefore, little reason for mediators to evaluate. However, this system meant that little attention was paid to what would happen if legal support – or evaluation – became inaccessible. The limited family mediator was taken for granted, and the problems with her conceptualization regularly overlooked.

It comes as no surprise that the limited mediator is too limited when the parties require further support. The rising number of people coming to mediation without formal legal support after LASPO has been well-documented in both empirical research and policy consultations.[16] However, it is easily forgotten that this population have always existed in some shape or form. For instance, some individuals may have chosen to not hire a solicitor. Others may have been unable to afford legal support, especially if there was a shortage of affordable legal services in their local area. Even if a person hired a lawyer, they may have been inappropriately referred to mediation. In any of these scenarios, mediation could become a breeding ground for unfair or unscrutinized outcomes. This is because the limited mediator type was restricted to facilitation, with no real opportunity to evaluate.

Family mediation is often regarded as inappropriate where more complex issues or party dynamics are present, particularly in instances of serious power imbalances or domestic abuse. Many of these power imbalances are gendered.

[16] See section 4.1.2.

In fact, a study into the purpose of family mediation would be incomplete without acknowledging the prominence of gendered power imbalances and abuse within private family disputes. While family mediation is premised on the assumption that parties have equal bargaining positions, this is rarely the case for separating couples (Meyers 1996: 859; Semple 2012: 207). The following discussion is focused on heterosexual couples, though power imbalances are also common within LGBTQIA+ relationships (Donovan et al 2006; Moscati 2020: 233).

The normative roles of men and women in the traditional family unit heavily influence the power dynamics that are present in mediation. The vision of absolute mediator neutrality and a strict facilitative framework requires mediators to treat parties equally. This stance is supposedly justified because the parties are of equal standing. However, it is dangerous to presume that the parties arrive at mediation from an 'equal playing field', possessing the same levels of autonomy, skills and expertise (Diduck 2013: 101). This is demonstrated through Guggenheimer's (1996: 148) theory of 'feminomics', described as 'the economic consequences of gender'. Guggenheimer argues that society places men and women into specific, economic roles. Men are typically the breadwinners who work to make an income, whereas women are the home carers who make non-monetary contributions to the family unit. The resources that are more likely to be held by the breadwinner, notably experience and income, are deemed more valuable by society, providing him with greater power and autonomy within the family unit. The values and skillsets of the home carer are, by comparison, deprioritized. These heavily entrenched roles often lead to gendered power imbalances that promote the interests of the male party (Semple 2012: 212). Gendered patterns of power can operate the other way around: a man taking on the role of the home carer can be disadvantaged compared to his female partner who provides the sole or main monetary income. There are also relationships where the parties equitably share both the breadwinner and home-caring responsibilities. Nonetheless, it would be inaccurate to ignore the standard societal context where men and women are assigned gendered roles that typically lead to significant power imbalances both during the relationship and upon relationship breakdown.

A mediator adopting a limited conceptualization of their role is unable to adapt to these dynamics. She may recognize a gendered power imbalance, but she cannot respond. This problem has been acknowledged by Meyers (1996: 860), who argues that a mediator may further 'the unconscionable exploitation of the weaker spouse'. While an absolute vision of mediator neutrality endorses formal equality (for example, a 50/50 split in relation to finances or property), this rigid view can lead to unfair outcomes in the family law context. To quote Lacey (1995: 12): 'gender neutrality' is not synonymous with 'equality'. This is because, as Fineman (2004: 273–274) argues in relation to government action, absolute neutrality is blind to 'underlying disparities in position'. The conceptualization of the limited mediator, a profession that favours inaction over action, does not take these structural inequalities into account. By refusing to intervene in the party dynamic or proposed settlement, the limited mediator deprioritizes the interests and views of the weaker party.[17] Davis (1983: 136) subsequently warns that a strictly neutral mediator could unintentionally support abusers and perpetrators of abuse. He questions why a mediator cannot confront a power imbalance, so long as her concerns are voiced to both parties.

3.3.1 The neutrality dilemma

To reiterate, the limited mediator type cannot respond to any challenges within the mediation setting. If she attempts to combat a power imbalance, she departs from the absolute vision of her neutrality (Meyers 1996: 863–864; Mulcahy 2001: 510). Inaction is subsequently viewed as neutral, even when it leads to an unfair or unjust outcome for the weaker party.

However, the decision to do nothing – to be complicit in one party's dominance within the mediation setting – is an unneutral act in itself. By refraining to respond, the mediator indirectly prioritizes the empowered party. The same could be said of a mediator who does not critique a proposed settlement where that outcome favours one party. To speak promotes the interests of the weaker party, but to not speak implicitly supports the stronger disputant. Mediators are barred from influencing the outcome, yet their passivity inevitably has some impact.

The limited mediator finds herself in a very difficult position. She is, in fact, caught in a neutrality dilemma. On the one hand, a mediator cannot react as it is considered unneutral. Yet to do nothing is an unneutral act in many circumstances. If a mediator does not appropriately respond to a power imbalance, mediation may result in an unfair or unjust outcome. Remaining firmly neutral can thus violate the pursuit of fairness in family law (Exon 2006: 416). Similar concerns have already been voiced in the mediation literature. Bogdanoski (2009: 27), for example, discusses 'the mediator's perennial dilemma' when confronted with a power imbalance. The dilemma has also been described as a 'double bind' (Astor 2007: 226) that creates 'chaos for mediators' (Exon 2006: 416). To quote Becker (2013: 83), 'mediators are struggling to find where neutrality ends and departure begins'.

[17] Intervening, of course, could take on many different forms. Chapter 5 considers the meaning of 'mediator intervention', with particular reference to the ambiguity surrounding the function despite this monograph's empirical data.

This neutrality dilemma can cause parties to become disengaged with the mediation process. For instance, many families in the 1990s all-issues mediation pilots were frustrated that mediators did not take an active role in negotiations. Walker et al (1994: 56) felt that this reaction was foreseeable: if mediation was advertised as a settlement-orientated process that made a difference to negotiations, the parties would come to expect explicit support from the mediator. The authors subsequently criticized the lack of research on how mediators promoted agreement yet simultaneously upheld their neutrality (Walker et al 1994: 57). Davis (1988: 70) identified the same research gap several years prior.[18] In the seminal *Partisans and Mediators*, he argued that the role of the mediator was 'more complex than we might at first suppose'. He criticized the naivety in assuming that mediators are 'gifted, self-effacing facilitators', calling for further work into the credibility of mediator neutrality. Davis concluded that a 'skilled mediator' could, and should, support both parties. Even in the decades before LASPO, there was a clear demand for a nuanced – and *flexible* – understanding of family mediator practice.

Once again, the naivety of the limited mediator archetype comes to light. It is hoped that when confronted with a power imbalance, few mediators would do nothing and allow a case to take its course. Some mediators may encourage the weaker party to speak up or move the parties into separate rooms. Others might decide that they cannot adequately deal with the problem and end the mediation. All of these actions, even if they lead to termination, involve some form of evaluation. The image of the limited mediator is therefore not an ideal, but an aspiration that can never be achieved.

Such criticisms reveal a significant shortcoming of the limited mediator archetype: that her existence, and the explanations underpinning her role, are at best underdeveloped. How do mediator remain neutral, yet still engender settlement in a way that upholds the autonomy of the parties? When confronted with a power imbalance, does the mediator *really* just sit there and refuse to act? What exact steps does a mediator take in this situation? Unfortunately, the limited mediator type conceals the reality of mediator practice: there is little to no evidence on what mediator actions are facilitative, let alone what actions are evaluative and thus prohibited. This problem is a key reason for the evolution of the flexible mediator type, as detailed in Chapter 4. It also justifies the empirical work on (contemporary) mediator practice detailed in Part II of this monograph. Without such investigations, the practices of the flexible mediator will remain concealed.[19]

---

18 For further discussion on Davis' work, see Blakey (2023b).

19 It must be recognized that the empirical data detailed in the monograph is premised on a content analysis of regulatory documents and interviews with family mediators. Later sections of Part II, particularly sections 5.6 and 8.3, acknowledge that this data does not

3.3.2 A turning point for family mediator practice

All-issues mediation signalled a change in direction for family mediator practice, with Sims (2020: 297) describing its introduction as a 'defining moment' in mediation's history. The development signified increased trust in mediators from a variety of stakeholders, including policy makers and the legal profession, to mediate beyond children's matters. Family mediation became a more comprehensive process, with financial disputes no longer reserved to the lawyers' arena.

Walker et al (1994: 122) predicted that family mediators would no longer see a small and homogeneous client base if all-issues mediation was launched across England and Wales. They commented that if state support were to continue, mediation would 'need to be accessible to a wider range of separating and divorcing couples'. Soon after the all-issues pilots, the Family Law Act 1996 introduced legal aid for family mediation.[20] In a bid to encourage uptake, section 29 mandated that legal aid applicants to private family court proceedings must first attend an intake meeting. This intake meeting would be conducted by a mediator and enable parties to learn about the mediation process. The government subsequently commissioned a three-year pilot on the impact of the mandatory intake meetings under section 29 (Parkinson 2020: 328). The pilot, led by Davis et al (2000: 58), found that two-thirds of people attending a section 29 meeting were deemed suitable for family mediation. This development had caused a change in mediation clientele. The standard mediation user before the pilot was described as 'articulate' and 'rational', reflecting the ideal demographic. By contrast, the clients under the new scheme were 'less interested, less knowledgeable, and less motivated' (Davis et al 2000: 202–203). These parties were not that different to the general separating population, though Davis et al (2000: 203) admitted: 'mediation services were not, by and large, used to handling the mainstream'. Family mediators were under pressure to adjust their practices as a result, a preliminary sign that the profession was to go beyond their limited conceptualization.

The variation in clientele meant that mediators were increasingly responsible for screening parties into mediation (Davis et al 2000: 208). The reforms brought by the Family Law Act 1996 had placed pressure on mediators to deal with a variety of clients, even if these parties only attended the section 29 meetings. However, the challenge with this extended – and evaluative – role was that mediators lacked the proper training to screen or

comprehensively capture the practices of the flexible mediator type, and that observational data is required to make an even more substantial contributions to ongoing discussions.

[20] See section 2.2.3.

deal with more difficult disputes. In Davis et al's (2000: 58) study, just under half of cases where one party feared their ex-partner were deemed appropriate for mediation. While this finding suggests that many complex cases were being excluded from mediation, it also shows that a sizeable proportion were now being handled by mediators. Another study by Hester et al (1997: 40, 44) revealed that court welfare officers (conducting in-court mediation) and out-of-court family mediators regularly adopted a narrow understanding of domestic abuse heavily premised on physical harm. It became clear that if mediators were to become the primary gatekeepers into mediation, adequate training had to be provided.

Challenges to the limited mediator archetype had begun only two decades after the first family mediation pilots. The belief that family mediators must be confined to a neutral position, a practice left unscrutinized by late 20th-century research, had clearly created problems as mediation was rolled out across the country. The limited mediator archetype was designed to support a small and niche market, yet cracks in her facilitative image appeared as her client base expanded. And so, the limited mediator was never as ideal nor realistic as first believed. Her narrow conceptualization distinguished her from the more evaluative lawyer or judge, a tactic which encouraged support for mediation throughout the political and legal spheres. However, her inability to move into evaluation – even if an action was only somewhat evaluative – was a noticeable problem for a growing number of complex disputes.

3.4 Conclusion

This chapter has traced the introduction of the limited mediator type. It showed that the limited mediator's strictly neutral and facilitative construction was not incidental, but rather an intentional choice to enable mediators to co-exist alongside evaluative lawyers. Initially, this limited conceptualization was justified because most parties had access to legal support. Furthermore, mediation was primarily used by a homogeneous clientele with straightforward disputes. There was, subsequently, little demand for mediators to evaluate and little appraisal of the limited mediator archetype.

However, the last section of this chapter revealed the various problems with the limited mediator, even in the late 20th century. It submitted that her conceptualization was underdeveloped and, regrettably, did not account for the intricacies of mediator practice. It also argued that the limited mediator archetype was problematic where power imbalances or abuse were present. Mediators have increasingly faced a neutrality dilemma in whether to respond to power imbalances, particularly after the introduction of all-issues mediation and legal aid funding in the 1990s. With a rapidly changing family justice system and no contingency plan set in place, mediators had little choice but to seek a more flexible archetype.

4

The Flexible Mediator

Chapter 3 uncovered the limited mediator archetype. It acknowledged that limited mediators are, unsurprisingly, limited in their ability to support parties and adapt to more complex disputes. This restriction, while it can have positive and negative repercussions for any family dispute, becomes a particular issue when the parties do not have an evaluative lawyer and depend on the facilitative mediator for additional support. A limited mediator must remain neutral at all times, despite the impact that her neutrality (or inaction) can have on negotiations. These predicaments have become increasingly common in the contemporary family justice system, leading to serious concerns around the effectiveness of the limited mediator type.

Chapter 4 argues that a second mediator archetype – the *flexible* mediator – has developed in response to the contemporary family justice landscape. Like the limited mediator, a flexible mediator is still largely facilitative. However, she differs in that she openly evaluates. Underpinning this more nuanced archetype is the realization that mediator neutrality is not an absolute or sacrosanct concept. As a result, flexible mediators can move across the facilitative and evaluative continuum of practices when appropriate. Viewing more evaluative actions as justifiably unneutral resolves the neutrality dilemma often faced by mediators and enables them to adopt more responsive strategies, two issues that were identified in Chapter 3. To clarify, the flexible mediator is not an unrestrained practitioner: she is still prohibited from conducting certain evaluative practices and behaviours. Nonetheless, evaluation is an authentic part of flexible mediator practice, making the archetype both more realistic and responsive to the contemporary landscape. Underpinning this archetype is the view that mediator evaluation has value in the family justice system after the Legal Aid, Sentencing and Punishment of Offenders Act 2012 (LASPO), so long as that evaluation is openly conducted and properly regulated.

This chapter uncovers the evolution of the flexible mediator by first highlighting the problems with the limited mediator type in contemporary times. It considers family mediation's position after LASPO in light of two factors: the withdrawal of legal support, and the subsequent diversification of mediation clientele. The discussion further shows that the limited mediator archetype could not effectively respond to these developments because she was confined to facilitation. Section 2 subsequently investigates the increasing demand for mediators to become more flexible. However, it is recognized that such flexibility is unattainable if the limited mediator archetype – reinforced by an absolute vision of mediator neutrality – continues to dominate discussions around the meaning and purpose of contemporary family mediation. The effect of this stalemate is illustrated by a recent debate on whether mediators should be permitted to draft consent orders, which shows that mediators are expected to adapt yet simultaneously prohibited from acting in light of their strictly neutral, facilitative and limited image. It is argued that the only way to move beyond this conundrum is to rethink the theory behind family mediation, specifically by adopting a more flexible conceptualization of the contemporary family mediator.

It is not the purpose of this chapter, nor the remainder of *Rethinking Family Mediation*, to argue that the role of the family mediator should be completely reformed. Rather, it seeks recognition that the flexible mediator archetype already exists and should, therefore, be developed and regulated. Section 3 presents evidence from as early as the 1980s that family mediators evaluate, though these behaviours are often hidden. Thus, it is not that mediators are incapable of adjusting to the post-LASPO landscape, nor that they have yet to adapt to it. Rather, the problem is that the flexible mediator type is concealed and not openly acknowledged. This limitation is, once again, attributed to the strict view of mediator neutrality, prompting the final part of this chapter to explore the ways in which mediator neutrality can be reframed. The chapter concludes that the flexible mediator archetype – one which responds to the issues in the post-LASPO landscape – can only be accepted if mediator neutrality is understood as a moderate, rather than absolute, concept.

4.1 Family mediation in the post-LASPO landscape

The end of Chapter 3 identified the 1990s as a turning point for family mediation and family mediator practice. At the start of the decade, family mediators were allowed to mediate finance and property disputes. The Family Law Act 1996 went on to introduce legal aid mediation, requiring mediators to screen incoming cases through formalized intake meetings. These reforms were part of a broader objective (held by both successive governments and mediation services) to increase family mediation uptake across England and Wales.

However, the number of parties attempting family mediation remained relatively low at the start of the 21st century. Between October 2004 and

March 2006, only one-fifth of individuals applying for legal aid in family breakdown matters had attempted mediation (Legal Services Commission 2007: para 1.11). A survey from the same study found that a third of respondents[1] did not discuss mediation with their solicitor or advisor, reducing the likelihood that they would attempt mediation later on (Legal Services Commission 2007: para 2.7). In another study on separating parents, only half of the divorced resident parents attempted mediation (Peacey and Hunt 2009: 138). None of the non-married resident parents had attempted mediation at any point in their dispute. Low uptake was attributed to a lack of public awareness around the process, an issue that Walker et al (1994: 6) originally recognized during the all-issues mediation pilots. Similar concerns continued into the 2010s (House of Commons Justice Committee 2015: para 144), though Barlow et al (2017: 207) have since counterargued that many couples simply view mediation as an unattractive option at the onset of separation.

Other empirical studies from this period continued to analyse the effectiveness of in-court conciliation. Trinder (2008: 338) acknowledges that in-court conciliation was increasingly promoted for children's matters in the 2000s, leading to the creation of the First Hearing and Dispute Resolution Appointment (FHDRA).[2] FHDRAs were, and still are, expected to occur five weeks after the issuing of a court application. As stipulated in Practice Direction 12B, 'the judge, working with the Cafcass Officer, or WFPO [Welsh Family Proceedings Officer] will seek to assist the parties in conciliation and in resolution of all or any of the issues between them'.[3] The Cafcass Officer (or Welsh Family Proceedings Officer) was 'to conciliate' the dispute, though the structure they adopted was to be determined 'by local arrangements'.[4] As a result, in-court conciliation continued to be provided in an 'ad hoc' manner (Cantwell 2006: 389). In a longitudinal quantitative survey of parents attending in-court conciliation for contact disputes, 76 per cent of participants reported reaching full or partial agreement through the process (Trinder et al 2006: ii). Nonetheless, Trinder (2008: 338) warned that conciliation failed to 'address or resolve embedded conflict', resulting in poor post-separation relationships regardless of whether a settlement was reached.

The LASPO reforms, by comparison, signalled a change in academic discussion. There had been some appraisal of family mediator practice outside of court from the 1980s,[5] but this line of thinking gained particular

[1] The respondents of this survey were legal aid recipients for family matters.

[2] A similar process is available for solely financial matters through Dispute Resolution Appointments.

[3] FPR PD 12B, r 14.11.

[4] FPR PD 12B, r 14.13.

[5] See section 3.3.1.

momentum in the 2010s. This shift can be attributed to two factors that had a significant impact on (out-of-court) family mediation after LASPO: the withdrawal of legal advice, and the subsequent change in mediation clientele. Combined, these developments give rise to a fundamental question: can the role of the family mediator be reformed to respond to the contemporary family justice climate?

4.1.1 The withdrawal of legal support

Chapter 2 covered policy's negative depiction of court in order to justify the withdrawal of legal aid. Building on this discussion, the legal profession was also portrayed as having a damaging impact on family disputes. Lewis (2000: 10) submits that solicitors were presented as aggressive third parties that reinforced adversarial notions of conflict and prevented settlement. Barlow et al (2017: 24) reach the same conclusion, identifying a long-standing discourse 'aimed at marginalising and discouraging the use of solicitors'. An example of such policy was the *Looking to the Future* White Paper, wherein the Lord Chancellor's Department (1995a: 6.21) criticized 'uncontrolled access to lawyer representation' in mediation. The paper contended that lawyers did not need to 'shadow' mediation, so long as 'suitable quality assurance mechanisms' were put in place. Mediation alongside legal advice was depicted as superfluous, though there was no explanation of what these quality assurance mechanisms entailed nor how they were a suitable replacement for advice. Funding for legal support was, as identified throughout Chapter 2, only warranted in cases of need.

The withdrawal of solicitors in family justice was well documented around the time of LASPO, as demonstrated by the Mapping Paths to Family Justice project. Led by Barlow et al (2017), Mapping Paths was an extensive study into English and Welsh family dispute resolution from late 2011 to early 2014. It examined three family justice procedures: mediation, collaborative law and solicitor negotiation. The research design comprised a national survey, party and practitioner interviews, as well as observations. Barlow et al's (2017: 165) findings corroborated earlier research on the significance of settlement within family mediation. However, the researchers discovered that the context in which this objective operated had drastically changed. While solicitors were originally commonplace within family disputes, 47 per cent of Barlow et al's (2017: 71) questionnaire sample[6] had not obtained legal advice. This finding was supported by the interview data, with many legal professionals expressing a concern that the cuts to legal aid under LASPO would render advice even more inaccessible (Barlow et al 2017: 134).

6 This sample comprised separating couples from 1996 to 2011.

These apprehensions were well warranted. In the year after LASPO's implementation, the number of legal help and controlled legal representation matters for family disputes started under legal aid dropped 78.9 percentage points from 204,247 to 43,106 (Ministry of Justice 2024b: table 5.1). This number has continued to decline, reaching a worrying low of 24,784 in 2022–2023, and only a slight improvement of 26,453 by 2023–2024. Hitchings et al's (2023: 105–106) Fair Shares project also provides a fully representative picture of the financial and property arrangements made upon divorce after LASPO. In a survey of 2,415 divorcees,[7] only a third of respondents used legal support in relation to their dispute. Out of those who had not sought support from a lawyer or legal service, two-fifths cited cost as a key reason for this decision (Hitchings et al 2023: 113). Thus, a large population of divorcing and separating couples are no longer obtaining legal advice following LASPO.

Research commissioned by the Ministry of Justice on the use of Mediation, Information and Assessment Meetings (MIAMs) confirms the decline of legal support within family mediation. The first report by Bloch et al (2014: 7) considered the perceptions, experiences and impact of MIAMs. Their findings revealed that solicitor referrals into mediation diminished after LASPO as fewer individuals were obtaining legal advice at the beginning of, and during, their family dispute (Bloch et al 2014: 12–13). Solicitors were no longer the first port of call for private family matters, and unmet legal need increased as a result.

Legal support supposedly remains available to those receiving legal aid via the Help with Family Mediation scheme, whereby a lawyer receives a fee for advising a party during mediation or drafting a (financial) consent order once a settlement has been reached.[8] However, the benefits of Help with Family Mediation have failed to materialize. Hitchings and Miles (2016: 178) acknowledge that the scheme has done little to prevent unmet legal need, describing the Help with Family Mediation statistics as 'disturbing'. An in-depth study by the author of this monograph reveals that only 78 individuals received legal support via a solicitor through Help with Family Mediation in the year after LASPO (Blakey 2024: 89). This number rose to 302 the following year, possibly influenced by the introduction of mandatory MIAMs. However, the number of Help with Family Mediation cases subsequently declined, dropping to 95 in 2021–2022 and 76 in 2022–2023.

---

7 All participants had obtained a decree absolute in England and Wales in the last five years, with the survey conducted from August to September 2022 (Hitchings et al 2023: 52).

8 Civil Legal Aid (Remuneration) Regulations 2013, SI 2013/422, sch 1 pt 1 para 3; Civil Legal Aid (Procedure) Regulations, 2012, SI 2012/3098, reg 8.

Parties can continue to seek support through advice agencies, such as Citizens Advice Bureaux. However, the funding available for these organizations has been drastically cut since the 2000s, a fact that the Ministry of Justice failed to acknowledge when first proposing LASPO (Cookson 2011: paras 5.4.1–5.4.11). In the year after the LASPO's enactment, nine Law Centres closed and the number of clients seen by the Citizens Advice Bureaux fell by 8 per cent (Low Commission 2015: 20). Free advice has become particularly inaccessible for family matters, with only eight out of 41 Law Centres being listed as providing advice for family matters as of July 2024 (Law Centres Network 2024). The decline of advice services has intensified the 'legal advice vacuum', identified by Smith et al (2017: 81), in which legal support is only available in concentrated parts of England and Wales.

Various other initiatives to support disputants have materialized in recent years, including self-help guides, pro bono schemes and a rising number of professional McKenzie Friends (Smith et al 2017; Maclean and Eekelaar 2019; Smith and Hitchings 2023).[9] Even so, both 'non-lawyer legal services' and 'extra-legal support services' remain massively understudied, with family justice reforms remaining heavily 'lawyer-centric' (Smith and Hitchings 2023: 661, 675). The utility and value of non-lawyer services, particularly where family law disputants often lack the emotional capacity to take in information, is subsequently unclear. The availability of these schemes across England and Wales is also unknown. While the accessibility of legal support through lawyers and advice services has massively declined since LASPO, the rise of alternative family law services may have helped to resolve the legal advice vacuum across the two countries. Smith and Hitchings (2023) consequently argue that there is value in investigating the full range of services, including family mediation, that are now offered to family law disputants.

Even if these non-lawyer and extra-legal services go some way to resolve the legal advice crisis, the historic separation of powers between lawyers and mediators creates a problem for the latter after LASPO. Traditionally, a limited mediator *facilitated*, whereas a partisan lawyer *evaluated*. This distinction meant that mediators heavily depended on lawyers (or other professionals) to advise and provide more direct support to clients. However, the sharp separation of powers is both unrealistic and problematic in the contemporary climate. Fewer parties receive evaluative support from a lawyer, and, in many instances, only one party in a dispute has legal advice (Hitchings et al 2013: 124–125). Hitchings and Miles (2016: 175) express the same concern, arguing that the

9 Section 8.1 returns to the rising hybridity of family law services.

ability of mediators to provide information but not advice has placed them in an awkward position after LASPO.

4.1.2 A rising heterogeneity within family mediation's clientele

The second consequence of LASPO was the diversification of family mediation's clientele. Returning to the Ministry of Justice's MIAM reports, the second paper by Hamlyn et al (2015: 20–21) revealed that more parties were self-referring to mediation after LASPO because they did not have a solicitor. These findings corroborated the first MIAM report which noted that mediators were also doing more to market and advertise their services (Bloch et al 2014: 14–15). As a result, 'a greater variety of clients' were attending MIAMs. Similar to the mandatory intake meetings under section 29 of the Family Law Act 1996,[10] people who self-referred into mediation were not properly screened before the MIAM and therefore had less knowledge of the process. In concluding their report, Bloch et al (2014: 39) called on mediators 'to adapt their skills and approaches' to meet different parties' needs. The demand for a new type of mediator – a flexible mediator – was becoming increasingly apparent.

The knock-on effects of LASPO meant that mediators became the primary gatekeepers to family mediation. With fewer people seeing a lawyer, fewer attended mediation with any prior screening. Thus, an additional burden was placed on mediators: to extend their safeguarding responsibilities and screen out cases that were unsuitable for mediation. In many instances, a mediator would be the first – if not only – professional to decide if mediation was appropriate.

This increase in responsibility came about despite evidence that mediators were still not properly screening parties for domestic abuse. As part of a broader study on mediator practice, Morris (2013: 452–453) analysed 22 sole MIAMs (attended by one party) and 13 joint MIAMs (attended by both parties). She found that most mediators continued to adopt a narrow interpretation of abuse and spent very little time screening the parties for suitability. Instead, their focus was on determining the parties' financial assets and whether the parties were eligible for legal aid (Morris 2013: 455). Similarly, ten of 56 mediation clients interviewed by Barlow et al (2017: 98) reported that their mediator did not discuss domestic abuse with them during the MIAM. Hamlyn et al (2015: 43) highlight the need for mediators to be more aware of the party dynamics that could render mediation inappropriate, particularly after the introduction of mandatory

[10] See section 3.3.2.

MIAMs in 2014. Unfortunately, no further data on the effectiveness of mediator screening has been collected.

At the same time, empirical evidence suggests that many mediators are taking on more complex matters that were originally deemed unsuitable for mediation. Bloch et al (2014: 27) identify a 'variance in mediator approach' to MIAMs and mediation in their sample of 20 family mediators. They outline three distinct approaches after LASPO (Bloch et al 2014: 16–17). First, some mediators adopt a 'purist' approach and rarely take on complex cases. This group feel unable to mediate more difficult disputes, adhering to the traditional understanding of their role. In this sense, purist mediators align with the limited archetype. By contrast, most mediators in Bloch et al's sample took the second 'realist' approach, whereby they mediate more difficult disputes on the basis that mediation is often the only viable option for parties without legal representation in the post-LASPO climate. Finally, 'optimist' mediators also mediate more complex cases but for different reasons than the realists. Rather than mediate on the grounds of necessity, optimist mediators feel that mediation is appropriate so long as the parties are willing to engage with the process. Bloch et al (2014: 30–31) warn that this 'relaxed' approach could lead to 'negative outcomes', though they do not provide any detail as to why. Interestingly, the optimist approach (and to some extent the realist approach) reveals a growing view among mediators that they can handle more difficult power dynamics, once again alluding to the flexible archetype.

Effective family mediation continues to be associated with a number of factors, such as the emotional readiness of both parties and relatively equal footing (Barlow et al 2014: 25). In the Mapping Paths study, mediation was more likely to result in full or partial settlement where there were high levels of trust between the parties, as well as low levels of conflict (Hunter et al 2014: 1408). The limited mediator type is, largely speaking, well-equipped to deal with this population. However, disputes involving more complex issues or difficult party dynamics, even if they only make up a minority of cases screened into mediation, pose a significant problem for the limited mediator. Hamlyn et al (2015: 23) predict that between 66 to 76 per cent of privately funded MIAMs lead to mediation. While it is unclear how many of these cases would have been screened out of mediation before LASPO, the high conversion rate raises serious questions about the ability of limited mediators to effectively mediate a variety of disputes in the contemporary landscape. As Barlow and Hunter (2020: 15) explain, family mediation has transformed from a 'relatively niche service' for low-conflict cases to a 'mass service' for the entire separating population. The contextual justification behind the limited mediator is therefore not only weakened, but increasingly problematic in the post-LASPO landscape.

4.2 The calls for a flexible mediator practice

To summarize, the family justice system is drastically different after LASPO compared to when family mediation was first piloted in the late 20th century. From the 1970s to 1990s, the majority of separating couples accessed a solicitor (Walker 1996: 61). These lawyers provided assistance, as well as flexibility, to the dispute at hand. Post-LASPO, more parties attend mediation without first consulting a solicitor or legal advisor. This population is also more heterogeneous and often come to mediation with complex or difficult family matters. The limited mediator, who is unable to engage in any form of evaluation, is poorly suited to this clientele. However, self-representation in court is also inappropriate as the court system has not accommodated the needs of Litigants in Person after LASPO (Mant 2022). With no other viable alternative, disputants are practically forced into mediation (Hunter et al 2017: 247). Barlow et al (2014: 33) make several proposals to close the LASPO gap, including a lawyer-assisted model of family mediation for more complex cases. Unfortunately, this proposal has yet to be piloted or implemented at a national level.

Much of the contemporary family justice literature on mediation subsequently seeks to explore how mediation could respond to the post-LASPO climate. Barlow et al (2014: 25) summarize their position: 'In a context in which mediation is effectively the only choice, mediation needs to adapt to provide more tailored and specialised services.' They reiterate this argument in the concluding paragraph of their monograph: 'There is an urgent need to consider how mediation can be re-designed to operate more effectively and can re-establish the interdisciplinary linkages it needs to provide a better service in these neoliberal times' (Barlow et al 2017: 211).

Parkinson (2016: 110), one of the founders of family mediation in England and Wales, makes the same realization. She writes that the traditional approach to family mediation cannot adequately respond to the rising number of complex disputes, and that mediators must subsequently adopt a 'flexible practice'. Similarly, Hitchings and Miles (2016: 179) raise a crucial question: 'If there is no legal advice for those mediating, what, if anything, can mediators do about that?' Clearly, the demand for mediators to adapt has only intensified in the contemporary landscape.

However, these calls have led to little change. This is because flexible mediator practice remains a far-fetched idea so long as the profession is bound to its original and limited archetype. The absolute understanding of mediator neutrality puts mediators in a bind, unable to react or adjust the mediation setting in light of the parties' needs. If legal support is to remain inaccessible, the only viable solution is to modify the role of the family mediator. Unfortunately, this realization is missing from the dominant discussions around family mediation reform, creating a stagnancy of sorts. A recent debate on whether mediators can draft consent orders demonstrates the severity of this problem.

4.2.1 The stagnant debate on mediators drafting consent orders

The drafting of consent orders, while not a reserved activity, is usually carried out by a solicitor because of its legal significance.[11] While family mediators have never been explicitly prohibited from drafting, doing so could be perceived as an unneutral action that also encroaches on the work of lawyers. However, this long-standing perspective has since been called into question. Two years after LASPO's implementation, the Solicitors Regulation Authority (2015) confirmed that a lawyer mediator could draft a consent order: 'In limited circumstances where you are not advising the clients as to their legal position but simply reflecting the agreement they have reached it may be possible to agree a very specific and defined retainer [to draft a consent order].'

This brief paragraph sparked intense debate within the family mediation community. On one hand, anecdotal evidence suggested that the profession had come under increasing pressure to draft consent orders after LASPO. Edwards (2016: 1169) argued that mediation services must be 'consumer-driven' and respond to the withdrawal of legal advice, though acknowledged that the guidance published by the Solicitors Regulation Authority raised doubts as to whether mediators were even qualified to draft consent orders in the first place. By contrast, mediators such as Braithwaite (2016: 1362) argued that the unavailability of legal support was not a 'viable reason to move away from the need for separate legal advice'. She submitted that while mediators should meet the 'needs' of clients, this demand alone should not determine what was 'professionally ethically correct'. The drafting of a consent order posed a significant risk to a mediator's neutrality, rendering the action unethical from Braithwaite's perspective.

The Family Mediation Council (FMC) went on to consult its members about the issue. Its 2016 consultation set out the 'traditional model of family mediation' in which a mediator could inform the parties about the law but was prohibited from explaining how it applied to a dispute (FMC 2016a: 1).

---

11 Reserved activities are outlined in the Legal Services Act 2007, s 12 and sch 2. For further information on the Legal Services Act, see section 7.3.

The FMC (2016a: 2) acknowledged that clients were increasingly asking mediators to prepare consent orders, and asked three questions:

1. Would the role of a mediator as an impartial third party in mediation be jeopardised by that mediator drafting a consent order, once a mediated agreement has been reached?
2. Is it possible to draft a consent order without giving advice on its terms?
3. Is it appropriate to draft a consent order without giving parties advice on its terms? (FMC 2016a: 5)

These questions suggest that the limited mediator type continued to dominate (and stifle) debate after LASPO. Looking at each question in order, the first question emphasized the importance of mediator neutrality (or impartiality). Its phrasing ('*Would* the role of a mediator as an impartial third party in mediation be jeopardised') hints that mediator neutrality may be infringed by drafting a consent order. The second question insinuated that any action beyond facilitative information was problematic and must be avoided. Regrettably, the FMC did not ask respondents whether information could have the same impact as advice, a possibility that will be examined in section 4.3.1. The third and final question reiterated that family mediators were prohibited from giving advice, limiting the types of evaluation that they could perform. Combined, the image of the limited mediator underpinned all three questions. There was no consideration as to whether mediators *could* or *should* do more in the post-LASPO landscape. Rather, the FMC appeared to assume that mediators were facilitative neutrals with little – if any – ability to intervene.

Table 4.1 summarizes the responses to the two-month consultation, published in May 2017 (FMC 2017: 2). Out of 53 responses, over half (57 per cent) of respondents[12] agreed that drafting jeopardized a mediator's neutrality. Only a third (34 per cent) felt the opposite, suggesting that the majority of respondents did not believe that mediators should draft consent orders. The second question saw a similar distribution of responses, with nearly half (49 per cent) of respondents submitting that a consent order could not be drafted without giving legal advice. There was no clear consensus on whether drafting a consent order without giving advice was appropriate: 42 per cent agreed, and 45 per cent disagreed.

The low number of responses to the consultation is, in many ways, disappointing. Notwithstanding the validity of the findings, the fact that only 53 mediators answered the consultation suggests that the members of the FMC are largely disengaged from the discussions around mediation reform.

[12] Respondents were family mediators and trainee family mediators.

Table 4.1: Responses to the Family Mediation Council consultation on mediators drafting consent orders

Consultation question	Yes	No	Not answered
Q1. Does drafting jeopardize the role of the impartial mediator?	30	18	5
Q2. Is it possible to draft without giving advice?	20	26	7
Q3. Is it appropriate to draft without giving advice?	22	24	7

Source: FMC 2017

Nonetheless, it is worth considering the official responses from four Member Organizations: National Family Mediation (NFM), the Family Mediators Association (FMA), Resolution and the Law Society.[13]

Both NFM and the FMA upheld the traditional conceptualization of family mediation. NFM argued that a mediator could not comment on a proposed settlement without providing advice (FMC 2017: 10). While the organization acknowledged the need for a 'more holistic service', it felt that allowing mediators to draft orders was neither appropriate nor a comprehensive replacement for legal support (FMC 2017: 16–17). The FMA adopted a similar stance, arguing that any reform to family mediation should consider how the process 'can be supported by (cost) effective advice by lawyers' (FMC 2017: 17). It argued that neutrality sat at 'the heart and soul of mediation', rendering mediators unable to draft consent orders in any way that would be helpful or effective. From examining both submissions, it appears that neither NFM nor the FMA sought to alter the role of the family mediator in the post-LASPO landscape. They preferred her traditional conceptualization, seeking reform that protected the limited archetype.

By contrast, Resolution (2017: paras 3–4) acknowledged that the full representation model was unavailable to most disputants after LASPO. The organization argued that, so long as a 'framework of standards' was put in place, a mediator would not automatically depart from her neutrality by drafting a consent order. Resolution concluded that with further guidance and regulation, the family mediator could become a 'neutral draftsperson'. The Law Society (2017: para 19) agreed, though it emphasized that mediators must explain to their clients that only a lawyer can provide legal advice.[14]

13 The Law Society and Resolution originally published their responses on their official websites. However, these documents have since been removed.

14 It should be recognized that this comment is particularly lawyer-centric as legal advice is not a reserved activity under the Legal Services Act 2007. For further information, see section 7.3.1. Also see Smith and Hitchings (2023: 660).

The organization appeared somewhat pragmatic in its answer, recognizing that many mediators were already drafting consent orders. The question for the Law Society was not whether to prohibit this action, but how to regulate it:

> [I]t may be too late to seek to turn back the clock: whatever the formal position of the FMC organisations, individual mediators are already writing consent orders. Mediators draft memorandums of understanding that are agreed to by both parties at the end of successful mediations. The practical question is how to regulate an activity which is already happening, and how to protect clients who after mediation may not go to a lawyer and go to court with a MoU [Memorandum of Understanding] which is insufficient for the purpose of securing a consent order. (FMC 2017: 17)

The divide in opinion among the four organizations is unsurprising when considering the usual professional backgrounds of their members. NFM, which began as the National Family Conciliation Council in the 1980s, typically represents not-for-profit mediation services and therapeutic mediators. The FMA was established around the time of all-issues mediation, though its members still tend to originate from a therapeutic background. Mediators from either of these organizations are unlikely to have much legal training, and thus may feel uncomfortable drafting a consent order that could become legally binding. By comparison, both Resolution and the Law Society are regarded as Member Organizations for lawyer mediators. Most, if not all, of their members will have drafted consent orders in the past. This backdrop, along with the fact that the consultation was triggered by guidance from the Solicitors Regulation Authority, alludes to increasing interest among lawyer mediators and their representatives to depart from the limited mediator archetype.

Nevertheless, it must be recognized that Resolution and the Law Society still adhered to an absolute understanding of mediator neutrality. While the consultation received a variety of responses as to whether mediators should draft consent orders, the majority of respondents continued to support the idea that a mediator could not give any form of advice, let alone do anything to go against their neutrality. There was a clear demand for a flexible type of family mediator, though the consensus was that she should remain constrained in some shape or form.

4.2.2 Published guidance on drafting consent orders

While the FMC's consultation was largely inconclusive as to whether, and if so, how, mediators should draft consent orders, the Law Society and Resolution (2019) published joint guidance on the matter two years later. Approved by the FMC, the guidance states that it applies to 'all mediators regardless of professional origin', including those without a legal background (Law Society and Resolution 2019: para 2). It then lists three principles for mediators to follow when preparing an outcome document (Law Society and Resolution 2019: para 3). Interestingly, these principles largely replicate the three questions from the FMC's consultation. First, the guidance states that mediators must remain 'impartial'. Second, it establishes that mediators must not give 'advice'. Third, it confirms that mediators must reiterate to the parties 'the importance of taking independent legal advice'. After setting out these principles, the Law Society and Resolution (2019: para 9) emphasize that mediators must work within their 'professional boundaries and expertise'. However, they explain that mediators can add 'greater detail' to a Memorandum of Understanding in such a way that it becomes a draft consent order, so long as this outcome is sought by both parties (Law Society and Resolution 2019: paras 12–14). If a mediator does draft a consent order, they must remind the parties that the document is not an endorsement of the mediated settlement.

The guidance subsequently maintains a strict separation of powers between lawyers and mediators, stipulating that the latter can only draft a consent order if they remain neutral. By doing so, it continues to constrain family mediator practice. The fact the guidance was even published shows that mediators are expected to adapt to the post-LASPO landscape. And yet, that same guidance bars the profession from going beyond its limited archetype. The FMC's consultation, as well as the guidance released by the Law Society and Resolution, stipulates that mediators can only draft consent orders within the strict confines of information and neutrality. It may be that the guidance was designed to be more of a constriction, rather than a widening, of the mediator's remit. Nonetheless, a consent order drafted under this guidance is simply a duplication of the Memorandum of Understanding. While this approach renders a mediator facilitative and neutral, she is not flexible. The sole purpose of her consent order would be to allow parties to turn their settlement into legally binding agreements, albeit with no evaluative oversight. To this extent, a mediator drafting a consent order could be more damaging than it is responsive, leading to binding orders that lack any legal scrutiny.

On the other hand, a small section of the Law Society and Resolution's (2019: para 17) guidance alludes to a growing evaluative task for mediators. The guidance notes that mediators should consider if certain tasks 'blur the lines' of their professional role, giving the example of whether a mediator should 'prepare or assist' parties with the D81 financial summary. This document, outlining the parties' financial situation, is sent to court alongside the draft consent order. However, helping parties to write a financial summary places a new responsibility on mediators to guide parties throughout a dispute, not just within mediation. Furthermore, the guidance does not expressly stop mediators from completing the financial summary on the parties' behalf. It is up to the mediator to decide if this task, in the words of the Law Society and Resolution, blurs the lines between mediator and lawyer. That decision will depend on various factors, including the mediators' skills, expertise and their own understanding of what tasks they are allowed to perform. Consequently, mediators may take different approaches to this task, particularly where they originate from various professional backgrounds. Most parties will be oblivious to this potential variance when deciding which mediator to hire: they will be unaware that some mediators may provide a very light touch to the D81 form, whereas others may complete the document. The lack of clear guidance from regulatory bodies is extremely concerning, and makes mediators solely responsible for deciding whether they should provide the flexibility that is now necessitated in many disputes. While a mediator is well within their right to help parties with the D81 form, another mediator (or even a regulatory body) may consider her actions to be unjustifiably evaluative. A mediator could subsequently be condemned for drafting a consent order, despite exercising the very discretion that she was given by her regulatory bodies. This situation is no different to what was expected of mediators when the Solicitors Regulatory Authority first released their guidance, and continues – if not intensifies – mediators' neutrality dilemma.

The consent order debate is strong evidence that the general understanding of family mediator practice remains underdeveloped, regardless of major developments to the family justice system. Throughout various publications, the family mediator is described in the same way as when she was first introduced in the late 20th century. She is conceptualized as a strictly neutral facilitator, unable to provide anything close to advice. Yet if the context surrounding mediation has changed, surely the powers and responsibilities of its professionals should follow. This is, of course, a pivotal question for debate to consider well beyond this monograph. At present, the discussions around family mediation reform have become circular. On the one hand, there is a growing demand for flexible mediator practice. This change is only possible if mediators are allowed to depart from their traditional and limited archetype. To refuse reform hinders the effectiveness of contemporary family mediation, but to permit it violates the role of the mediator as it was traditionally conceived. A mediator who is open about their evaluation risks being seen as a bad mediator, even if this action is necessary to continue dispute resolution. And so, reform that would recognize the flexible mediator archetype becomes unfeasible.

4.2.3 Moving towards a flexible mediator archetype

How exactly can this stagnancy be resolved? The demand for a flexible mediator clearly exists. However, simply calling for flexibility only considers family mediator practice at a surface level. Furthermore, prohibiting mediators from drafting consent orders, or only permitting such action so long as the mediator does not provide anything analogous to advice, will not ensure anything close to the level of flexibility that is desired after LASPO. Without a drastic change in approach, family mediation reform remains at a dead-end.

A sophisticated understanding of the family mediator is urgently needed. In its response to the consultation on consent orders, the FMA criticized the 'unsatisfactory state of the wider jurisprudential debate' around family mediators' practice after LASPO (FMC 2017: 20). The organization noted that there had been no real consideration as to whether mediators gave non-partisan advice, nor how the profession dealt with legal disputes.[15] While the FMC did not consider this line of thinking throughout the rest of the consultation, this fleeting reference alludes to some recognition that reform is ineffective without an extensive reassessment of what family mediation can (and perhaps already does) achieve.

In actuality, the calls for mediators to adapt signal a demand to reinstate the facilitative to evaluative continuum of mediator practice that was considered in Chapter 3. Riskin (1996) originally argued that a mediator conducted both facilitative and evaluative behaviours. However, the fluidity of Riskin's framework was quickly lost under the traditional conceptualization of family mediation. The limited mediator became trapped in the facilitative realm, unable to move into evaluation without jeopardizing an absolute vision of her neutrality. Yet mediators can only respond to the LASPO gap if they are allowed to evaluate. This development is far from perfect, nor will it render family mediation a panacea for all disputes. However, what is the alternative? To leave family mediation reform dormant and provide no support for the family justice disputant? In the words of Hitchings and Miles (2016: 188), a contemporary family justice system dependent on accessible legal support through a lawyer is 'doomed to fail'. Reinstating the continuum of mediator practice, despite its potential drawbacks, is a pragmatic solution to the post-LASPO landscape.

The *flexible mediator* archetype reinstates the fluidity of Riskin's continuum. For a flexible mediator, facilitation continues to sit at the heart of her work. However, this approach is now balanced alongside the demand for evaluation. And so, the flexible mediator is a facilitative third party that assists but also conducts more evaluative actions. In this sense, discovering

---

[15] According to the FMC (2017: 20), 'a small number of other respondents' voiced the same concern.

the flexible mediator archetype is more about what the mediator can do in the contemporary era alongside her traditional role, rather than suggesting that she has completely departed from her limited conceptualization. Instead of completely changing her skillset, the flexible mediator has expanded it. Mediator facilitation is thus balanced with – not replaced by – mediator evaluation.

This is not to say that a flexible mediator can conduct the most evaluative actions. She still cannot decide an outcome like a judge. Perhaps she cannot advise, though the strict divide between advice and information has come under scrutiny in recent years (as considered in section 4.3.2). Nonetheless, a flexible mediator is permitted to go beyond the provision of neutral information, where appropriate, to provide an advisory assistance of sorts. This conceptualization recognizes that many actions – including information-provision and drafting outcome documents – can be used by mediators to influence settlement. It also recognizes that these evaluative behaviours are a natural part of mediator practice, resolving the naivety that underpins the limited mediator archetype.

The key question, of course, is when and whether such intervention is appropriate. Without adequate checks and balances, a flexible mediator could completely dictate the mediation setting. If she is going to act in a way that inevitably influences the outcome, that outcome must be fair and perhaps even just. This task inevitably means that more is expected of the mediator. She will have to determine when a case requires more oversight – for example, where there is a severe power imbalance, domestic abuse or the parties have limited legal support. Furthermore, she must have the legal knowledge and skills to determine whether an outcome is fair and just in the first place. These widening responsibilities have significant implications for whether family mediators can ensure family justice and what that family justice entails, two questions that will be revisited in Chapter 6. Regardless of the outcome of these discussions, it is clear that becoming a flexible mediator is no easy task.

4.3 Does the flexible mediator already operate?

In the 1990s, Riskin faced heavy criticism for suggesting that mediators could evaluate. However, readjusting mediation theory does not necessarily mean changing mediator practice. In fact, evidence suggests that many mediators already take on a contemporary conceptualization of their role. Riskin (2003: 7) made the same realization, arguing that his thesis was descriptive rather than normative. It was, in his words, 'too late' to argue that mediators could not evaluate.

Riskin's statement holds true in the post-LASPO landscape. The empirical work covered in Part II of this book shows that the flexible mediator type is already accepted, albeit implicitly or subconsciously, by both family mediation's regulatory bodies and their members. Mediators adopt a number of functions across the facilitative to evaluative continuum of practice (Chapter 5) that reveal an increasingly quasi-legal role for the profession (Chapter 6). Before moving onto this original empirical investigation, it is worth setting out the previous literature that begins to uncover the flexible mediator archetype. This body of work suggests that mediators regularly go beyond a purely facilitative framework, actively guiding parties towards certain discussions or outcomes.

The promotion of child welfare is a clear example of mediator evaluation. Historically, family mediation could only be used in child-related disputes. Policy praised the process for reducing not only the bitterness between separating parties, but also the harm caused to children by parental conflict. Family mediators were not supposed to dictate a particular outcome in light of a child's welfare, though they could encourage the parties to focus on specific issues. This response is evaluative as a mediator must have first decided that the parties had not focused enough on the needs and wishes of their child. A mediator thus promotes the interests of one particular individual – the child – above all other concerns. Davis (1988: 53) subsequently describes child welfare as the 'pillar' of family mediation.

This form of evaluation has been evidenced for some time. Clients at the Bromley Conciliation Bureau pilot, studied by Davis (1988: 66) in the early 1980s, mentioned that mediators were 'active' in discussions. In particular, they felt that the mediators gave a voice to the children, reminding parents to concentrate on the needs of their child (Davis 1988: 80). More recent evidence shows that mediators continue to prioritize and promote child welfare in the contemporary family justice landscape (Barlow et al 2017: 135–136). This form of evaluation, even if it is widely seen as justified, still contradicts the absolute vision of mediator neutrality. Dingwall (1986: 18) argues that the promotion of child welfare causes mediators to have a 'dual role' in negotiations: first, as 'facilitator of a two-party agreement' and, second, 'as agents of third parties'. This position can lead to 'an internal contradiction' of sorts, whereby mediators are expected to uphold the autonomy of the parties and simultaneously speak for any children or affected individuals who are not part of the negotiations.[16] Smoron (1998: 269) acknowledges the same paradox in the American context, identifying a conflict between a mediator's neutrality and her 'duty' to promote children's best interests. While evaluating to uphold child welfare departs from the limited mediator archetype, this action is widely accepted as good practice.

16 Also see Simpson (1989: 265).

Mediators have also been known to evaluate for concerns beyond child welfare. However, such evaluation is regularly conducted under a facilitative guise. This cover-up is illustrated through two pieces of research. In the first paper, Rifkin et al (1991: 154–155) describe how mediators introduce themselves as neutral third parties who cannot influence the outcome of the case. However, they adopt a 'supportive' role in private conversations with each party. Mediators thus support both parties to refine their arguments, as well as encourage the disclosure of information. Rifkin et al label this action 'equidistance'.[17] While equidistance may encourage communication by empowering the parties to state their own views, it still requires a mediator to evaluate. Of course, this action goes against mediator neutrality. A party may even interpret equidistance as a sign that they have a personal and open relationship with the mediator. And so, if a party goes on to seek further approval for their stance, the mediator retreats to their neutral and facilitative role. Once the party has stopped seeking further support, the mediator can revert to equidistance to gain additional information. Consequently, the mediator is trapped in a never-ending 'paradox', secretly moving between facilitation and evaluation in an attempt to maintain their neutral image (Rifkin et al 1991: 159).

In the second paper, Greatbatch and Dingwall (1989: 636) set out the process of 'selective facilitation'. Through analysing recorded mediation sessions, they learn that mediators move parties towards a particular outcome by making it the focus of discussions. This focus is often secured by allowing one party to speak more than the other. Greatbatch and Dingwall (1989: 637) argue that selective facilitation can also be used to challenge the strength and plausibility of a proposed settlement. The researchers do not have an issue with this approach, arguing that it is often logical, and at times preferable, for mediators to encourage certain outcomes. However, they warn that 'mediator influence' – in essence, mediator evaluation – becomes problematic when it is 'invisible' to the parties involved (Greatbatch and Dingwall 1989: 639).

With the exception of child welfare, mediator evaluation has been historically concealed by a facilitative proxy. Family mediators appear facilitative, but they regularly evaluate to advance negotiations. These evaluative actions are hidden to uphold the limited mediator archetype and her absolute commitment to neutrality. This lack of transparency has always been troublesome to the extent that disputants do not fully understand what the process involves. However, the post-LASPO landscape amplifies this problem significantly. Family mediators are increasingly expected to adapt in light of parties' needs, but are prevented by their neutral and limited

[17] The writers use one case study from 32 mediated cases to illustrate equidistance.

image. While a mediator may take a more flexible approach and evaluate throughout a dispute, the lack of transparency around these practices prevents the flexible archetype from being realized.

4.3.1 The unrealistic distinction between information and advice

Initial evidence of the flexible mediator archetype can also be found in two recent studies on the strict divide between information and advice. Combined, the research suggests that mediators regularly use information in a way that directs parties to a certain conversation or outcome. Technically, information-provision in this format is not facilitative because it requires the mediator to first evaluate the party dynamic or proposed settlement. The findings subsequently indicate that the profession is taking a more flexible and responsive approach in the post-LASPO landscape.

Maclean and Eekelaar (2016: 92) observed and interviewed 25 family mediators as part of a study on the work of lawyers and mediators.[18] They outlined multiple instances in their observational data where mediators gave information that promoted the interests of one or both of the parties. On many occasions, this information had the same effect as advice (Maclean and Eekelaar 2016: 124–126). There were also a number of occasions where mediators gave advice in relation to the mediation process or the proposed outcome, despite being explicitly prohibited from doing so under their Codes of Practice. Maclean and Eekelaar concluded that the distinction between information and advice, as well as the separation of powers between mediators and solicitors, was challenging to maintain in practice.

Hitchings and Miles (2016: 183–185) then examined the different ways in which family mediators provide information. Their findings were based on interviews with 32 family justice practitioners, 16 of whom were trained mediators. Hitchings and Miles identified three approaches to information-provision among their mediator sample. First, most mediators said they only provided neutral information through 'overviews and open questioning'. They understood information as something 'more general', whereas advice was 'tailored to clients'. However, this broad form of information rested on the assumption that the parties could access legal advice. The second 'amplified' approach to information-giving was reality-testing. Here, a mediator could give information on specific issues and events. If the proposed settlement meant that one party would pay child maintenance, the mediator could ask if the proposed amount was affordable or realistic. Hitchings and Miles clarified that reality-testing was not advice because the

[18] Maclean and Eekelaar (2016: 92) acknowledge that this 'small qualitative study' was not statistically valid or representative.

mediator did not impose a stance on the parties, though this implicit nudge could have a similar effect to partisan support. This approach demonstrates the blurring between information and advice, as well as the problems with such a binary distinction. Finally, Hitchings and Miles outlined the 'viable options approach'. Through this strategy, a mediator made 'positive suggestions' that were not previously considered by the parties. Hitchings and Miles did not view this action as 'legal advice in the narrow sense' as the mediator encouraged parties to understand the issues around their dispute. Regardless, the viable options approach involved a more explicit form of mediator intervention: a mediator might not impose a settlement on the parties, but she still directs them towards a particular outcome.

Both studies demonstrate that information-provision is not an inherently neutral act. For instance, reality-testing and the viable options approach are more evaluative than the use of information to provide an overview or allow open questioning. The mediators in these studies were unmistakably evaluating; they took on a more active role in the mediation setting, guiding the parties towards a particular discussion or outcome. Together, this data is initial evidence of the flexible mediator archetype in the contemporary family justice landscape.

Part II of this monograph will show that evaluation is part and parcel of flexible mediator practice. However, this section already demonstrates that mediator practice has always been nuanced. As Maclean and Eekelaar (2016: 125) acknowledge, the mediators in their sample were not acting 'improperly or outside their remit' by giving information in a way that directed parties to certain outcomes. Evidence from as early as the 1980s shows that mediators evaluate. The main issue with this development, then, is the lack of transparency surrounding family mediators' evaluative strategies and their potential impact on the mediation outcome. The image of the limited mediator governs discussions, even though it no longer matches (and perhaps never matched) the reality for most family law disputants.

4.3.2 Recognizing the flexible mediator: readjusting neutrality

Why are the discussions around family mediation so heavily influenced by the image of a limited mediator? It comes back to the harsh and binary interpretation of mediator neutrality. To repeat the key arguments from Chapter 3, mediator neutrality has been perceived as an absolute and completely binding concept since family mediation was first piloted in England and Wales. Mediator facilitation is deemed neutral, whereas mediator evaluation is considered unneutral. Of course, evaluation can never be a purely neutral act. Thus, a family mediator must remain facilitative in order to be perceived as neutral and legitimate.

As Parkinson (2020: 48) warns, '[w]e need a theory to explain how mediation *actually* works, as opposed to how it *should* work' (original emphasis). Openly adopting a flexible understanding of family mediator practice would begin to resolve this issue. It would reduce the need for mediators to hide behind a facilitative proxy, and furthermore increase transparency in the mediation process. Accepting the flexible mediator type is also important in terms of recognizing mediator practice for what it truly is, as well as ensuring that disputants are properly informed about the family mediation process. However, the flexible mediator archetype cannot be properly recognized unless mediator neutrality is first reimagined.

To a growing number of academic commentators, mediator neutrality is 'folklore' and a myth that muddies, rather than illuminates, mediator practice (Rifkin et al 1991: 152). Section 3.1.1 previously set out three interpretations of mediator neutrality: neutrality as even-handedness, neutrality as to the outcome, and neutrality as non-bias. Each of these understandings can be criticized on the grounds of impracticality and ambiguity. For instance, neutrality as even-handedness can only be explained by first defining equal treatment. To treat the parties equally might mean prohibiting any kind of mediator intervention, but it could also allow the mediator to interrupt (and even criticize) provided she is equally harsh to both participants. The latter interpretation would, unsurprisingly, be rejected by most scholars as it gives the mediator unrestricted power in the face of party autonomy. However, prohibiting mediator intervention under the former approach removes most opportunities for the mediator to react, even when an evaluation is desirable. The second understanding of mediator neutrality, neutrality as to the outcome, overlooks the mediator's inevitable impact on negotiations. As recognized in Chapter 3, the mediator's presence alone establishes an expectation of negotiation and also settlement (Marshall 1990: 120; Douglas 2009: 42). If a mediator had no impact on the party dynamic or outcome, the value of mediation as a dispute resolution procedure would be non-existent. Furthermore, the idea of mediator neutrality as non-bias overlooks how a mediator's actions may favour one party, regardless of her intentions (Izumi 2010: 102–103). Micro-actions, such as pausing or a minor change in body language, can still be perceived as evidence of bias. This argument is summarized by Mayer (2012: 863), who writes: 'if we are perceived to be biased or non-neutral, then to a certain extent we are'. Serious concerns around the sacrosanct vision of mediator neutrality are thus apparent.

A potential solution is to completely disregard the concept of mediator neutrality from mediation theory. Exon (2006: 419) argues that the mediation could be redefined as 'a conciliatory process of using a third party to assist disputants to reach a desired goal'. However, this proposal is flawed. If Exon's recommendation were followed, mediator neutrality would simply be replaced with the idea of 'assistance' or 'conciliation', two subjective concepts that also lack clarity. Substituting neutrality for another concept could therefore create further inconsistency within mediator practice. Mediator neutrality should remain central to mediation theory, albeit re-envisioned in a way that renders the concept more flexible.

Alternatively, mediator neutrality could be viewed as an aspiration rather than an achievable goal. This approach is endorsed by Mayer (2012: 863) as the 'clearest and most meaningful' interpretation of mediator neutrality. Nonetheless, this approach would also create confusion (Astor 2007: 227–228). Mediators would struggle to prove that they upheld neutrality: what evidence would they provide, and how detailed would this evidence need to be? This evidentiary issue could be damaging to the mediation process, rendering mediators less accountable for their actions.

Another proposal, commonly found in the Australian mediation literature, is to re-envision mediator neutrality as mediator impartiality. Those favouring a shift towards impartiality, such as Boulle (2005: 23–26), argue that a neutral mediator is detached from the outcome and cannot support the weaker party. By contrast, an impartial mediator is interested in the outcome. While neutrality mandates disinterestedness, impartiality bestows fairness and allows mediators to intervene where acting otherwise could produce an unfair outcome (Kishore 2006: 221). To this extent, the concept of impartiality provides mediators with more space to adopt evaluative strategies (and thus be understood as flexible practitioners).

However, the concept of impartiality is just as obscure as neutrality. Crowe and Field (2019: 275–276) submit that neutrality and impartiality are used interchangeably in the mediation literature, rendering them 'more or less synonymous' in practice. They argue that the distinction between the two concepts is 'technical', making little difference to how people understand family mediation theory. Crowe and Field consequently describe impartiality as an 'empty' concept that provides no further explanation as to how a mediator should act. Astor (2007: 227), another Australian scholar, also contends that presenting impartiality as a 'solution' continues to hide the mediator's influence in negotiations. Whatever term is used to denote a mediator's stance, the concept needs to be understood in a way that permits mediators to evaluate.

Mediator neutrality is, in the words of Astor (2007: 236), 'firmly embedded in the theory and practice of mediation'. It sits at the heart of family mediation theory. To completely remove the concept would be incredibly controversial and potentially have little impact in practice. To view neutrality as an aspiration would recognize the importance of the concept, but possibly lead to poor practice. And so, mediator neutrality needs to be re-envisioned in a way that maintains its crucial position in family mediation theory and practice while simultaneously allowing mediator evaluation to occur. In essence, mediator neutrality must be reinterpreted in a way that makes some mediator evaluation *justifiably* unneutral.

The preferred approach is to reimagine mediator neutrality as a qualified concept. Much like mediator evaluation, neutrality is not inherently problematic. Rather, the issue is its purist interpretation that dominates discussions and prevents reform. Nolan-Haley (1998: 837) aptly summarizes this argument: rather than replace or remove neutrality altogether, the 'real question' is whether 'absolute neutrality' is justified. If mediator neutrality were reimagined as a moderate concept, mediator evaluation would become a legitimate action. There would, of course, need to be variouschecks and balances to reduce the risk of exploitation. Certain evaluative behaviours, such as determining an outcome or giving advice, should continue to be regarded as unjustifiably unneutral and outside the mediator's professional remit. However, by approaching neutrality as a moderate, not absolute, concept, the evaluative behaviours already practised by flexible mediators could be openly recognized and subject to appropriate regulation.

In general, the binaries that regularly dominate debate shroud contemporary mediator practice in ambiguity. First, a mediator is said to be neutral, not unneutral. This is despite numerous instances where omitting to act benefits one party over the other. Second, a mediator is allowed to provide information, not advice, yet the former often has the same effect as the latter. Finally, a mediator can be facilitative, but not evaluative. Such rigid (and limited) understandings of mediator practice are neither practical, nor desirable. This is because empirical data from both the late 20th century and post-LASPO family justice systems suggests that evaluation is part and parcel of the family mediator's remit. Nonetheless, it cannot be forgotten that this body of work is preliminary. The preceding research does not provide data on what types of evaluation mediators may perform, notwithstanding the professions' different approaches to information. Research must continue to study the existence of the flexible mediator archetype, as well as the impact of these harsh binaries on mediator practice.

4.4 Conclusion

Part I has tracked the development of family mediation through the limited and flexible mediator archetypes. This argument has been grounded in policy and theory, as well as previous empirical research. To no one's surprise, the limited mediator type heavily aligns with the context in which it was conceptualized: the orthodox family justice system. However, this archetype is not fit for purpose after LASPO. Chapter 4 has revealed how the limited mediator cannot adequately respond to the withdrawal of legal advice and subsequent heterogeneity of mediation clientele. At the same time, mediators are met with an ever-increasing demand to adapt – to become flexible and provide a more comprehensive service. And yet, the discussion on how to achieve flexibility is stagnant. Reform, unfortunately, appears to be at an impasse.

Rethinking Family Mediation responds to this problem by arguing that the purpose of family mediation needs to be reframed. Specifically, it calls for a transition from the limited mediator to the flexible mediator. Research shows that family mediators have evaluated for some time. Further evidence alludes to a greater variety of mediator practices in the contemporary landscape. The flexible mediator archetype is thus grounded in both long-standing and current mediator behaviours.

The key issue is the complete dearth of transparency surrounding contemporary mediator practice. The concept of the limited mediator is so enduring that most, if not all, mediator evaluation is hidden. Many mediators appear to carry out tasks that align with the flexible mediator archetype, though they conceal these practices to uphold their orthodox conceptualization. The lack of explicit recognition that mediators evaluate is a particular issue in the contemporary climate as it prevents the flexibility desired by many families who attend mediation with complex disputes and minimal legal support. Thus, the final section of this chapter proposed to reinterpret mediation theory, specifically by reimagining mediator neutrality as a qualified or moderate concept. If mediator neutrality is approached in this manner, the concept becomes compatible with the continuum of mediator practice. Mediators would consequently be permitted to move between facilitation and evaluation, ensuring flexibility. Without reform at a theoretical, intrinsic level, the demand for flexibility cannot be satisfied.

Part I, and the body of work it builds on, has provided a foundation from which to challenge the traditional conceptualization of family mediation in today's landscape. Yet just how does a flexible mediator operate? Furthermore, is there additional evidence that confirms her existence? Part II tests and further develops these arguments through an original study on how regulatory bodies and their members have understood the role of the family mediator.

PART II

An Empirical Study into the Flexible Mediator

5

The Four Mediator Functions

Part II of this monograph confirms the existence of the flexible family mediator archetype through an empirical project. It comprises three chapters. Chapter 6 considers the value of the flexible family mediator, specifically her quasi-legal remit, in relation to contemporary family justice. Chapter 7 adopts a broader lens and considers several problems external to family mediator practice that may limit the effectiveness of any reform. Before these discussions take place, Chapter 5 presents evidence of the flexible mediator type from the perspective of family mediation's regulatory bodies and their members. It specifically proposes a framework of four mediator functions to understand flexible mediator practice.[1] These four functions can be viewed as a typology, or, alternatively, broad descriptors of the various tasks conducted by flexible family mediators.

After briefly recapping the methods of the two-stage study in section 1, sections 2 to 5 outline the different mediator functions: mediators as *helpers*, *referrers*, *assessors* and *intervenors*. Each section describes a function and the tasks performed under it. Altogether, the findings show that family mediators are expected to be facilitative helpers but can also conduct a number of hidden evaluative practices via the other three functions. It is subsequently argued that family mediation's regulatory bodies and their members tacitly accept the use of mediator evaluation. These findings allude to a lack of clear guidance on how mediators should balance these contrasting expectations, placing the responsibility for the flexible archetype on mediators themselves.

In anticipation of Chapter 6, the final section of Chapter 5 considers the value of the four mediator functions in the post-Legal Aid, Sentencing and Punishment of Offenders Act 2012 (LASPO) climate. Echoing earlier

[1] This framework was originally published by the author in 2020 (Blakey 2020). It has since been updated for the purposes of this monograph. Whereas the article was solely premised on findings from the content analysis of Codes of Practice, this chapter also uses data from the interviews with family mediators.

chapters, the analysis reveals that it is the lack of transparency around contemporary mediator practice, not the flexible mediator herself, that is problematic. Combined, the four functions demonstrate the breadth of tasks that mediators feel they can conduct in certain situations, as well as the importance of further regulation.

5.1 Summary of research methods

Part II of *Rethinking Family Mediation* is based on findings from a two-stage empirical study, the methods of which were previously outlined in section 1.3. To summarize, the study comprised a content analysis of family mediation Codes of Practice in England and Wales, followed by semi-structured interviews with family mediators.

Extracts from the regulatory documents are quoted throughout this chapter. Six Codes of Practice were analysed, three of which were enforced in the 1980s and 1990s:

1. The National Family Conciliation Council (NFCC)'s (1985) Extended Code of Practice. This guidance followed the NFCC's original Code of Practice in 1984.
2. The National Family Mediation (NFM) and Family Mediators Association (FMA)'s Joint Code of Practice, released in 1994 (UKCFM 1997: A7).[2]
3. The UK College of Family Mediators (UKCFM)'s (1998) Code of Practice.

The three remaining Codes of Practice were implemented after LASPO:

4. The Family Mediation Council (FMC)'s (2018a) Code of Practice for Family Mediators. A newer version was released in September 2024, though only one section discussed in this monograph was modified (FMC 2024b).[3]
5. Resolution's (2018) Guide to Good Practice. This document is no longer publicly available.
6. The College of Mediators' (2019) Code of Practice for Mediators. This version is identical to the 2018 edition that was first studied, with the exception of new appendices.

---

[2] UKCFM is the cited author for the Joint Code of Practice because the document was sourced from its 1997 handbook. It appears that the UKCFM enforced the NFM and FMA's joint guidance before introducing its own Code of Practice in 1998.

[3] See section 6.1.

Figure 5.1: The four mediator functions on the continuum of mediator strategies

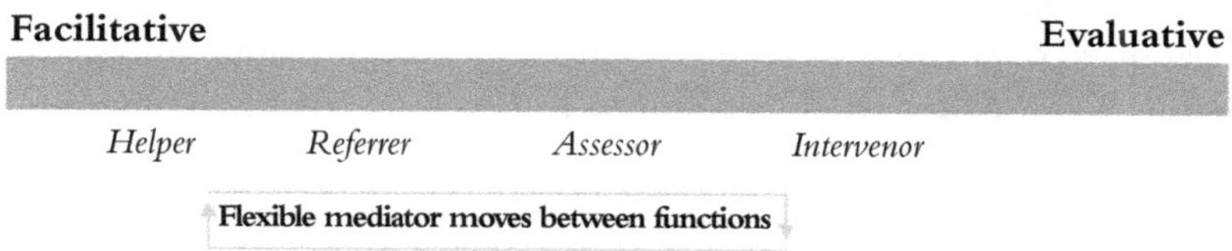

Seventeen family mediators were then interviewed. Five participants were lawyer mediators, and seven were therapeutic mediators. Another five participants were hybrid mediators; these mediators had legal backgrounds but took on additional training in a therapeutic field. To maintain anonymity, all interviewees are referred to by a pseudonym. Their pseudonyms are followed by a letter which denotes their professional background: L (lawyer), T (therapeutic) or H (hybrid).

Together, the two datasets reveal a framework of four mediator functions. Mediators can act as helpers, referrers, assessors and intervenors. Combined, these functions demonstrate the nuances and subtleties of contemporary mediator practice. They show that flexible mediators can move across the facilitative and evaluative continuum, as depicted in Figure 5.1. Moreover, they demonstrate an implicit acceptance by regulatory bodies (and a subconscious acceptance by their members) that mediators adopt a contemporary conceptualization of their role. While most of the mediator sample was not explicitly alert to the flexible archetype, many of their responses alluded to an evaluative role for the profession. Thus, the two-stage study provides ample evidence that most family mediators take on a flexible archetype in the post-LASPO landscape.

5.2 Mediators as helpers

The *helper* function is located towards the facilitative end of the continuum of mediator practice. Predictably, family mediation's regulatory bodies expect their mediators to help the parties work together and obtain a settlement. The NFCC wrote in its 1985 Extended Code of Practice: '[T]he conciliator helps the parties to explore possibilities of reaching agreement, without coercion. Where children are involved, the conciliator helps the parties to work out arrangements which balance their individual interests with those of their children' (NFCC 1985: s 2). Under this definition, the mediator provides support, particularly in relation to child welfare, to help the parties 'work out' their dispute. The same rhetoric was adopted in the 1990s:

> Family mediation is a process in which an impartial third person assists those involved in family breakdown, and in particular separating or

> divorcing couples, to communicate better with one another and reach their own agreed and informed decisions about some or all of the issues relating to or arising from the separation, divorce, children, finance or property. (*NFM and FMA* in UKCFM 1997: s 1.2; UKCFM 1998: s 1.2)

Similar descriptions can be found in more recent Codes of Practice:

> Mediation is a process in which those involved in family relationship breakdown, change, transitions or disputes, whether or not they are a couple or other family members, appoint an impartial third person, a Mediator, to assist them to communicate better with one another and reach their own agreed and informed decisions typically relating to some, or all, of the issues relating to separation, divorce, children, finance or property by negotiation. (FMC 2018a: s 1.3)

> Family mediation is a process in which those involved in family breakdown, whether or not they're a couple or other family members, appoint an impartial third person to assist them to communicate better with one another and reach their own agreed and informed decisions concerning some, or all, of the issues relating to separation, divorce, children, finance or property by negotiation. (Resolution 2018: 13)

> Mediation is a process in which an impartial third person assists those involved in conflict to communicate better with one another and reach their own agreed and informed decisions concerning some, or all, of the issues in dispute. (College of Mediators 2019: s 1.2)

Across these definitions, the mediator is presented as an 'impartial third person'.[4] She 'assists' the parties with the settlement, and the party dynamic. In other words, she is a *helper* – a professional who provides facilitative support.

The helper function is, in essence, the cornerstone of the limited mediator archetype. Under the traditional conceptualization of mediator practice, a mediator cannot do anything that goes against her helper function if she wants to be regarded as an impartial third party. By comparison, the helper function remains fundamental to the flexible mediator archetype, but is just one of many functions balanced by the profession. It continues to influence contemporary mediator practice, often leading more evaluative strategies to be restricted in their scope. Yet while flexible mediators conduct a careful balancing exercise between the various functions, the image of them as helpers continues to dictate discussion around mediation reform. As a result,

[4] The meaning of mediator neutrality (or impartiality) will be returned to in section 6.2.

a mediator's more evaluative functions become concealed, particularly under the guise of providing information.

5.2.1 The limitations of the helper function and information-provision

Throughout the two-stage study, regulatory bodies and their mediators regularly referred to the use of information. Mediators could use information for a variety of purposes, including more evaluative strategies. For this reason, information-provision is discussed under each mediator function. The forthcoming sections of this chapter demonstrate not only the centrality of information-provision within the conceptualization of family mediation, even in the contemporary landscape, but also its regularly evaluative nature.

A facilitative approach to information-provision underpins mediators' helper function. In fact, the ability to inform but not advise is central to the conceptualization of the family mediator. The NFCC originally hinted at this limitation in its Extended Code of Practice, recognizing that mediation did not replace advice: 'while offering a different approach from the legal process of negotiation by solicitors or adjudication by the court, conciliation should not be seen as a substitute for legal advice' (NFCC 1985: s 6).

In the 1990s, regulatory guidance stipulated that a mediator 'must not give legal or other advice' (UKCFM 1997: s 5.9; 1998: s 6.10). The College of Mediators (2019: s 6.11) adopts the same phrasing in its current guidance, while the FMC and Resolution place some onus on the mediator to clarify that she can only give information:

> The Mediator may inform Participants of possible courses of action, their legal or other implications, and assist them to explore these, but must make it clear that he or she is not giving advice. (FMC 2018a: s 6.2)

> Mediators will provide information about the legal process, general legal principles and associated matters ... but won't provide any individualised advice. (Resolution 2018: 54–55)

Throughout these provisions, the regulatory bodies emphasize that mediators cannot give – and cannot be perceived to give – legal advice. To return to the discussion in section 3.2.2, mediators can provide information in relation to numerous areas, including the law, because both parties are said to have equal access to that support. By comparison, advice is an unneutral and partisan act. There is no space within these excerpts for a fluid interpretation of information and advice, confirming the harsh binary between the two concepts. With mediators only being permitted to give information, they must act as facilitative helpers.

Similar findings emerged from the mediator interviews. In general, the sample made a clear distinction between information and advice:

> Obviously, I can't give legal advice, but I can give legal information. (*Emma [L]*)

> As mediators, we can't give legal advice. (*Jessica [T]*)

> [W]e [mediators] make it clear right at the beginning that we're not able to give advice. I feel most of them [the parties] respect that. ... Obviously, we're quite free to give information rather than advice. (*Megan [T]*)

Most mediators in the study, including those from a therapeutic background, thought they could give information about the law. They felt they could provide information on the legal rules and norms surrounding family disputes, including the factors outlined in section 25 of the Matrimonial Causes Act 1973. However, some interviewees doubted whether they were allowed to apply this information to the specific circumstances of a case. Victoria explained:

> What I would say is there are five orders the court has the power to make. When they make a decision, they apply the section 25 factors. ... I'll give them legal information. For example, would an inheritance be taken into account? The legal information on that is if it's sufficient, certain and proximate. But I would avoid applying the legal information to their set of circumstances. What I would do is put 'two plus two equals', and then it's up to them to make 'four', or to go to their solicitors to make four. (*Victoria [H]*)

Victoria presented information-provision as a formula. She would provide information ('two plus two') but the parties were responsible for applying it to their dispute to reach the answer ('four').

While a party can use the information provided by a mediator to resolve their dispute, many will lack the skillset or capacity to do so. These individuals are subsequently dependent on more explicit professional support to receive an evaluation. If a mediator is limited to being a helper, evaluative support (especially advice) can only be provided by another professional. The helper function is thus premised on the assumption that many individuals receive legal advice or another form of evaluative support outside the mediation setting, reinforcing family mediation's traditional conceptualization.

5.2.2 Mediators' perceptions of their role

Towards the start of the interviews, mediators were asked to describe their role in three words or phrases. Some participants provided three separate nouns or adjectives, whereas others used three words to form a statement. Altogether, their responses reveal a strong association with the helper function throughout the sample. However, further examination of these responses uncovers a more nuanced and somewhat evaluative (as well as flexible) understanding of family mediator practice.

All 17 mediators selected at least one word that indicated a preference for facilitation. Answers included 'neutrality' (*Judith [H]*), 'assistance' (*Mary [H]*), 'guidance' (*Lydia [T]*) and 'impartial' (*Jessica [T]; Megan [T]*). *Victoria [H]* chose 'non-judgmental'. *Lauren [T]* took a similar stance by responding with 'empathy'.[5] A small group of participants selected phrases that portrayed the mediator as someone who ensured a facilitative environment: *Emma [L]* discussed 'providing parties with a safe place', *Michael [L]* mentioned 'holding the space', and *Harley [T]* said his role was about 'giving people an opportunity'. Three mediators (*Amy [L]*; *Charlotte [T]*; *Kate [H]*) chose the word 'helping', and another four participants (*Rebecca [L]; Jane [T]; David [H]; Rosie [L]*) selected 'facilitator'.

The participants were asked to explain these terms, providing an insight into the dominant helper function:

> As a mediator, you are helping them solve their problems together. … You're helping them hear each other and listen to each other. (*Kate [H]*)

> I think I'm a facilitator. I facilitate discussion and conservation. I think I try to be a supporter, in that I try to support equally each of them. … There's something about supporting and working with people. And there's also something about being an impartial guide. (*David [H]*)

> I'm helping them to make the decisions for the family, otherwise who else is going to do it for them? Usually what happens is nobody makes the decision for them. So, facilitating a way forward and reducing the conflict for the future. (*Rosie [L]*)

To the sample, a family mediator was responsible for facilitating party autonomy and supporting settlement. *Jessica [T]* aimed to 'empower [parties]

5 *Lauren [T]* described empathy as: 'Being able to receive and take on board without being seen as judgmental etcetera and communicating back in a way that makes the person feel understood and able to continue communicating and look for a solution.'

with guidance to make their own decisions'. Charlotte expressed the same view and wanted the parties to realize they could reach a settlement:

> I think as soon as they [the parties] start the process of separation and divorce, they feel somehow there is kind of a legal system that is going to tell them what to do. They forget actually that it's entirely, really, a lot of it is up to them. If they want it to be. It's [mediation] maybe helping them see the freedom that they have to make decisions. (*Charlotte [T]*)

Across the entire sample, family mediation was understood to give parties the autonomy to resolve their disputes. A mediator supported parties in achieving this goal, but only through facilitation. Altogether, these extracts heavily reinforce the long-standing definition of family mediation as a process in which a third party *helps* parties reach an outcome.

While all 17 participants undoubtedly associated their work with the helper function, their views on what it meant to be a family mediator were much more complex. In fact, an evaluative remit could be identified throughout many of their responses. When asked to explain the words they affiliated with their role, two mediators who selected 'facilitator' appeared to take a somewhat evaluative approach. First, *Rebecca [L]* said that mediators were 'taught to be leaders'. While a leader may conduct a variety of tasks, their status alone suggests that they can direct and perhaps even control the mediation setting. Second, Jane felt able to interrupt:

> I guess you're managing the meeting but facilitating is a better word. You're helping them have communication and sort of trying to eliminate the bad conversations and trying to get them to focus on the future. You're facilitating – you're picking and choosing what's being said and sort of ignoring what shouldn't be said. I guess that's what I mean by being a facilitator. Kind of taking control of what is being said, really. (*Jane [T]*)

Jane said she would go beyond her role as a limited helper to eliminate any 'bad conversations'. She took control of discussions to focus the parties on the future, perhaps even intervening when necessary. Despite Jane's supposedly limited approach, she was not as facilitative as her initial words suggested.

Other mediators selected words that were more directly related to evaluation. Mary picked the term 'awareness'. She explained that mediated agreements should be both practical and able to withstand legal scrutiny in court:

> Awareness of what is really going on. Awareness of what the law is and what is going to get through the courts. There is no point in

> getting them to agree something which the court won't sanction. Also, awareness of any children who are with us in the room, as it were. Awareness of what the unit can stand. Again, getting them to agreements that are going to last. (*Mary [H]*)

Mary claimed that she would use different techniques to increase awareness, from promoting the best interests of the child to following legal norms. These strategies served as benchmarks to assess – and therefore evaluate – the proposed agreement. In a similar vein, *Kate [H]* explained that 'the mediator has to make sure that whatever they decide is workable in practice'. She hinted at the use of reality-testing, considered in section 5.4.2, whereby mediators assess the feasibility of a proposal. These responses indicated that much of the sample conducted more evaluative tasks, alluding to the flexible archetype.

Some participants appeared to understand (albeit perhaps subconsciously) that they could move between facilitation and evaluation by selecting words that encompassed different strategies. *Rosie [L]*, for instance, selected 'facilitator', 'reality-tester' and 'solution-focused'. *Megan [T]* described her role as 'impartial', but also set out her responsibility to 'keep parties focused' and 'manage their discussions'. Both of Rosie and Megan's first words – 'facilitator' and 'impartial' – alluded to a facilitative framework. However, their second and third phrases depicted a more settlement-oriented role that went well beyond the confines of the limited helper function. While neither mediator explicitly acknowledged that their chosen words depicted both facilitative and evaluative strategies, their responses gave the impression that they felt capable of moving between the two frameworks.

Thus, there was evidence early on in the interviews that mediators did not view themselves as unconditional helpers. The helper function was a starting point for mediators, as well as a benchmark from which to measure whether a more evaluative approach was justified. However, it was not the only function available to mediators. The sample heavily associated their work with assistance, yet understood that they could move along the continuum of mediator practices – represented by the other three functions – when necessary. They were flexible, not limited, practitioners.

Neither the regulatory bodies studied, nor the mediators interviewed, recognized the complexity of this situation. As will be revealed throughout this chapter, regulatory guidance lacked direction on how a mediator should balance their facilitative and evaluative strategies. The sample, as a whole, did not openly acknowledge that their role involved the balancing of conflicting responsibilities and obligations. This limited understanding was prevalent throughout the study, reinforcing the argument made towards the end of Part I that family mediators either conceal their evaluative remit or are unaware of its existence. Both inferences explain the obscurity around the flexible mediator type, once again alluding to a concerning lack of transparency around contemporary family mediator practice.

5.3 Mediators as referrers

If a mediator exhausts all facilitative techniques at her disposal, she is, under her limited conceptualization, prohibited from moving into evaluation. However, the *referrer* function enables mediators to signpost parties to a service outside mediation for this exact type of support. For example, a mediator can refer an individual to support services in light of alleged abuse (FMC 2018a: s 5.4.2, s 6.6.4). If a mediator does not have a legal aid contract and one or both parties are eligible for public funding, she can refer them to another mediation service (FMC 2018a: s 8.9). In effect, a mediator can refer parties to any service that would be beneficial to their dispute.

The central purpose of the referrer function, however, is to signpost parties to legal advice. Research by Hitchings et al (2013: 97) previously showed that mediators emphasized the need for parties to understand their legal rights and obligations. The same finding emerged from the current interviews, with the entire mediator sample reinforcing the need for legal advice. They felt that referral was particularly important when dealing with financial or property disputes:

> I think one of our roles is to make sure people have access to advice. We encourage people to seek advice. Certainly, in property and finance matters, it's about saying, 'Go and get advice'. What you don't want to happen is four, ten, whatever years down the line you think, 'Why did I do that?' Go and take advice. It's worth it. (*Harley [T]*)

> Finance and property, I'd probably push it [legal advice] a bit more. It's always important to have legal advice, especially when we've done a financial disclosure in mediation and then they've had a meeting where they've considered the different options. (*Emma [L]*)

The interviewees frequently associated the referrer function with their ability to give information, but not advice. This was a standard response across the sample, regardless of a participant's professional background. Two mediators explained:

> I can't tell them [the parties] what's right and wrong. I can't say, 'Oh you can't do that, that's not fair'. That's not my job. I'm not allowed to. So, what I say is, 'Right, there's your proposals. Here's the information.

> This is what you need to sort out. Now go get your solicitor to look at it and check that they're okay, and you feel you're fully protected, and everything's been thought through.' (*Jessica [T]*)

> [I]t's very difficult to explain to people what their legal rights are, because they're different, without sounding partial. And I'm absolutely not going to do that. So, for example, if you have an unmarried couple with a child. The unmarried couple won't be claiming any spousal maintenance because they're not spouses. The child will only be supported by the child support system which is quite rigid. How else will you deal with X? Sometimes you need to say to them, 'Go off and talk to your lawyer about this'. (*Judith [H]*)

These mediators adopted a facilitative reading of the referrer function. They were not assessing the proposed settlement, but instead encouraged the parties to see a lawyer to confirm whether the proposal was workable, fair or legally correct. Their referral moved legal advice – or evaluation – outside the mediation process, reinforcing the limited role of the family mediator.

However, referring is not an inherently facilitative action. In many instances, a mediator will only refer after evaluating the settlement or party dynamic. Returning to the previous quotes, *Jessica [T]* said she 'can't tell them [the parties] what's right and wrong', but can provide information and refer clients to a solicitor. *Judith [H]* would similarly tell an unmarried couple who could only claim child maintenance through the child support system to 'talk to [their] lawyer about this'. In order for both mediators to conclude that a referral was needed, they first needed to evaluate. As another example, *Charlotte [T]* said she always recommended legal advice but would 'push it more when somebody has a really unrealistic idea of what they want'. This response required Charlotte to be aware of the issues with one party's view or proposal, something which she could only accomplish through an evaluation. Her recommendation was a warning signal that a party's suggestion was problematic and therefore should be changed with the assistance of a lawyer. These mediators were encouraging a settlement of a certain quality, though it appeared that they would return to their dominant helper function upon referral.[6] This form of evaluation, even if small in scope, is preliminary evidence of the flexible mediator archetype.

Turning to the Codes of Practice, regulatory bodies have implicitly accepted the evaluative aspect of mediator referral over time. The NFCC originally expected all parties to obtain legal support: 'The parties should be warned against entering into any agreement without first obtaining legal advice on its terms. They should be encouraged to seek legal advice

6 The 'quality' of agreement is returned to in Chapter 6.

in all cases' (NFCC 1985: s 3, original emphasis). This blanket rule required mediators to refer every single party to legal advice. The risk of mediator evaluation, specifically when determining if legal advice is appropriate, was thus eliminated. However, from 1994, NFM and FMA required mediators to 'advise participants that it is desirable in their own interests to seek independent legal advice' (UKCFM 1997: s 6.4). The UKCFM expanded on this guidance four years later:

> Mediators must inform participants of the advantages of seeking independent legal advice whenever this appears desirable during the course of the mediation. Mediators must advise participants that it is desirable in their own interests to seek independent legal advice before reaching any final agreement and warn them of the risks and disadvantages if they decide not to do so. (UKCFM 1998: s 6.11)

The FMC and College of Mediators replicate this section in their current Codes of Practice:

> The Mediator must inform the Participants of the advantages of seeking independent legal or other appropriate advice whenever this appears desirable during the course of the Mediation. The Mediator must advise the Participants that it is in their own interests to seek independent legal advice before reaching any final agreement, and warn them of the risks and disadvantages if they do not do so. (FMC 2018a: s 8.14)

> Mediators must inform participants of the advantages of seeking independent legal or other advice whenever this appears desirable during mediation. (College of Mediators 2019: s 6.12)

These provisions allude to a more sophisticated interpretation of the referrer function. In the contemporary landscape, family mediators are not expected to refer every individual to legal advice. Instead, they must decide whether legal advice is 'desirable'.[7] In order to determine the desirability of such support, the mediator must first evaluate the proposed settlement or party dynamic. By doing so, she departs from the orthodox and absolute facilitative framework. This alteration in Codes of Practice is evidence of the flexible mediator archetype, a practitioner who uses both facilitative and evaluative strategies. Furthermore, it suggests that regulatory bodies have increasingly allowed mediators to evaluate over time.

---

7 Resolution (2018: 17) likewise requires that mediators should refer parties to legal advice when 'helpful'.

Interestingly, the evaluation that underpins the referrer function goes against the limited mediator archetype. This is because referring the parties to further support can benefit one party over the other. In these instances, referral sits at odds with an absolute understanding of mediator neutrality and, thus, the limited mediator archetype.[8] Why, then, is the referrer function openly permitted by regulatory bodies? A potential reason is that the evaluation which underpins a referral largely operates to move any other form of evaluation outside the mediation setting. After notifying the parties that they should seek legal advice, a mediator can revert back to their helper function. Her evaluative remit is restricted as a result. This sequence begins to mirror Rifkin et al's (1991) concept of 'equidistance', as covered in section 4.3, whereby mediators take on an active role in discussions yet retreat to their strictly neutral conceptualization when the parties seek approval for their stance. And so, while the contemporary approach to the referrer function suggests that mediator evaluation is becoming increasingly permitted, it appears that regulatory bodies may only explicitly permit referral because it enables mediators' limited image to continue.

Mediator evaluation is, once again, concealed by the dominant image of mediators as strictly neutral third parties. This facilitative proxy hides the flexible mediator archetype, despite her evaluative actions being of potential value in the post-LASPO landscape. Nevertheless, the remaining two mediator functions – mediators as assessors and intervenors – demonstrate how evaluation is no longer left to lawyers and is increasingly conducted within the mediation setting.

5.4 Mediators as assessors

Compared to helping and referring, assessing is a much more evaluative task. The function has gained traction over time, particularly within Codes of Practice, and again signals a shift towards the flexible mediator archetype. It envisages a diverse role for mediators whereby they assess several elements of the dispute, such as the proposed settlement and the dynamic between the parties. Following assessment, a mediator can respond in a variety of ways, including intervention as covered in section 5.5. Altogether, the assessor function demonstrates the breadth of flexible mediator practice, as well as the archetype's ability to adapt to the case at hand.

The assessment function includes mediators' ability to screen, a role that has become increasingly prominent in the contemporary family justice landscape. Screening is covered in section 6.1 in relation to how flexible mediators may or may not support a contemporary vision of family justice. For now,

8 At the same time, omitting to refer could benefit one party and thus also be perceived as unneutral. The decision to refer or not to refer is another example of the neutrality dilemma often faced by (limited) mediators, as highlighted in section 3.3.2.

the discussion will focus on two different forms of assessments: predicting court outcomes and reality-testing.

5.4.1 Predicting the likely outcome in court

Predicting court outcomes is a customary practice for family law practitioners (Sarat and Felstiner 1995: 122). However, there was initially no basis in family mediation Codes of Practice for mediators to perform this action. The NFCC (1985: s 2) did not consider whether its members should be able to discuss the likely outcome in court, though stipulated that a conciliator must help parties 'without imposing the conciliator's own values on them or directing them towards an outcome preferred by the conciliator'. Mediators were explicitly prohibited from predicting court outcomes in the 1990s: '[Mediators] must not predict the outcome of court proceedings in such a way as to indicate or influence the participants towards the outcome preferred by the mediators' (*NFM and FMA* in UKCFM 1997: s 5.9; UKCFM 1998: s 6.10). By contrast, the FMC now allows a mediator to notify clients that she feels a judge may not approve the proposed settlement:

> The Mediator must not seek to impose any preferred outcome on Participants, or to influence them to adopt it, whether by attempting to predict the outcome of court proceedings or otherwise. However, if the Participants consent, the Mediator may inform them (if it be the case) that he or she considers that the resolution they are considering might fall outside the parameters which a court might approve or order. (FMC 2018a: s 6.2)

Section 6.2 emphasizes that a mediator cannot 'impose any preferred outcome' or 'influence' the settlement. It warns mediators about straying too far into evaluation, reiterating the importance of the helper function. The FMC then permits mediators to inform the parties that a proposed outcome may fall outside the ambit of what a court would order. This action is evaluative in the sense that a mediator must first predict the likely outcome in court. If they decide to notify the parties about that assessment, they intend to influence the settlement. Similar to the evaluation that underpins mediators' referrer function, this response, while standard for contemporary (and flexible) mediator practice, would technically contravene an absolute reading of mediator neutrality as it could advantage one party over the other. This contradiction, once again, highlights the difficulties with a binary and strict understanding of mediator practice. It demonstrates the naivety of a limited mediator archetype and, likewise, the authenticity of its flexible counterpart.

Section 6.2 permits and simultaneously restrains mediator evaluation. It originates from family mediation guidance published by the Law Society in the 2000s, studied by Webley (2010: 168), which encouraged mediators to notify parties if the proposed solution was likely to fall outside the typical outcome approved by court. Webley (2010: 157) described a mediator following this guidance as a 'legal informer and backstop', reflecting a somewhat partisan (and evaluative) role that was usually reserved for solicitors. The FMC replicates this section in its Code of Practice, though it inserts a facilitative prerequisite into the assessment by including the need for party consent. However, it is unclear how a mediator can obtain this consent without hinting that there may be an issue with the proposed settlement.[9] Even if a mediator asks for permission when mediation begins, one party may still interpret this request as a sign of partisanship.

It should be recognized that informing parties about the likely outcome in court is different to imposing an outcome not previously considered by the parties. This is because the former action is less evaluative than the latter and maintains focus on the parties' own negotiations. Nonetheless, even if the mediator limits their assessment to the proposals that the parties themselves have made, informing them that their settlement may not be approved by court inadvertently tells them what kind of settlement may be accepted. A party may then use this information as a 'bargaining chip' to alter the agreement in their favour (Mnookin and Kornhauser 1979: 968).[10] To this extent, the distinction between informing and imposing (or influencing) is not clear-cut, similar to the distinction between advice and information itself. The FMC thus appears to place some constraints on mediator evaluation, possibly to maintain mediators' neutral image, yet their approach inevitably enables mediators to go beyond their limited archetype.

Inconsistencies within the three current Codes of Practice exacerbate this problem even further. Under section 4.2 of the College of Mediators' guidance: 'They [mediators] must not attempt to move the participants towards the mediator's own preferred outcome or to predict the outcome of court or formal proceedings' (College of Mediators 2019: s 4.2). In comparison to the FMC, the College of Mediators does not permit its mediators to speak to parties about the likely outcome in court.[11] By

9 Maclean and Eekelaar (2016: 80) also raise the issue where only one party consents to the assessment.

10 The use of legal information to bargain in the shadow of the law is returned to in section 6.3.2.

11 The College of Mediators (2019: s 6.11) stipulates in a later section: 'They [mediators] must not predict the outcome of court or formal proceedings in such a way as to indicate or influence the participants towards their own preferred outcome.' The wording of section 6.11 suggests that mediators can predict the likely outcome in court so long as they do not advance their own preferred outcome. It is closer aligned with the FMC's Code of Practice but contradicts section 4.2 of the College of Mediators' guidance, which completely bars mediators from predicting court outcomes.

contrast, Resolution writes: 'Resolution mediators do have a responsibility, however, to inform clients if they think that the outcomes they are considering might (or would) fall outside that which a court might approve or order' (Resolution 2018: 17). Rather than asking the parties for permission, a mediator following Resolution's guidance must notify parties if the agreement may fall outside what would be approved in court. Resolution subsequently presents assessment as a mandatory task for its mediators.[12] The varying approaches within the three Codes of Practice were previously recognized by Maclean and Eekelaar (2016: 80), as well as Barlow et al (2017: 109). However, these issues have yet to be resolved.[13] This could lead to significant inconsistencies in mediation practice, particularly where predicting court outcomes involves an evaluative assessment of the proposed settlement.

Family mediators receive little direction from their regulatory bodies on how to navigate their conflicting obligations. They are not told when it is desirable to discuss the likely outcome in court, placing further responsibility on the profession to juggle its dogmatic and limited image with the increasing demand for evaluation. Rather than clarify how the helper and assessor functions could or should work together (and in what circumstances one function should be prioritized over another), the regulatory bodies continue to portray mediators as facilitative helpers. As a result, the profession is said to only provide information about the likely outcome in court, despite the evaluation that regularly underpins their actions. This concealment obscures the flexible mediator type, once again alluding to a lack of transparency in contemporary mediator practice.

Despite minimal guidance, the mediator sample appeared to balance the helper and assessor functions. The balance adopted, however, varied among the participants. Interviewees appeared to separate predicting court outcomes into two tasks, as summarized by Rebecca:

> I suppose when somebody is really trying to almost sabotage the process by saying, 'I've come to mediation, but actually I haven't come in good faith. It's my way or the highway. My way is over there away from all reasonable proposals'. You have to sort of think, well, is this right for

[12] Resolution's stance is to be expected as its membership primarily consists of lawyer mediators, many of whom practice as solicitors or barristers. The presence of legal norms in mediation is perhaps more important to this group of mediators, though further research is required to corroborate this claim.

[13] It is important to reiterate that Resolution no longer appears to enforce its Guide to Good Practice, though the inconsistency between the FMC's and College of Mediators' guidance remains.

> mediation? You might then start talking about the parameters, the way that family law works and start vaguely. Depending on how difficult it is you then could start to have to be really explicit and say, 'Well, a judge is probably not going to accept that'. (*Rebecca [L]*)

First, a mediator can 'vaguely' outline the parameters of family law. Second, she can explicitly talk to the parties about the likely outcome in court. These tasks will now be considered separately.

5.4.1.1 Predicting as a form of information-provision

Much of the sample conflated predicting court outcomes with their ability to provide legal information. At first glance, this approach appears to reinforce the strict divide between information and advice. A small number of respondents, including *Charlotte [T]*, felt unable to give any explicit guidance on the likely outcome in court: 'I mean, I always talk about the section 25 factors [points to a poster on the wall]. They can see how a court would look at any decision. ... But I wouldn't say, "The court would do this or that". I wouldn't do that at all.' From Charlotte's perspective, giving information was completely different to predicting court outcomes. She took a very facilitative approach to information-provision, one which ultimately portrayed her as a limited helper.

However, as argued in Chapter 4, information is not intrinsically facilitative. Rather, mediators may use information in order to guide parties towards a particular discussion or outcome. If a mediator informs parties about the likely outcomes in court, this action still involves a form of assessment. Similar developments have been recognized in the family justice literature for some time, with Barlow et al (2017: 184) arguing that mediators use information to strengthen the shadow of the law. Section 4.3.1 previously referred to work by Maclean and Eekelaar (2016: 126), who observed multiple instances where mediators used information to influence the final settlement. The same section considered Hitchings and Miles' (2016: 185) 'viable options' approach, whereby a mediator directs parties towards a particular settlement or supports them in understanding a proposal.

The present study corroborates these findings. Most interviewees acknowledged that they would use legal information to move parties towards a particular outcome. Both Lydia and Jessica felt that the ability to give information enabled them to speak to the parties about their options:

> They [the parties] phone up and ask for advice, or during the mediation. Just asking, 'What would you do?' They're always asking for advice. You have to say clearly to them, 'I can't give you advice,

> but I can give you some information. This is what would happen, these are the choices, these are your options'. (*Lydia [T]*)

> Finances are a bit easier in that sense because they're a bit more systematic. You can actually say, 'These are your options with pensions. These are your options with the property. These are your options with your savings. This is what the law says about debts'. You can actually give a lot more practical information on finances. (*Jessica [T]*)

Lydia and Jessica refused to give advice. However, by setting out the 'options' available to parties, they gave information that could significantly alter the outcome of negotiations. These mediators did not claim that they would explicitly discuss the probable outcome in court, yet their actions remained evaluative. By presenting this task as merely an offer of information, these mediators concealed their assessor function behind an image of helping.

Two interviewees appeared to recognize that these actions were evaluative. The start of this chapter referred to an extract from *Victoria [H]*'s interview. She claimed she would give parties the formula of 'two plus two equals', with the intention being that parties reached the solution, 'four', themselves. She later commented that mediators should only 'get parties so far' as 'somebody who has been listening carefully can make a reasonable judgment'. In this later excerpt, Victoria understood that she influenced mediation if a party responded to her prompts. *Jessica [T]* likewise said that she 'can guide them [the parties] with information. … But it's very much what they need to do'. Both Victoria and Jessica were aware that the information they provided could alter the proposed settlement, but stressed that the responsibility for such change was on the parties themselves. They took on a flexible understanding of their role, albeit one that was restricted in the sense that they could not command or directly impose an outcome.

The majority of interviewees did not demonstrate this level of reflexivity. They continued to present information as a facilitative action, even when it was used to influence negotiations. For example, David was asked whether his mediation clients understood the difference between information and advice. He explained:

> Yes. I think we make it clear. I think that it's less relevant in children's cases than it is in finance. But I think because we make it clear then eventually – some people it takes a lot of time for the penny to drop. Maybe I'm repeating what I said earlier, but my position is you can give as much detailed information about the law as you know. You can go as far as you know. But you give it in a way which is objective and impartial, as you might read it in a book or article. In the sense that it can be applied. So, I will say to people, you can talk about a range of

> things. You can give it in an objective and impartial way. You can be very detailed. (*David [H]*)

From David's response, it appeared that he would give legal information that was not tailored to the case at hand. He framed this approach as 'objective and impartial'. Nevertheless, David mentioned that this information could be 'very detailed'. He did not consider how this information could still direct parties towards a particular outcome; instead, he reiterated his commitment to impartiality. Despite David's depiction of himself as a limited information-giver, evaluation underpinned his work. This statement was true for much of the sample – if a mediator truly had no impact on a case, there would be little point in giving information in the first place. Most interviewees did not acknowledge this reality when discussing how they predicted the likely outcomes in court, once more suggesting that the evaluative tasks employed by flexible mediators were regularly hidden or unacknowledged.

5.4.1.2 Predicting as a form of explicit evaluation

Both the FMC and Resolution allow their members to discuss whether the proposed agreement matched what would be upheld in court. However, the mediators interviewed only discussed this approach occasionally. The reluctance among the sample to perform this action was unexpected, and suggests that mediators regularly limit their evaluative functions. The responses of those who claimed that they would explicitly discuss the probable outcome in court provide further support for this hypothesis.

It appeared that some participants reassured parties that they were not giving advice (continuing to conceptualize their work as information-based) but would still explicitly evaluate any proposals made by the parties. *Emma [L]* would say to her clients: 'Look. I'm not giving you legal advice, but I'm telling you as a matter of fact that there is absolutely no way that you're going to have a 20/80 split.' Emma's conceptualization of her role remained heavily dependent on the divide between information and advice, though this distinction was blurred in her response. She was confined to giving information, yet also felt obliged to provide more evaluative support. This perspective suggests that Emma actually adopted the flexible mediator archetype.

Other participants would predict court outcomes more openly. They did not conflate this action with providing information:

> If people are proposing something that is outside what a court would order, we are able to say that. To say, 'I believe it's unlikely a court would approve that'. And they'll say, 'Really?' Yes, you need to check. (*Lauren [T]*)

> I don't think I've ever had one [mediation case] that is so kind of extreme in their differences that I feel, 'Oh this is not going to work'. If I did think that then I would probably say, 'Look, this might be outside what a judge would see as fair and acceptable'. (*Megan [T]*)

> It [the agreement] also has to be approvable by the court, if it's then going to become a consent order in divorce proceedings. So, an important role of the mediator is to make sure that people don't leave with a completely unworkable or an agreement that is not going to be approved by the court. You have to flag it up, and that's one of my roles: 'I'm not 100 per cent sure that would be approved, so I strongly recommend that you speak to your solicitors to get their view on it'. (*Kate [H]*)

> You can say, 'Well, if the court were looking at this, they might think it is a bit unfair'. You can do that kind of thing. (*Amy [L]*)

This small group of participants, comprising mediators from all three professional backgrounds, felt that they could assess the proposed agreement and determine whether a similar outcome would be reached in court. Of course, these mediators would need to understand various legal rules and norms in order for their assessments to be legitimate. For instance, Amy would not only have to understand what orders have been considered 'unfair', but be able to apply that knowledge to the parties' situation. This explicit prediction enabled Amy to actively participate in negotiations, providing her with a quasi-legal remit that could prove useful in the post-LASPO climate. This evidence further supports the claim that contemporary family mediation has become more concerned with justice, a proposition that is elaborated upon towards the end of this current chapter and in Chapter 6.

5.4.2 Reality-testing

Reality-testing also involves an assessment of the proposed settlement or party dynamic. A mediator can reality-test whether a proposal follows legal norms or upholds the welfare of the child, in addition to its feasibility.

Neither the NFCC, NFM and FMA, nor the UKCFM discussed reality-testing in their guidance. By comparison, the three current regulatory bodies accept reality-testing in some shape or form.[14] The College of Mediators

[14] While the study shows that reality-testing was not mentioned in late 20th-century Codes of Practice, it is unclear if the action was first permitted in the 2000s or the 2010s.

and Resolution specifically consider reality-testing in relation to legal norms and the likely legal outcome:[15]

> In contexts where mediators are operating within a legislative framework they should reality test the workability of proposals put forward by the participants to be clear whether they fall within legal parameters. (College of Mediators 2019: s 4.2)

> As clients work towards achieving an outcome, their preferred option should be carefully reality-checked and information given where an option being considered may fall outside that which a court would approve. (Resolution 2018: 40)

While the FMC does not cover reality-testing in its Code of Practice, the organization gives further information in its *Manual of Professional Standards and Self-Regulatory Framework*.[16] Section C9 outlines various expectations of mediators when producing an outcome statement at the end of mediation. These responsibilities include 'ensuring that all mediated outcomes follow a clear rationale, are reality-tested, and are approved by both participants' (FMC 2022a: 19).

Despite these provisions, the reach of reality-testing is unclear. None of the three regulatory bodies clarify how far the parties themselves are responsible for reality-testing. On the one hand, reality-testing may only allow a mediator to inquire. She may be able to ask about the consequences of a proposed settlement, but cannot explain them herself. Alternatively, reality-testing may cover the viability and longevity of an agreement. This reading would allow mediators to explicitly tell parties (or guide them to the conclusion) that their proposal was unworkable in the long term, widening the function's remit. The lack of detail in regulatory guidance leaves the nature of reality-testing ambiguous, albeit adaptable.

While the mediator sample appeared to restrict their ability to predict probable court outcomes, they were much more comfortable with reality-testing. Most mediators said they reality-tested when a proposed agreement did not match the parties' situation. *Mary [H]*, for example, explained that reality-testing was about 'getting them [the parties] to imagine what it's going to be like'. *Jessica [T]* emphasized that it was essential that a mediator 'questioned [the parties] on things that might happen in the future that they

[15] Resolution (2018: 37–38) additionally asks mediators to help parties in 'reality testing arrangements they are considering in the context of their growing children's needs'.

[16] Version 1.4 of this manual was introduced in September 2014 and last updated in March 2022. Version 1.5 was introduced in September 2024, though no modifications were made that affected the contents of this monograph (FMC 2024d).

haven't thought about'. *Lauren [T]* likewise claimed that reality-testing 'was not telling people that they're wrong, but it's about understanding and getting them to clarify it for each other, as well as themselves'.

Several mediators thought that this assessment was particularly important when a proposal benefitted one party over the other. As discussed by Kate and Rosie:

> The clients have to believe you are there for them both. So, your behaviour and everything you say, the language that's used, has to be constantly worded in a way that's mutual. That doesn't mean you can't reality-test and say, 'I know you're saying that, but what would happen if you did that and where would she then live?' ... You should make sure that you are completely balanced in your language. (*Kate [H]*)

> You can have one that turns up with their Mac laptop and the Excel spreadsheet, and the other who has been looking after the kids for 25 years. The first one will say, 'Well she can get a job now'. Right, okay, you were happy for 25 years for her not to work, but suddenly ... and realistically, what is she going to get? She's a bit old to start her training. She's not going to be earning the 35, 40 thousand you may like her to. You will need to give her some support. (*Rosie [L]*)

Kate did not think that reality-testing compromised her neutrality because it enabled the views of both parties to be reflected in any proposals. Rosie similarly felt that she could give more support to a weaker party through reality-testing, though she did not clarify what this meant in practice. What became clear from these excerpts, even if mediators did not recognize it themselves, was that reality-testing could be incredibly evaluative. This form of assessment weakened the traditional helper function, demonstrating how the mediator sample took on a contemporary conceptualization of their role.

The interview data indicates that more mediators are reality-testing after LASPO. In a pre-LASPO study, Hitchings and Miles (2016: 184) found that a 'smaller number of interviewees', comprising 16 family mediators, mentioned reality-testing. By contrast, reality-testing was discussed by roughly two-thirds of the current mediator sample. The increased interest in reality-testing indicates that the practice – and more evaluative tools in general – have become more prevalent within family mediator practice. This finding, once again, alludes to the rise of the flexible mediator archetype. Regulatory bodies appear to accept this development, with recent Codes of Practice openly allowing mediators to reality-test.

While mediators appear more open to reality-testing compared to predicting court outcomes, it remains to be seen exactly how the profession restricts its use. Some mediators may take a very limited approach to reality-testing, whereas others may reality-test every aspect of a proposal. At this moment in time, mediator assessment is unpredictable. This ambiguity contributes to the lack of understanding surrounding the flexible mediator type. However, it must not be forgotten that such variance is an inevitable – and perhaps even welcome – part of contemporary mediator practice. The flexible mediator archetype, as her name suggests, adapts to the case at hand. Thus, it is actually preferable for mediators to adapt their approach to reality-testing so long as the action stays within pre-determined limits. The real issue, then, is that this flexibility is not properly recognized or regulated. If it were, the general understanding of flexible mediator practice would improve, and limitations could be placed on her conceptualization where it was felt that an assessment went too far. While the nuances behind contemporary mediator practice have understandably generated apprehension, hiding these actions behind a facilitative proxy does little to mitigate the issues associated with the flexible archetype.

5.5 Mediators as intervenors

The fourth function, mediators as *intervenors*, involves the mediator intervening by acting in a way that alters the discussion or the mediation setting. There was ample evidence within both regulatory guidance and the interview data that intervention has become a common practice for family mediators after LASPO. However, similar to the assessor function, intervention was often restricted. Various examples of intervention, including stopping the parties from acting in a certain way, will be set out in the following subsections. The present study does not reveal the specifics of these interventions, revealing the need for further research and data on the flexible mediator archetype.

Intervention typically follows assessment. In this scenario, a mediator identifies a problem with the settlement or party dynamic and intervenes in an attempt to alleviate the situation. As this section will go on to show, many actions that are considered to be interventions may also fall under another function. For instance, predicting court outcomes and reality-testing have been discussed as forms of assessment, yet those strategies may turn into interventions once a mediator uses them to intentionally direct the outcome. While this fluidity may obscure the different mediator functions, it should not be regarded as a drawback of the theory. Rather, it demonstrates the versatility of the contemporary mediator, a factor which should be welcomed in the post-LASPO landscape.

Mediators can intervene in response to a power imbalance, though regulatory bodies did not always permit this action. In 1985, the NFCC only mentioned the risk of harm in a section on confidentiality. It stated that if a mediator felt 'a person's life or safety is endangered' or 'there is substantial danger, particularly to a child', she was expected to signpost the parties onto the relevant support service (NFCC 1985: s 4). The NFM and FMA released a similar provision the following decade, stipulating that mediators were required to 'advise the participants to seek help from the appropriate agency' if there had been (or was a risk of) significant harm to a child (*NFM and FMA* in UKCFM 1997: ss 8.3–8.4). Mediators were additionally required to contact the 'appropriate agency' themselves if it was 'necessary or desirable' to protect a child from significant harm. While a mediator following either Code of Practice still had to evaluate the party dynamic to determine the risk of harm, she was barred from intervening. Instead, she could only refer the parties to additional support. And so, mediators' ability to evaluate was heavily restrained, reinforcing the limited archetype.

However, the NFM and FMA also introduced a new section in their Joint Code of Practice to address problematic 'behaviour': 'Mediators must at all times remain impartial as between the participants. They must conduct the process in such a way as to redress, as far as possible, any imbalance in power between the participants. They must seek to prevent manipulative, threatening or intimidating behaviour by any participant' (*NFM and FMA* in UKCFM 1997: s 4.4). Several years later, the UKCFM (1998: s 4.20) explicitly referred to 'violence or any other harm'. Section 4.4 built on the NFM and FMA's previous guidance:

> Mediators must seek to prevent manipulative, threatening or intimidating behaviour by any participant. Mediators must conduct the process in such a way as to redress, as far as possible, any imbalance in power between the participants. If such behaviour or any other imbalance seems likely to render mediation unfair or ineffective, the mediator must take appropriate steps to try to prevent this, terminating mediation as necessary. (UKCFM 1998: s 4.4)

The FMC (2018a: s 6.3.2) repeats this section, though the final sentence now reads 'including terminating the Mediation *if* necessary' [emphasis added].[17] For this provision to apply, a mediator must first recognize that one party's behaviour is 'manipulative, threatening or intimidating'. Following this assessment, she must intervene in three broad ways. She must, first, prevent abusive behaviour and, second, alter the mediation process to redress power imbalances. These responses are considered in section 5.5.1. Third, a mediator must take appropriate steps to prevent mediation from becoming unfair or ineffective, as discussed in section 5.5.2.

[17] Similar phrasing is used by the College of Mediators (2019: s 4.3.2) and Resolution (2018: 14). Both organizations confirm that 'appropriate steps' include termination.

5.5.1 Preventing abusive behaviour and redressing power imbalances

Preventative measures can be relatively straightforward. For instance, a mediator can set ground rules for all the parties involved (Parkinson 2020: 267). A mediator can specify that no one should interrupt while another person is speaking, repeating these rules if they are not followed (Gulliver 1979: 223). Such reminders can help the parties stay focused on a particular task and potentially reduce the risk of abusive behaviour.

In a similar line of thinking, *Jane [T]* said that power imbalances were often prevented through 'the preparation work'. She explained that she would 'empower' the weaker party 'to speak up', and also felt that the Agreement to Mediate, a document which set out how both the parties and the mediator were expected to act in mediation, gave reassurance that inappropriate behaviour would be dealt with. Four other participants mentioned the Agreement to Mediate. *Judith [H]* felt the section on safeguarding in her Agreement to Mediate was particularly important as it clarified to the parties that she would still refer the case to the appropriate authorities if a child had been harmed. *Harley [T]* similarly mentioned that his Agreement to Mediate placed a particular focus on 'taking into account the needs of each other and the children'. Both Judith and Harley claimed they would return to these expectations to keep the parties on track. Nonetheless, it is inevitable that some parties would ignore these preventative measures.

The FMC additionally expects mediators to conduct the mediation process to redress any imbalances between the parties. This could involve changing who speaks in what order, as well as increasing (or decreasing) the number of breaks in a mediation session. In her interview, *Jessica [T]* specifically spoke about 'practical things, such as obviously room arrangement, chairs, where they sit'. *Emma [L]* recalled a case where she immediately took one client to the mediation room when they arrived instead of having them 'sit in reception'. These adjustments may appear relatively small in terms of their impact, but can be crucial in supporting a vulnerable or nervous individual.

A mediator can adjust the mediation setting even if neither of the parties has raised a concern. This action is emphasized by Roberts (2014a: 270), who mentions that mediators should speak to the parties individually at the start of every session to determine if additional support is needed. The number of private conversations can increase if the mediator feels that it would support the weaker party to explain or develop their view. Adjustments can also be made during the mediation session: for example, *Charlotte [T]* spoke about giving one party 'more time to understand something or to speak up when the other person has a tendency to speak more or dominate in that area'. *Rosie [L]* shared a similar situation where one party continuously shut down the other person's attempts to understand what financial assets were available. Rosie's response would involve 'making sure you went through everything carefully, making sure she [the disempowered party] had all the information'.

One way a mediator can seek to prevent or redress power imbalances is by switching to a different family mediation model. Eight interviewees mentioned shuttle mediation, whereby the parties sit in separate rooms and the mediator moves between them. Some participants felt that shuttle mediation gave a voice to weaker parties:

> They [a party] might not be vocal in what they want to get out. If you feel like there is something they're not saying, or possibly depending on the dynamics, caucusing and actually splitting them up. They might be able to speak then when they're with just you. They might answer questions better in a shuttle mediation. (*Megan [T]*)

> If I feel that there's any power imbalance I'll say, 'I think we need a break'. And I'll caucus that meeting then. Just invite them for some time out until the mediation can start again. (*Jane [T]*)

Despite the flexibility that shuttle mediation provided, most of the interviewees who mentioned the model had reservations about its effectiveness. For example, *Charlotte [T]* felt that shuttle mediation could be 'inefficient'. She explained that many parties wanted to try shuttle mediation 'but also want it [mediation] done really quickly, and that's just not realistic'. Kate also thought that shuttle mediation prevented open discussion between the parties:

> Well, the whole beauty of mediation is that people are hearing things directly. The mediator will help them unravel really important things that they need to discuss. … If they can't hear that and are getting my summary of what the other said, it's in my voice. It's not coming from each person's voice and their body language and visual expressions. That's often what makes mediation work. … Whereas in a shuttle … I always say it's not true mediation. It's the next best thing. (*Kate [H]*)

A recurring theme emerged in the data: family mediators were only comfortable intervening when they felt that it was appropriate and necessary for mediation to continue. To Kate, shuttle mediation was the 'next best thing' as the model limited the opportunity to foster a positive relationship between the parties. By the same token, *Lauren [T]* spoke about how she would offer 'separate appointments on different days' for cases with significant safety concerns. She mentioned that the model was not 'productive', but sometimes the only way that mediation could work.

These findings suggest that family mediators use a wide variety of interventions in complex disputes. This variance is, of course, to be expected of the flexible mediator archetype. The limited mediator was well suited to straightforward disputes with legal support on both sides, as argued in Chapter 3. However, Chapter 4 recognized that family mediation's clientele became more heterogeneous and complex after LASPO. The demand for mediators to be flexible – in other words, intervene – intensified as a result. The interview data suggest that family mediators now regularly adopt a contemporary understanding of their role, implicitly or subconsciously accepting evaluation as an important, albeit restricted, part of their work.

5.5.2 Taking appropriate steps

The third way that the FMC expects mediators to respond to power imbalances is the use of 'appropriate steps' when mediation becomes 'unfair or ineffective'. The FMC does not explain the meaning of either phrase: it is the responsibility of each mediator to determine when mediation becomes unfair or ineffective, whether they are allowed to intervene, and what appropriate steps they should take.

Termination is a clear example of intervention. However, the interview data indicated that mediators rarely stop mediation. *Harley [T]* mentioned that he had only terminated mediation 'once or twice' in the 20 years that he had been a mediator because the weaker party was unable to 'say whatever [they] wanted'. In fact, only a third of the sample mentioned termination, most of whom viewed it as a last resort when all other options had been exhausted. This view was advanced by *Emma [L]*, who felt that it was 'inappropriate to continue' mediation when one party kept trying to exert control over the other individual. *Jessica [T]* would likewise threaten to stop mediation in order to keep one or both of the parties on track, though it was unclear when she would actually follow through with this warning.[18]

What other steps can a mediator take when mediation becomes unfair or ineffective? The FMC adjusted its guidance to clarify that intervention *included* termination, implying that mediators could now intervene in a variety of ways. Parkinson (2020: 267) provides some examples of interventions in her practitioner textbook. She explains that a 'pro-active mediator' – in effect, a mediator taking on a flexible conceptualization of her role – could 'acknowledge and respond to the dynamics in the room'. Parkinson also suggests that a mediator can 'offer suggestions' or 'raise questions that neither participant has raised'.[19] In a similar vein,

---

[18] Jessica stated: 'If they [the parties] are having an argument about something, I'm very clear in saying, "Look, if you can't keep your voices down or discuss this civilly around the table, then mediation is not right for you".'

[19] Gulliver (1979: 225) similarly comments that a mediator can make 'suggestions' that they think 'a party would like to make', where that individual appears unable to do so.

Charlotte [T] claimed that she would 'occasionally interrupt or reframe' discussions, but did so to 'try to create a space for the other person to speak'. This was the preferred approach for much of the sample. Interviewees would use questioning tactics to encourage the parties, rather than act on their behalf:

> [O]ne person might be very clued up with the finances. Again, let's talk about it. 'What I'm picking up here is you're really up to date with it: you can do it straight away. You're not, so you're going to need more time. That is probably going to be frustrating for you. Is it okay if we, if we go forward?' You're bringing them with you. Rather than not talking about it and one person might be thinking, 'You've given that person all that time. God, I'm already there!' Anticipate what they might be feeling. Get their permission. You're treating them with huge respect when you say, 'Is it okay if we do it like that?' Asking questions all the time rather than making statements for them. (*Harley [T]*)

> [Y]ou have to really address that [power imbalances]. When she'd sort of say, 'Oh well, you [the other party] used to do all the finance and that kind of thing'. Okay. Let's draw this out. Sometimes you have to ask more of the questions. (*Amy [L]*)

> [T]rying to really keep engaging and asking questions and keep checking with the person who isn't so vocal. (*Megan [T]*)

> You make sure that Dad has the space to talk. By giving him the space, you've redressed the potential power imbalance in the room. (*Kate [H]*)

> I will encourage them [the parties] to say what is on their mind. However foolish they may think it is, I would rather know. It doesn't matter. They can't use it against you. If I think there is an important point they're trying to make, then I will help advocate that point for them. (*Michael [L]*)

For the majority of participants, intervention was about giving the weaker party the space to advocate for themselves. While this tactic was still a form of evaluation as the mediator had to determine that one party needed more support, the sample's responses suggest that they placed restrictions on their intervenor function. They attempted to empower the weaker party, an action which, if successful, could reduce the need for mediator evaluation later on.

A handful of participants spoke about more direct techniques that influenced negotiations. These actions were still centred on the use of information, though the way in which the information was used would render mediator evaluation more explicit.[20] Judith said that she would provide more support to someone without legal representation (in effect, a Litigant in Person in mediation) if the other party had legal advice:

> If I know that he or she has got legal advice I will probably be a little more protective of the other one [without legal advice] … I mustn't be partial, but I will probably be a little more protective of the other one. Just to say, 'Have you thought this out?' That's usually when I get very firm recommending legal advice. (*Judith [H]*)

Harley admitted that he 'can be a bit blunt'. He would openly explain to the parties that one individual was compromising more than the other:

> Of course, the danger if there's domestic abuse issues is that one person might do all the giving and one person might do all the taking. I like having open conversations. If someone does get through a block, I'll say, 'Right, this person has just given something!' If it happens again, I'll say, 'Oh! This person has given again'. I will basically let them know that, actually, it's not okay for one person to keep doing it. That doesn't work. So it's about articulating. (*Harley [T]*)

At first glance, these strategies are not that different to those used by purely facilitative limited mediators. Both limited and flexible mediators can make statements or raise questions throughout a mediation session. However, the flexible mediator differs because she actively participates in discussions to support one or both of the parties. A limited mediator seeks to continue discussions, regardless of the subsequent outcome. Meanwhile, a flexible mediator intervenes because she feels it will improve the party dynamic or proposed settlement. Her strategy is flexible, though the specifics of these interventions remain somewhat unclear.

[20] Parkinson (2020: 268) similarly suggests that mediators can manage power imbalances by obtaining and sharing information between the parties, as well as exploring 'all available options' for settlement. This strategy was adopted by *Lydia [T]*, who mentioned: 'If there is a power imbalance and we get to mediation … I suppose it's the giving of information that's useful, in those circumstances. Because people do need to be aware of what courts might consider.'

5.5.3 The scope of mediator intervention

All three obligations set out by the FMC involve an evaluation of, and interference with, the party dynamic. After a mediator has realized that the parties are of unequal standing, she must determine the best course of action and then put this plan into fruition. Mediation may be suspended or terminated, though most mediators regard this action as a last resort. The focal point of these provisions is that a mediator must take certain steps to reshape the party dynamic: she is *required* to change the process in light of the parties' needs. Yet with little guidance from regulatory bodies, it is up to the mediator to determine what level of intervention is appropriate.

The way that regulatory guidance deals with the intervenor function amplifies mediators' neutrality dilemma. The neutral image underpinning the helper function, as well as the original conceptualization of family mediation, means that a flexible mediator's evaluations are regarded as radical and consequently inappropriate. Yet Codes of Practice also permit, and at times mandate, evaluation through the intervenor function. Regulatory bodies do not resolve these conflicting messages, let alone acknowledge them.

There exists a haziness, or perhaps a cognitive dissonance, around the breadth of interventions available to family mediators. The mediator sample did not provide many concrete examples of how they intervened, nor were their explanations very thorough. In this sense, the strategies and techniques of a flexible mediator might be so instinctual that the sample was largely unaware of their interventionist behaviours. This unfamiliarity is not helped by the lack of detailed guidance on how mediators should intervene, nor the absence of discussions around contemporary mediator practice in the post-LASPO landscape. Consequently, there is a pressing need to explore the types of intervention undertaken by mediators. Further empirical work would help to clarify whether these interventions are justifiably unneutral, and perhaps even reduce the apprehension around the flexible mediator archetype.

5.6 The value of the different functions in contemporary times

The four-function framework shows that family mediator practice has become more flexible over time. It demonstrates how mediators feel able to adopt a number of different strategies, particularly after LASPO. This flexibility is evident within Codes of Practice, as well as mediators' understanding of their role and the mediation process. Even when the mediator sample viewed their work as facilitative, they claimed to use techniques that guided parties towards particular outcomes. Evaluation underpinned many of these actions. Thus, there was ample evidence in the study that mediators move across the continuum of mediator functions to adapt to the case at hand. The final section of this chapter connects these four functions to the transition from the limited to the flexible mediator archetype, and, in anticipation of Chapter 6, begins to consider how the latter can provide more effective support in the contemporary family justice system.

The helper function embodies the traditional conceptualization of the limited family mediator. Mediators have long been understood as neutral assistants with little power to command the mediation outcome. This stance was encapsulated by the NFCC (1985: s 3), which stated that mediators 'must never give an evaluation or subjective appraisal of either party to either solicitor'. While this excerpt relates to communications between mediators and lawyers, it illustrates how mediators could not openly assess the parties involved in a dispute. If a mediator was prohibited from performing this evaluation outside of mediation, it is likely that they were also prevented from doing so during negotiations. Mediators were limited to the facilitative realm, expected to act as helpers at all times.

Assessment and intervention were only permitted where there was harm (or likely harm) to a child. If such harm occurred, the mediator was required to refer the parties to legal or other advice. Notwithstanding this scenario, all other parties were referred for legal support, reducing the potential for mediator evaluation. The referrer function was thus designed to protect mediators' limited conceptualization. This approach was relatively effective in the late 20th century where, as discussed in Chapter 3, family mediators saw a generally homogeneous clientele with regular access to a solicitor. The prominence of lawyers and legal aid within the traditional family justice system meant there was not only little demand for mediators to move beyond the helper function, but little justification for doing so.

In the 1990s, the referrer function became conditional. Family mediators were still required to refer parties to additional support, but only when it was 'desirable'. The profession was subsequently expected to evaluate the party dynamic or the dispute to determine if further support was needed. Regulatory bodies still include this prerequisite in their contemporary Codes of Practice. While the interview data suggests that mediators emphasize the importance of legal advice in many situations, relying on other family dispute professionals to provide more direct support is impractical in the post-LASPO landscape. A stagnancy of sorts arises as a result, whereby mediators are increasingly expected to adapt but prohibited from moving beyond their traditional and limited archetype. As mentioned by Resolution:

> An increasing percentage of people are not seeking legal advice on family legal issues. This may be because they don't have the means to afford it or that they have made a choice not to do so. … Whilst you may have considerable concerns for those who cannot afford legal advice, you must ensure you work within the requirements of the FMC Code of

> Practice and must not provide partial advice, as to do so would breach your neutrality and the impartiality of any mediation process. (Resolution 2018: 17–18)

It is understandable that regulatory bodies are hesitant to allow mediators to go beyond their helper function. However, it is unlikely that mediators will ever be allowed to provide advice.[21] Openly giving advice is an unjustifiable departure from neutrality, even for the flexible mediator. However, prohibiting mediators from conducting less radical forms of evaluation does little to aid the profession in supporting the rising number of disputants with no other support. If mediators are increasingly expected to adapt, they must be permitted to go beyond their helper and referral functions.

Regulatory bodies' growing acceptance of the assessor function reveals an increasingly evaluative remit for family mediators, again confirming the emergence of the flexible mediator archetype. Over time, regulatory guidance has been changed to allow mediators to predict the probable outcome of a dispute were it heard in court (notwithstanding the FMC's requirement for party consent). Mediators are also explicitly allowed to reality-test. The sample appeared to take a reserved approach to the former task by first providing information about legal norms, though several interviewees said that they would explicitly discuss the probable court outcome with their clients. The sample was, by comparison, much more comfortable with the idea of reality-testing. Even so, both strategies first required family mediators to be aware of the legality and viability of different proposals. Once an assessment took place, a mediator must have been able to apply those norms to the case at hand. A limited mediator, bound to her strictly facilitative framework, would be prohibited from performing these actions.

The final intervenor function is further evidence of the flexible mediator archetype. Through intervention, a mediator directs the mediated outcome. By doing so, she provides additional support to the rising number of self-representing disputants within mediation. While the intervenor function is frequently associated with termination, this action alone does not provide the desired level of flexibility post-LASPO. Unfortunately, the specifics of other techniques and strategies under this function remain unclear. Regulatory bodies expect mediators to respond to power imbalances, yet provide no concrete examples of good practice within their published guidance. The mediator sample regularly spoke about how they would intervene,

21 If such reform were introduced, mediators would probably only be permitted to give advice through an alternative mediation procedure. A similar idea was discussed by Maclean and Eekelaar (2016: 132) who propose a model of 'legally assisted family mediation'. For further information, see section 8.2.

though many of their responses were underdeveloped and only revealed the intervenor function at a foundational level. The techniques they described were often analogous, if not identical, to those employed through the other functions, such as information-provision and questioning. The intervenor function is ambiguous, making it incredibly difficult to understand the intricacies of contemporary (and flexible) mediator practice.

This problem is not aided by the fact that the flexible mediator type is often hidden to uphold absolute mediator neutrality. The expectation that mediators remain facilitative helpers – and only become referrers when necessary – means that mediator evaluation is still disregarded as poor practice. In order for a mediator to be flexible yet maintain her limited image, she must evaluate discreetly. And so, mediators are portrayed as a group of strictly facilitative helpers, despite being allowed to assess and intervene. Gulliver (1979: 226) acknowledges this adaptability and comments that mediators do not 'adopt a single role' during negotiations. Instead, they adjust their work 'to fit the changing circumstances'. Kate recognized this fluidity in her interview:

> I think the role of the mediator is a lot more than in a way one can describe, because it's very subtle in terms of how you are helping them move forward. Just the way you say something back, you reframe it in a different way. Whatever skills the mediator will use, it involves you thinking on your feet all the time, because you never know what will happen in the room. But at the end of the day, that's what our main role is. It's to help them. (*Kate [H]*)

A limited mediator must remain within the facilitative realm, only evaluating to refer parties to further support. However, this conceptualization is dogmatic and impractical in today's family justice system. Flexible mediators are still helpers and adopt this function throughout most negotiations. They remain alert to any shifts in the party dynamics and take on a number of other functions (including referral, assessment and intervention) in response. Neutrality thus appears to be prioritized at the start of mediation, but balanced alongside flexibility as negotiations continue.

Perhaps the more facilitative mediator functions are best understood as the starting point for contemporary mediator practice. As acknowledged in section 4.2.2, the flexible mediator is more an extension of the limited archetype, rather than an outright departure from it. To *Kate [H]*, the 'main role' of the mediator was to help parties create an agreement that worked for their particular situation. However, she recognized that mediators adopted 'subtle' techniques to promote settlement, improve party communication or manage conflict. And so, as a mediator evaluates, she adopts a contemporary conceptualization of her role. This format enables the mediator to, where necessary, be flexible and provide more direct support, all while promoting her facilitative and neutral image.

This approach has interesting implications for the debate about whether mediators should be allowed to do more in the post-LASPO landscape. Section 3.1.3 recognized that mediator evaluation had been criticized as unfettered and uncontrollable. However, the content analysis and interview data both show that mediator evaluation is actively constrained by its performers and their regulators. This regulation ensures that some degree of facilitation is maintained. Many, if not all, of these constraints are also imposed by mediators themselves. It is thus apparent that evaluation has become a critical component of contemporary mediator practice, though it is governed by various checks and balances to ensure that mediators keep within their professional boundaries. The flexible mediator is, by default, a facilitative helper, yet she conducts constrained forms of evaluation when required. The problem, then, is that mediators are unable to be open about their evaluative practices, concealing their flexible conceptualization in the process.

The lack of direction from regulatory bodies on this matter is concerning. With little published guidance, mediators are left to grapple with the intricate task of balancing the four different functions and deciding when to move between them. Of course, regulatory bodies cannot be expected to provide comprehensive guidance on how a mediator should act in every instance. Such rigidity would absolve the very flexibility that contemporary mediator practice seeks to provide. However, this chapter has cited numerous parts of current guidance that echo and sometimes adopt the exact same wording found in earlier Codes of Practice. As a whole, regulatory guidance is yet to undergo any significant revisions in light of the post-LASPO landscape.

The key issue, once again, is the absence of transparency around the transition to the flexible mediator archetype. There is a lack of openness among regulatory bodies and their members as to how mediators adopt a variety of facilitative and evaluative strategies. This cover-up has, in turn, prevented the proper regulation of flexible mediators, leaving much of their work unscrutinized. While the flexible mediator type could play a key role in supporting family law disputants after LASPO, her value can only be realized with further recognition and reform. The dominant image of the limited mediator has massively constrained scholars' and practitioners' understanding of the profession, stifling debate and reform.

5.7 Conclusion

Family mediators are regularly portrayed as information-giving facilitators. They are expected to be limited neutrals at all times. Yet there are cracks in the facilitative façade within not only Codes of Practice, but also in the responses of mediators themselves. The findings from the two-stage empirical project show that mediators are tacitly understood to take on a contemporary conceptualization of their role. Regulatory bodies allow their members to carry out tasks that are often more evaluative than they are facilitative. Family mediators themselves are habitually aware of these different techniques. However, it is still rare for mediator evaluation to be openly permitted, with such acceptance usually being hidden or implicit.

Through examining four different functions, this chapter has shown how flexible mediators adapt their strategy to the case at hand. Mediators are known to be *helpers*, but they often evaluate the settlement or party dynamic to determine if a *referral* to other support is desirable. They also *assess* and *intervene*. These latter two functions enable mediators to begin to provide the flexibility that is highly sought after in the post-LASPO family justice system. However, a lack of data on the specific techniques employed under these functions renders our understanding of the flexible mediator archetype somewhat underdeveloped.

For the flexible mediator to be openly accepted, her evaluative techniques must be transparently used, properly recognized and effectively regulated. At present, none of these strands are satisfied. The study indicates that regulatory bodies only allude to mediator evaluation, and family mediators struggle to recognize the intricacies of their role. For these reasons, the debate around family mediation reform urgently needs to acknowledge the presence and fluidity of the four mediator functions. This development could have significant implications for the post-LASPO era; open use of the assessor and intervenor functions could promote a contemporary vision of family justice and, ultimately, a contemporary mediation model where mediator evaluation is regulated. Chapter 6 investigates this line of thinking by returning to the question of whether family mediation can be viewed as a family justice apparatus.

6

Flexible Mediators and Family Justice

Earlier parts of this monograph argued that the contemporary conceptualization of family mediation aligns with a contemporary vision of family justice. In Chapter 1, it was submitted that access to justice is no longer strictly associated with access to court and that family mediation has evolved into a potential family justice apparatus. This was followed by the claim in Chapter 2 that the Legal Aid, Sentencing and Punishment of Offenders Act 2012 (LASPO), despite its significant drawbacks, provided an opportunity to rethink the meaning of family justice in the contemporary landscape. Combined, these chapters advanced the idea that the purpose of family mediation and family justice had developed more widely over time. The remainder of Part I parked the discussion of family justice and instead tracked the development from the limited to the flexible mediator archetype. This transition was then evidenced by a framework of mediator functions, as set out in Chapter 5.

Chapter 6 combines these discussions and reflects on the value of the flexible mediator type in supporting contemporary family justice. Its arguments are again based on data from the content analysis of family mediation Codes of Practice and semi-structured interviews with family mediators, though more reference is made to the latter.

This investigation is in three parts. The chapter begins by examining mediators' ability to screen parties into mediation. The data suggests that while mediators do not feel they can mediate every single dispute, LASPO does not provide an adjudication safety net for more complex matters. These findings are considered in relation to the concern, as identified throughout Part I, that mediators are not well-positioned to resolve the complicated cases now being funnelled into mediation. Section 2 goes on to consider how regulatory bodies and their members perceive mediator neutrality, particularly when a mediator is confronted with a difficult party dynamic. Unsurprisingly, neutrality remained central to the conceptualization of family mediation. At the same time, all the mediators who were interviewed felt permitted, if not required, to respond to power imbalances, even when they understood their neutrality as unconditional. Section 3 subsequently examines the impact of these practices on flexible mediators' ability to support family justice. It is revealed that the mediator sample did not explicitly associate family mediation with access to justice, yet still felt that mediation should ensure settlement of a certain quality. This section builds on prior literature around the use of legal norms in mediation and argues that some mediators now *mediate in the shadow of the law*. The chapter concludes by considering the implications of flexible mediators' often quasi-legal role.

6.1 Screening for suitability

Family mediators have become increasingly responsible for screening parties out of mediation since the late 1990s, despite concerns that the profession does not adequately assess for power imbalances or abuse (Hester et al 1997; Morris 2013). Post-LASPO, mediators are the first point of contact for many disputants in the private family law system. The following discussion reveals that screening, operating as a form of assessment under the four-function framework proposed in Chapter 5, is a critical component of flexible mediator practice.

Turning to family mediation Codes of Practice, the ability to screen for domestic violence was outlined in 1998: 'In all cases, mediators must discover through a screening procedure whether or not there is fear of violence or any other harm and whether or not it is alleged that any participant has been or is likely to be violent towards another' (UKCFM 1998: s 4.20). The Family Mediation Council (FMC) broadens this criterion to abuse: 'In all cases, the mediator must seek to discover through a screening procedure whether or not there is fear of abuse or any other harm and whether or not it is alleged that any Participant has been or is likely to be abusive towards another (or towards a child)' (FMC 2018a: s 5.4.2). If a mediator must determine whether abuse is feared, has occurred or is likely to occur, she has to consider the parties' relative standing. This task inevitably involves an evaluative assessment of whether mediation is appropriate for the dispute. Screening thus positions mediators as the gatekeepers to mediation. This gatekeeping role is particularly visible when a mediator conducts a Mediation, Information and Assessment Meeting (MIAM), as she is required to 'assess whether a mediation process may be suitable in the circumstances' (FMC 2018a: s 2.4).

Both the FMC and the College of Mediators highlight the importance of mediator screening in their recent Codes of Practice. In 2018, the FMC introduced section 3.7: 'Mediators must have appropriate safeguarding policies and procedures in place' (FMC 2018a: s 3.7). The FMC does not explain what is meant by 'appropriate safeguarding policies', though further guidance was published via its newsletter (FMC 2018b):

> Paragraph 3.7 reinforces that family mediators are responsible for making sure that they take appropriate measures that protect clients from harm or damage throughout the family mediation process. It applies to all family mediators, though mediators who see children as part of the mediation process may have different policies and procedures in place to those who do not. (FMC 2018c)

The College of Mediators (2019: 8–9) also introduced new provisions on screening in 2019. Appendix C, titled 'Assessing Suitability to Mediate', stipulates that '[c]onsideration of suitability must be grounded in the core principles of mediation'. The guidance then lists several factors for mediators to take into account when screening, including whether the parties are 'willing to engage in mediation', 'feel safe, not intimated' and 'are free to make decisions'. Another part of Appendix C specifically covers the safety of participants, identifying 'coercive control' as a form of domestic abuse.

Both section 3.7 and Appendix C require mediators to assess for any power imbalances. The FMC presents screening as mediators' 'responsibility', whereas the College of Mediators stipulates that appropriate safeguarding procedures 'must' be put in place. Together, these two provisions indicate that mediator screening is no longer reserved for specific cases. Every party must be screened before mediation commences, preferably through an individual MIAM.[1] Mediators must also screen the parties throughout the mediation process.[2] This heightened responsibility suggests that mediators are continuously evaluating the party dynamic, underscoring their role as gatekeepers to mediation and possibly even court.[3]

Section 2.3.4 previously covered the Children and Families Act 2014, which made MIAMs mandatory for most private family law applicants.

---

1 Under the FMC's (2018a: s 7) Code of Practice, mediators could conduct a joint MIAM and see both parties at once. However, the MIAM had to involve an 'individual element' so the mediator could screen for domestic abuse. As of September 2024, the FMC (2024b: s 7) now stipulates that all MIAMs 'must be conducted separately'.

2 Appendix C of the College of Mediators' (2019: 8) guidance reads: 'Suitability for mediation should be considered at the initial/assessment stage and, if mediation goes ahead, throughout the process.'

3 Interesting, this form of mediator evaluation is not concealed. When a mediator screens for suitability, there is no facilitative proxy to hide her evaluation. If the mediator feels mediation is inappropriate, she can refuse to mediate. This openness reflects a procedural gatekeeping role as the mediator is supposedly not evaluating any proposed settlement; she is assessing the parties (both individually and collectively) to decide if mediation is appropriate.

Following the legislation, mediators have (theoretically) played a critical role in deciding whether a case should be resolved through mediation or court. However, there are conflicting opinions on whether this task also renders mediators the gatekeepers to court, and, therefore, key players in family justice. On the one hand, Doughty and Murch (2012: 342) argue that mediators have a significant influence over how a case progresses through the family justice system. By requiring court applicants to attend a MIAM, the mediator decides whether mediation is the most appropriate forum for child welfare without speaking to or seeing any relevant children. This reality leads Doughty and Murch to question if mediators can adjust their role in a way that enables them to become 'part of the access to justice apparatus'. They ask whether mediators should come under 'a broad conception of a family justice system', or continue to provide 'an administrative service' outside the justice sphere (Doughty and Murch 2012: 344). By comparison, Parkinson (2013: 207) posits that mandatory MIAMs do not render mediators the gatekeepers to court. The objective of a MIAM, from Parkinson's perspective, is not to prevent individuals from going to court, but to ensure that they are aware of their alternatives. While participation in a MIAM is often required or expected, mediation is not mandated. Mediator screening consequently does not hinder justice through the courts. Nevertheless, it is submitted that mediator screening cannot be viewed in isolation from all the other developments in the family justice system. The role of family mediators has expanded over several decades, as demonstrated by the rise of the flexible archetype. Furthermore, mandatory MIAMs, even if they have value in informing parties about mediation, remain part of a state-led agenda to move disputes away from court. When screening is considered alongside the many other evaluative tasks conducted by flexible mediators, as well as the rationale behind the Children and Families Act 2014, it becomes apparent that family mediation is no longer isolated from court and formal decision-making. Rather, mediation is an integral part of the family justice system.

If this is the case, it is logical that the family mediation process aims to ensure that some form of family justice is obtained by the parties. However, it is worth considering if family mediation can really provide the form of justice that was advocated for in Part I of this monograph. Family mediators have taken on additional tasks and responsibilities over time, particularly in the post-LASPO landscape. This expansion prompts a consideration as to whether flexible family mediators actively contribute to the administration of family justice, or if their efforts inadvertently hinder it. The answer hinges on several factors, including the types of disputes being screened into mediation, as well as the ability of flexible mediators to handle these disputes effectively.

6.1.1 The growing task of mediator screening

The interview data provide valuable insight into mediators' perceptions of their screening role, as well as the types of cases they feel capable of mediating. It also begins to shed light on whether more complex disputes are screened out of mediation through the exemptions to rules around both legal aid proceedings (as enshrined in LASPO) and mandatory MIAMs (as found under Practice Direction 3A of the Family Procedure Rules).[4] These findings are a useful, albeit preliminary, indicator as to how the exemptions to mandatory mediation may have been applied (or, for a better word, disregarded) had the 2023 proposals been introduced.

It was to be expected that a small number of interviewees would view screening as a minor part of their role. These mediators tended to rely on lawyers to screen parties out of mediation:

> I don't do a huge amount about safeguarding because most of my referrals are through solicitors. I'm aware of it. But having worked in a different sort of more legally aided area then it was highly, highly relevant. Usually if there's something coming through with those sorts of issues, I've already had a heads-up from the person who referred it. (*Emma [L]*)

> I think they've [the parties] probably screened themselves out previously, to be honest. I think most who come are nowadays recommended. They want to resolve it, one way or the other. (*Michael [L]*)

Emma and Michael followed a traditional conceptualization of family mediation whereby the demand for mediator assessment was weakened because the parties could access legal support – in other words, evaluation – outside the mediation process. Interestingly, both mediators used to provide family mediation through legal aid but stopped after LASPO. Emma, who worked at a private law firm, acknowledged that screening was 'highly relevant' when she worked in legal aid. These responses suggest that some mediators saw gatekeeping as a relatively minor part of their role. However, this finding was expected because the interview sample was designed to be purposive, and some of the interviewees primarily dealt with clients who continued to acquire legal support through a lawyer after LASPO. It was anticipated that these mediators would feel that they did not have to screen as much in comparison to their peers because their clients' lawyers would determine whether mediation was appropriate well before a MIAM took place.

[4] See section 2.3.4 for further information.

In comparison, the standard response from the interviews was that screening had become a fundamental part of mediators' workload. Interviewees said they screened for domestic abuse and other power imbalances. Rebecca explained:

> So, obviously there can be communication imbalances. There can be intelligence imbalances and emotional imbalances. Emotional intelligence imbalances. Often the woman, sorry to say, is typically much more emotionally intelligent, and, the man comes across maybe as being kind of quite harsh but is in actual fact unable to get out what they want to say. The emotions might come out as anger or, 'I'm fed up with this'. But it's because they're not able to articulate or be fully … feel comfortable in the process. Then obviously we look at whether there has been any domestic abuse and that's the screening you do at the beginning. That doesn't necessarily mean screening out. You have to ask people what has happened and whether or not that prevents them from coming to mediation. (*Rebecca [L]*)

The interviews cannot generate data on the quality of mediator screening, but uncover a general view among participants that they were required to screen for several different factors. Rebecca, for instance, recognized the gendered dimension in disputes and how these disparities provided parties with different forms of negotiating power. She cited a number of imbalances relating to communication, intelligence and emotional capabilities. Charlotte took a similar view:

> Obviously I screen for domestic violence. Not that if there is, that means that it's not suitable, but it's about the current mindset and how able either party is to sit in a room or feel free to express an opinion or negotiation… in most cases, I would encourage at least to try one session. You never really know what's going to happen. (*Charlotte [T]*)

While neither Rebecca nor Charlotte claimed that mediation was a panacea for family matters, they were keen to mediate. Both mediators adopted a flexible approach towards screening by considering how the parties' previous relationship impacted the current negotiations. They also took into account the parties' individual circumstances, history and overall dynamics. Their responses suggest that screening was a detailed and thorough exercise for some mediators in the post-LASPO landscape, an argument originally advanced in Chapter 4. Nonetheless, further research on mediator screening would be needed to determine if the majority of family mediators took this approach.

These quotes convey another important message: domestic abuse and other serious power imbalances do not automatically render mediation unsuitable to most mediators. The sample as a whole thought that mediation should be attempted in most cases. Megan believed it was more appropriate to screen parties *into*, rather than out of, mediation:

> I remember from our training they said it as in, 'You can screen in or you can screen out'. So it depends on how you're looking at it. You can think, you know, you actually want to get everyone involved in mediation, as many as you possibly can. You'd always think, 'Well (pause) how can I make this work?'. Or, you could be like, 'Hm, actually, that's a bit difficult'. Be more about screening out. I suppose for me as a mediator I'm more of a screen in person. I always want to try. I think mediation can help in the majority of cases. (*Megan [T]*)

Rosie gave a similar response when asked how she decided whether mediation was appropriate:

> Often I look at what their options are going to be. Sometimes perhaps we're too cautious. Because [pause] my view of mediation, even if it only sorts out one thing, it's still done something. It may not resolve everything, but if you can narrow it down, then great. If there are issues about safety, you can deal with the mediation in a way to make sure that people are going to be safe. There are ways around, I think. If it's clearly one person who is very manipulative and they're just not going to listen, then there's no point. But the important thing is that you sit with them, tell that one to shut up and then encourage the other one to talk. (*Rosie [L]*)

The majority of interviewees agreed with these mediators. They felt that mediation had merit in most instances, even if it only resulted in a partial settlement. The sample appeared to screen in a large number of cases into mediation after LASPO, possibly perceiving themselves as competent and able to mediate these more complex disputes.

This finding is particularly significant when it is recognized that LASPO and the introduction of mandatory MIAMs were not intended, at least in theory, to restrict access to court for certain cases. Under LASPO, legal aid for a private family law matter in court remains available where there has been, or is a risk of, domestic abuse.[5] Implicit within this legal framework is an understanding that cases involving domestic abuse should be screened

---

[5] Legal Aid, Sentencing and Punishment of Offenders Act 2012, sch 1, para 12(1); The Civil Legal Aid (Procedure) Regulations 2012, 2012/3098 reg 33. See Chapter 2 for further discussion.

out of mediation. Victims of abuse are also not required to attend a MIAM under the Family Procedure Rules. While the present study can only allude to the operation of these exemptions, its findings appear to be out of sync with the legislative framework. Altogether, the interview data infers that neither framework guarantees an adjudication safety net for victims of domestic abuse.

6.1.2 Mediators' approaches to screening post-LASPO

It is important to recognize that family mediators will mediate certain cases for a myriad of reasons. Some may feel well-equipped to handle more complex disputes, whereas others may do so because they think mediation is the only viable option for their clients. With this divergence in mind, the study investigated the sample's reasoning for screening cases in or out of mediation.

Section 4.1.2 previously outlined mediators' different approaches to MIAMs. In Bloch et al's (2014: 16) study, most mediators were 'realists' who screened more cases into mediation in light of the post-LASPO landscape. These mediators felt that if mediation was not attempted, the alternatives for most clients (namely to self-represent in court or attempt to resolve the dispute themselves with little oversight) were poor. 'Optimist' mediators also took on more complex or difficult cases, but did so because they felt able to mediate those disputes. These two groups differed from the 'purist' mediators who remained reluctant to mediate certain cases, regardless of the problems within the contemporary family justice system.

All three approaches were evident in the current mediator sample. Some interviewees could be described as purists, though they were relatively few in number. *Jessica [T]* was a purist mediator who felt that more complicated cases should still go to court. She admitted that most litigants were self-representing after LASPO, but said: 'at least they have legal people around them'. *Lydia [T]* was similarly reluctant to mediate where one party had mental health issues: 'Mental health issues are quite hard because people who do actually have mental health issues that will affect mediation don't often say. You know you try and question, but if they're really withholding it, it's very hard. Very difficult.' Lydia leaned towards a purist construction of her role, admitting that certain party characteristics rendered mediation more difficult. Harley, by contrast, approached the same problem as an optimist:

> I think there is a danger if somebody has a mental health issue in mediation, people will think, '[panicked] What do you do?' You just work with what's there. You can ask them, 'Hang on, what do I need to know? What do I need to know in order to be helpful here? Do I need to be concerned about anything? Are there any signs I need

> to be aware of?' Just to destigmatize it. To demystify it and make it something ... how many people have mental health issues? It's a lot of us. The social work course training, again, gave me a lot of grounding. (*Harley [T]*)

Harley warned that screening out parties with poor mental health stigmatized the condition further.[6] He spoke highly of his previous background in mental health work, suggesting that this experience improved his practice as a mediator. Harley also appeared somewhat critical of purist mediators, like Lydia, who were more apprehensive about mediating these cases.

Echoing Bloch et al's findings, the majority of interviewees in the present study were realist mediators. This group recognized that they screened more cases into mediation because they felt it was the most viable option for parties after LASPO. To provide three examples, Jessica was first apprehensive about screening cases out of mediation where the parties had few alternatives:

> It's a very difficult one because there's some people that you know shouldn't really be doing mediation. But a lot of them can't afford to resolve it any other way, so they're stuck. You don't want to say, 'No you can't do it', unless there's something glaringly ... you know, mental health issues but, again, where is that line? There's a lot of people going through divorce that have some mental health issues. (*Jessica [H]*)

Rebecca spoke about the pressure to mediate after LASPO:

> [B]efore LASPO I was very happy with doing that [screening out]. People could go and get their own solicitors. Then it would go to court and probably they'd settle. ... Post-LASPO [pause] I've really worried about closing down mediations like that. I probably have carried on too long trying to drag situations ... it can be about the children or finances. The difficulty, particularly in the early days, when the courts were not used to the Litigants in Person, particularly about finances. Where else are the parties going to go? (*Rebecca [L]*)

Finally, Victoria discussed the difficult situation where one party was eligible for legal aid and the other person could not afford mediation.

6 For a discussion on whether mediation is effective where one or both parties have mental health issues, see Barlow et al (2017: 97).

She said she would sometimes meet with a client for free to ensure that mediation continued:

> Well, invariably, the other person who doesn't qualify [for legal aid], actually their income isn't that high. In order to ensure their engagement, I sometimes see them for free. [Another mediator] said, 'Well, good luck to you, because you could afford to do that'. I can't afford to do that, actually. But I do because I want to complete the process. … I feel very strongly that we're a rural area and everybody should have access to mediation. You do now get a lot more Litigants in Person going to court, and actually you want to try to avoid that. It's stressful for them and the family. And it's the public purse. Well, where do those people go? And actually, the only place they can go where they don't have to pay and they can actually get legal information and be screened for domestic abuse is mediation. So, I'm really keen. (*Victoria [H]*)

When examined together, these three responses illustrate how many mediators take on certain cases, even if they feel that mediation is not the most appropriate choice for themselves or the parties involved. They believe that mediation, despite its potential drawbacks, is the only feasible option for many clients after LASPO.

The standard reaction among the sample is strong evidence that the flexible mediator archetype has partially developed out of necessity. It cannot be forgotten that decades of reform have drastically changed the family justice landscape. The post-LASPO climate has clearly placed more pressure on mediators to intervene and evaluate. And so, family mediators have taken on a flexible conceptualization of their role in order to adapt. The flexible mediator archetype is, in many ways, not a perfect construct, but a pragmatic development.

Of course, this development raises serious questions about how many mediated disputes end in a fair or just outcome. Family mediation was not designed to deal with more difficult disputes. And yet, a significant proportion of the mediator sample felt that there was sufficient flexibility in their role to adapt. For example, there was evidence that many interviewees would assess and intervene if one party downplayed the other side's views. They would also stop mediation momentarily or terminate the process in extreme circumstances. Nonetheless, it is questioned how far these mediators could uphold a form of family justice when mediation continued, and what exactly that justice looked like. It is vital to approach this discussion with caution, and refrain from placing 'excessive faith in the value of the mediation process' (Barlow et al 2017: 108).

The rising use of mediator screening underscores the need for a pragmatic consensus on what disputes are appropriate for mediation. To a large extent, the flexible mediator type has arisen in response to the changing family justice system. However, the issue remains that few individuals can access traditional forms of legal support post-LASPO. More complex cases are channelled into mediation due to a lack of feasible alternatives, yet the limited mediator type is confined to neutral assistance and referral when dealing with these disputes. A flexible mediator can assess and intervene, though her conceptualization remains hidden and understudied. To risk this monograph sounding repetitive, the discussions around improving contemporary family justice must be pragmatic, not idealistic.

Such pragmatism first requires the flexible mediator type to be explicitly recognized. From there, the debate around family mediation reform can begin to consider what kinds of disputes the *flexible* mediator – not the limited mediator – can support. If the flexible mediator and her screening abilities were properly acknowledged, clearer rules could be put in place to ensure that mediation did not occur when the process was detrimental to the parties involved. Without further recognition and subsequent regulation, there is a considerable risk that the more complicated disputes coming to mediation will not obtain anything close to justice. Once again, acknowledging the flexible mediator archetype is crucial to ensuring the appropriate and effective use of mediation in the contemporary family justice landscape.

6.2 Balancing mediator neutrality and flexibility

Part I acknowledged the primacy of neutrality within family mediation theory. Chapter 3 revealed a dominant and absolute interpretation of mediator neutrality that restricted family mediators to facilitative practices. Chapter 4 then proposed that mediator neutrality should not necessarily be abandoned or replaced, but approached as a qualified concept that enabled some mediator evaluation to occur. This reconceptualization is the foundation of the flexible mediator type, a professional who justifiably departs from her neutrality to provide additional support. Section 6.2 returns to this argument by examining how family mediation's regulatory bodies and their mediators understand 'neutrality'.

Starting with regulatory guidance, the National Family Conciliation Council (NFCC 1985) did not explicitly mention mediator neutrality in its Extended Code of Practice. Instead, the organization emphasized conciliators' responsibility to help parties 'without imposing [their] own values' (NFCC 1985: s 2). Guidance from the mid-1990s included dedicated sections on mediator neutrality, covering all three interpretations of the concept.[7] First, a mediator had to be even-handed: 'They [mediators] must conduct the process in a fair and even-handed way' (UKCFM 1998: s 4.3).

[7] See section 3.1.1.

Second, a mediator must be neutral as to the outcome: 'Mediators must at all times remain neutral as to the outcome of mediation. They must not seek to move participants to an outcome which the mediator prefers' (*NFM and FMA* in UKCFM 1997: ss 2.3–2.4). Third, a mediator was neutral in terms of non-bias:

> Take care not to become (or be perceived to have become) partial to the view of one client rather than the objectives and aspirations of both. (Resolution 2018: 24)

> They should also be aware of the impact of unconscious bias towards participants in mediation. (College of Mediators 2019: s 4.9.1)

The FMC summarizes all three interpretations in its current guidance: 'The Mediator must remain neutral as to the outcome of the Mediation at all times … [she] must at all times remain impartial as between the Participants and conduct the Mediation process in a fair and even-handed way' (FMC 2018a: ss 6.2–6.3.1).

The lack of precision around what it means to be 'neutral', 'impartial' or 'even-handed' is not surprising given the limited direction within regulatory guidance.[8] However, this vagueness creates a particular problem in the sections on mediator neutrality as the concept is already heavily criticized for its ambiguity.[9] None of the regulatory bodies clarify when a mediator can depart from her neutrality, suggesting that a strict and rigid interpretation is preferred. On the other hand, the lack of precision may reflect the elusiveness of mediator neutrality itself. It could be that the concept is so complex that it cannot be defined in a brief paragraph or sentence. Nevertheless, if the provisions are read in isolation, it is apparent that the regulatory bodies portray mediator neutrality as an absolute gold standard. A critical line of investigation, then, is how family mediators themselves perceive their neutrality.

6.2.1 Mediators' understanding of their neutrality

The interview data revealed two broad conceptualizations of mediator neutrality, each accounting for roughly half of the sample.[10] The first

8 Cooks and Hale (1994: 63) reach a similar conclusion when studying American Codes of Practice for mediators.

9 See section 4.3.2.

10 All mediators except *Jane [T]* were asked what they understood by 'mediator neutrality'. Her interview was cut short due to an issue with a client before their mediation session.

approach was the traditional, absolute interpretation of neutrality identified in Chapter 3. Judith commented:

> It's [mediator neutrality] really important. It's almost like being an actor. It's really important. If you feel the other person is turning towards the other person too much. Being neutral, you have to be really careful. It's not quite like somebody holding a talking stick, you know you can only talk when you hold the stick. But it's really important for them [the parties] not to feel that you're spending too much time with the other person or that you're ignoring them. (*Judith [H]*)

Amy [L] adopted a similar stance by stating that mediator neutrality meant 'you don't take sides'. Kate agreed with this idea of even-handedness, though admitted that it could be challenging to maintain in practice. She spoke about a MIAM where a woman was separating from her long-term partner:

> There are words that we use, so 'you both', 'each of you', etcetera. If you are listening to one [party] for any length of time, you have to make sure the other one has got the chance to respond. To me, it means being very balanced and being absolutely non-judgmental. That's really testing. The story I heard this morning. … It was outrageous what I heard. But I know that she wouldn't have known I was thinking that, because, although I'm a terrible poker player, I'd like to think I'm experienced enough to ensure that she had no idea what I was thinking in my head. They will have no idea that I think his behaviour is really quite despicable. Anyone would agree that his behaviour was not appropriate, but he won't know that. (*Kate [H]*)

Kate was shocked by the ex-partner's alleged behaviour. She felt she could mask these feelings and remain neutral, though the task was 'testing'. Several other mediators also acknowledged the difficulties in upholding an absolute vision of neutrality, particularly when negotiations reached a standstill. Jessica said her neutrality meant 'you always just have to sit back'. She then explained:

> It [negotiations] can get very heated. I might take one [party] out for five minutes which I have to be very careful with because of my neutrality. You can't really, once you've started mediation, carry on separate conversations. But they need a coffee, or they may just need five minutes. (*Jessica [T]*)

The participants who adopted an orthodox understanding of their neutrality gave responses that read almost like textbook answers. They heavily underscored the need for a mediator to be strictly neutral and treat both parties equally at all times. However, many of these interviewees acknowledged that this approach did not account for the subtleties of mediator practice. Thus, a mediator may appear to follow a limited conceptualization of their role, but this does not mean they are blind to the neutrality dilemma that often arises.

The other half of the sample rejected the traditional interpretation of mediator neutrality. They distinguished the concept from impartiality:

> Neutrality seems to signify something more passive to me. There is a kind of, just letting it happen. Whereas I think impartiality is about allowing something to happen, without having an investment in the outcome, other than that outcome is something that will be helpful to the clients. … I mean it's just a word-banding exercise in some senses. Neutrality can mean that you don't have a particular investment as well. Thinking about the Swiss. [Laughs] It's a very big term … the reality is that we're never really neutral. (*Mary [H]*)

> I'd distinguish between neutrality and impartiality. Neutrality would mean having no values. That wouldn't accord with the principles of mediation where Codes of Practice say mediators have a special responsibility with children. That again needs a whole load of unpacking as to what that means, but it's not value-free. … That's not neutral, but that's different, trying to retain impartiality so that both parents feel that you're trying to help the whole family and not one more than the other. (*Lauren [T]*)

Central to this alternative conceptualization was the notion that mediators provided some kind of support beyond their neutrality. *David [H]* was against the term neutrality because he had 'two focuses': 'the welfare of the child' and 'keeping the family out of court'. He was one of few mediators in the sample who appeared more aware of his evaluative remit. *Megan [T]* likewise discussed the concept of multi-partiality. She said an impartial mediator was 'removed', whereas multi-partiality meant mediators were 'a bit more drawn into it'. She took the latter approach, describing it as being 'on both of their sides, rather than on anyone's side'. For many mediators, their neutrality (or impartiality) did not mean that they were passive third parties with no interest in the mediated outcome. Rather, they supported both parties and were actively involved in negotiations to ensure that an effective agreement was reached.

Before considering the impact of these different conceptualizations, it is worth revisiting the concept of impartiality. Section 4.3.2 explained that mediator impartiality is premised on even-handedness regarding the process, but not the outcome. By contrast, neutrality requires mediators to be disinterested in the outcome at all times (Boulle 2005). It was questioned whether these terms were largely synonymous in practice: if the intention behind adopting the term 'impartiality' was to avoid contradictions in mediation theory, this could also be achieved by redefining and sharpening the meaning of 'neutrality' itself (Crowe and Field 2019). And so, it was argued that the problem was not necessarily the terminology used, but the mass ambiguity as to when and how a mediator balances their facilitative image with the demand for evaluation. However, this argument must be considered alongside the fact that nearly half of the mediator sample opted to describe themselves as impartial. These mediators were often more aware of – and open to – their evaluative framework than their neutral counterparts. It also should not be forgotten that regulatory bodies use the term 'impartial' rather than 'neutral' when defining family mediation in their Codes of Practice.[11] There was a clear preference for impartiality within much of the data, alluding to a distinction between the two concepts. This finding should be taken into account when reforming family mediation, particularly when considering whether to replace mediator neutrality with the concept of mediator impartiality. Regardless, the argument still stands that the chosen concept should be understood as a moderate (not absolute) standard in order to permit mediator evaluation and, therefore, the flexible mediator archetype.

6.2.2 Mediator neutrality, professional background and intervention

While it was to be expected that family mediators would have different views on their neutrality, an unanticipated trend emerged during the data analysis. In fact, there was a strong correlation between a participant's interpretation of their neutrality and their professional background. All lawyer mediators followed the traditional understanding of the concept, whereas therapeutic mediators tended to adopt an alternative conceptualization. The responses were more mixed among hybrid mediators, with three out of five adopting an alternative interpretation of neutrality. Table 6.1 summarizes the sample's responses.

While there was no definitive explanation as to why the mediator sub-groups held different views on their neutrality, there was some indication that the participants were influenced by the training, culture and ethos of their professional background(s). Three mediators mentioned reflexivity in their interviews. David ran a training course for family mediators and noticed that lawyer mediators struggled to reflect on their work:

> I think one of the things that is really difficult about mediation is when mediation begins and two people walk into the room, you have no idea

[11] See section 5.2.

Table 6.1: Mediators' conceptualization of mediator neutrality by professional background

Conceptualization of mediator neutrality	Lawyer mediators	Therapeutic mediators	Hybrid mediators
Traditional *(neutrality)*	5	2	2
Alternative *(impartiality, multi-partial)*	0	4	3

> where it is going to go. You may have had a couple who seemed to be fairly calm and together in session one. But in session two, they've completely changed. Lawyers find that quite difficult to handle, and to work reflectively. (*David [H]*)

This argument is illustrated by Mary and Emma's contrasting statements:

> I think it [therapeutic training] helps you to reflect. But, also, perhaps to manage your work. If you feel … if you feel anxious in the room or angry with one of your clients. … Those will impede the work. I sometimes think that some of the resistance in the mediation room is the mediators themselves. (*Mary [H]*)

> I suppose it's [mediator accreditation] really about trying to get people to have experience. … It's a much better thing than doing these ridiculous reflective – I can't begin to tell you what a load of rubbish I thought that reflective bit of work was. (*Emma [L]*)

Mary, a hybrid mediator, preferred the term impartiality. Throughout her interview, she emphasized the need for mediators to consider the therapeutic benefits of family mediation. She promoted reflexivity, claiming that it helped to remove the mediator from any ill feelings they held towards the parties. By comparison, Emma, a lawyer mediator, adopted a traditional understanding of neutrality. She was frustrated about the reflective tasks required for FMC accreditation, describing it as a 'load of rubbish'. These conflicting views are preliminary evidence that mediators from different professional sub-groups have different views on concepts, such as neutrality and reflexivity. However, further data is required to confirm this hypothesis.

Regardless of the interpretation adopted, none of the interviewees saw their neutrality as a barrier to intervention. When asked how mediator neutrality worked when there was a power imbalance between the parties, no one in the sample claimed that they could not react. Instead, all participants said that they would assess the situation and intervene.[12] *Charlotte [T]* followed the orthodox understanding of mediator neutrality, though acknowledged that it could be challenging to maintain in practice.[13] Nonetheless, she felt that she could still address power imbalances by giving the weaker party more time to speak. Charlotte said that while her neutrality may appear 'compromised', her clients 'understand' and rarely questioned her approach. *Rosie [L]* also adopted a strict interpretation of mediator neutrality but thought she could 'keep the balance' between the parties. She did not see this as 'favouring one [party] over the other', but rather 'keeping them both the same' in terms of power. *Megan [T]* differed from these mediators by preferring the term multi-partiality, yet also recognized that she could respond to a power imbalance. She explained that this intervention could involve 'focusing on one person' to make negotiations 'more equal'.

Altogether, the interview data shows that mediators' interpretation of neutrality has little to no impact on how they conceptualize the remainder of their role. None of the mediators, even those adopting the harshest views of neutrality, claimed that they did nothing if the parties were on unequal footing. As a whole, the sample felt able to respond. This approach enabled flexible mediators to do more in the post-LASPO landscape, and possibly even promote a just outcome.

6.3 Mediators' understanding of justice

A secondary objective of this monograph is to explore the value of family mediation in supporting contemporary family justice. This investigation raises the question of whether family mediation is even understood as a family justice apparatus to begin with. The following discussion provides the first empirical findings on family mediators' perceptions of access to justice in the post-LASPO era.

Towards the end of the interviews, mediators were asked to explain the meaning of 'access to justice'. Rather than discuss the concept in relation to mediation, the most common response was to draw attention to court. David and Lauren spoke about a 'right' to court:

> I think it means the right of individuals to go to court, if they feel they want to. (*David [H]*)

> I think it means the right ... the human right to go to court. You don't have to have a lawyer to represent you in court. ... I think access to

[12] See section 5.5 for further information on mediators' intervenor function.

[13] 'I'm also aware that it's [being neutral] impossible really. You have to project neutrality and be as neutral as you can.'

> justice is the human right to go to court on a justiciable issue. If there is one, you can't say only lawyers can appear in court. You have to then accept Litigants in Person. Then it's access to what kind of quality of justice. … There can be false expectations of what justice is and what is fair. But access to justice is access to a judiciary system. (*Lauren [T]*)

A number of mediators related the question back to mediation by suggesting that the process did not prevent access to court and, thereby, justice. David mentioned that 'mediation diverts people away from that access', yet 'offers an alternative'. Lauren differed to the extent that she felt mediation was not 'just an alternative', but 'a pathway that enables some people not to use the judicial system at all'. Other interviewees made similar comments:

> I think access to justice to me means if people want to, choose to go to court they can. So I do feel pretty strongly that attending mediation does not in any way interfere with anybody's access to justice. Because mediation is voluntary. If people come in and say they don't want to mediate, that's absolutely fine. They can go to court if they want to. Access to justice to me is all about the ability to access the family justice system, if they choose to do that. That doesn't mean they shouldn't be really informed and have mediation encouraged or pushed as a better alternative. (*Kate [H]*)

> ... you shouldn't need to have a high income if you need to use the legal system. I mean [pause] it feels a bit like a lost cause in terms of family law. There's no sufficient access to justice for criminal law, is there? So there isn't going to be any funding for family law. I suppose a lot of these things should be kept out of the courts, if possible, but as a last resort, you should be able to enter the system equally, irrespective of your income. (*Charlotte [T]*)

Kate emphasized the voluntary nature of mediation, arguing that this did not prevent access to justice. Charlotte similarly felt that court was 'a last resort', suggesting that access to justice would not be impeded if the parties went to another procedure beforehand. To this group of mediators, access to justice was synonymous with access to the courts, though not necessarily obstructed by family mediation if the process was voluntary.

Two mediators commented on the lack of justice in the contemporary family law system. They claimed that access to justice was:

> Something that we don't have at the moment. I'm, I'm horrified. I think it's absolutely appalling. There was a day – I am of that generation – there was a time when the green form for legal aid, you

> could do anything under the green form. It was only 25 quid and later went up to 50, but you could do anything on it. (*Emma [L]*)

> A bit of a joke. It doesn't exist. I see clients as a family lawyer who come for advice after they represented themselves in court and made a right mess of it. It doesn't help that a lot of the family decisions are made by Magistrates who are really unpredictable. … I feel a bit apocalyptic about it, I have to say. It's not going to get better, I don't think. (*Michael [L]*)

These responses again demonstrate the sample's association between justice, court and access to funding. This finding was anticipated given the general perceptions of court and mediation in the discourse around access to justice.[14] The ability to go to court is widely understood as a constitutional right that underpins the rule of law: article 6 of the Human Rights Act 1998 clarifies 'that everyone is entitled to a fair and public hearing within a reasonable time by an independent and impartial tribunal established by law'. By contrast, no one in the mediator sample referred to a right to mediate. This is because there is 'no right of access to a mediation' (Neuberger 2015: para 9). By viewing access to justice as 'access to a judiciary system', to quote Lauren, the interviewees (perhaps subconsciously) placed restrictions on what they thought they could achieve as mediators. From this perspective, it is difficult to perceive mediator evaluation as a method through which to secure contemporary family justice.

6.3.1 The 'quality of the agreement': measuring mediation outcomes

While the interviewees regularly conflated access to justice with court, this perspective did not necessarily match their broader views around the purpose of family mediation. When questioned on access to justice, the sample only considered mediation in terms of the process being an alternative to court. At the same time, they regularly emphasized family mediation's value in supporting disputants throughout their interviews. For instance, *Amy [L]* said that access to justice was 'the ability to be able to go to court (pause) and a lot of people don't'. Amy was asked how mediation fitted into that discussion, to which she replied that 'mediation is in a way about not going to court'. She expressed a concern that 'people don't know about mediation' and that MIAMs were not 'doing the job'. It was clear that Amy associated access to justice with court and even felt that justice was out of reach for many families. At the same time, she was disappointed that

[14] See section 1.2.

many people were oblivious to mediation, a process that was about moving disputes away from court (and thus, according to Amy, access to justice). Yet if mediation did not ensure access to justice, why was Amy so critical of a lack of awareness around the process? Of course, family mediation can have value even if the process does not secure justice. However, what then *does* mediation provide? And why did Amy think that mediation should be attempted in most cases if it could not ensure justice or anything close to the concept? This is a significant shortcoming in not only Amy's response but also the broader discussions around contemporary family mediation.

The same contradiction was evident throughout the interview data. Lauren was quoted earlier as emphasizing 'the human right to go to court on a justiciable issue'. This statement stood in stark contrast to an earlier section of her interview where she implied that mediation did more than simply engender settlement. She recalled a previous case where she worked with a trainee mediator, using the anecdote to emphasize the importance of securing high-quality outcomes:

> She [the trainee mediator] did the initial separate meetings and would tend to say the case was quite straightforward. There was a high-conflict couple who were agreeing to sell the house, and she just said, 'Good! You've agreed that'. And I'd just think 'Ah!' [Laughs] I would recognize, here is a man who is very keen to get his share now. She [the trainee mediator] really didn't seem to quite get it. I kept having to raise it and she decided not to carry on with mediation, which I think was a good thing. She just had a blind spot. She just thought an agreement was what we were looking for. It's the quality of the agreement. Yet we're not making judgments, but you can see what I mean. (*Lauren [T]*)

Within this excerpt, Lauren implicitly or subconsciously associated family mediation with a contemporary vision of family justice. She criticized the trainee for glossing over serious issues, hinting at a more active role for mediators beyond their facilitative image. The trainee sought 'an agreement', whereas Lauren wanted to secure an agreement of a certain 'quality'. From this extract, it was unclear what exact criteria Lauren used to determine if an agreement met her expectations. Barlow et al (2017: 6) suggest that family justice has a 'normative content', whereby certain standards are adopted to measure whether justice has been achieved. If a practitioner like Lauren uses similar norms to evaluate the quality of a mediated outcome, is she really providing something that different to justice? A mediator striving for a quality agreement may, in fact, encourage an outcome that mirrors justice itself.

The following discussion sheds some light on the criteria used by mediators to determine the quality of agreement. In particular, section

6.3.2 traces mediators' commitment to legal norms. While this monograph is focused on the prominence of those legal norms, it is important to recognize that mediators consider a variety of standards within mediation. This includes the norms and expectations brought by the parties themselves, such as the focus on needs that women often bring to financial disputes, as well as the notion of formal equality typically promoted by men (Barlow et al 2017: 177–180).

Child welfare remains a prevalent norm in family mediation and has already been referenced several times in this monograph.[15] For instance, section 4.3 considered how mediators are expected to uphold the welfare of any relevant children and evaluate in light of their needs. Section 5.5 further demonstrated how regulatory bodies originally understood harm as only relating to children. Under the FMC's (2018a: s 5.3) Code of Practice, mediators are now required to consider the welfare of the child 'at all times' and 'encourage the participants to focus on the needs and interests of the children'. *Lauren [T]* appeared to follow this provision rigorously. She described the role of the mediator as 'child-focused' and mentioned that 'children's feelings matter' within negotiations. She went on to reference Trinder et al's (2013) study on court orders in child contact cases and expressed a concern about the rising levels of poor mental health in younger populations. For Lauren, child welfare was the leading motivator in her professional work. In Dingwall's (1986: 18) words, she felt that she had a 'duty to speak for absent or weaker parties', specifically the children, to ensure that the mediated outcome was 'morally acceptable'. This norm may have led Lauren to become more direct, particularly if the proposed settlement did not reflect a high-quality agreement in relation to the child's wishes and feelings.

Other interviewees mentioned the need for parties to consider the welfare of the child, though this norm was not as decisive across the entire sample. For instance, *Rosie [L]* mentioned that mediation 'is all about the children' and 'what the children want'. *Jessica [T]* likewise described the welfare of the child as 'the fundamentals of family law'. In general, the sample recognized the importance of child welfare, though rarely went into further detail about what it entailed. In line with Barlow et al (2017: 181), these findings suggest that mediators were 'universally committed to children's welfare, but at a fairly abstract and procedural level'. The more prominent theme in the interview data was the use of legal norms, alluding to a quasi-legal role for the flexible mediator archetype.

[15] The welfare of the child in family mediation has also been researched by Davis (1988: 54), Trinder et al (2006), Smithson et al (2015) and Barlow et al (2017).

6.3.2 Mediating in the shadow of the law

In 1979, Mnookin and Kornhauser argued that disputes resolved outside of court are still influenced by legal norms. This is because disputants use the law as 'bargaining chips' and determine the likely outcome of their case had it been heard in court. Using this prediction, they attempt to leverage a more favourable settlement. In Mnookin and Kornhauser's (1979: 968) words, people 'bargain in the shadow of the law'. The two scholars claimed that the shadow of the law was only one factor that impacted settlement, with parental preferences, uncertainty in the law, transaction costs and strategic behaviour also coming into play. Several decades later, Batagol and Brown (2011: 217–218) argued that power dynamics also influenced negotiations. Following their study on family mediation, they found that a party's willingness to use legal procedures impacted the strength of various legal norms within mediation. This disparity was often gendered, meaning that the shadow of the law was much weaker for women who rarely used the threat of court to promote their own legal interests (Batagol and Brown 2011: 183–184).

Barlow et al (2017: 184–193) similarly investigated the shadow of the law through the Mapping Paths to Family Justice project. They found that family mediators, collaborative practitioners and lawyers brought the shadow of the law into their procedures in three main ways. First, the practitioners warned parties about the law or court process in order to encourage agreement. Second, they provided information about the law. Finally, some professionals measured any proposals against a case's likely outcome in court. All three tactics can be found in the regulatory guidance studied and were also discussed by the present family mediator sample, as detailed in Chapter 5.

The shadow of law through traditional legal advice and oversight has, of course, weakened after decades of reform to the private family law system. According to Barlow et al (2017: 194), 'solicitors played an important role in helping to bring the shadow of the law to bear'. However, the researchers warn that the law may have become 'less normative' within mediation after the LASPO reforms. Hunter et al (2017: 244), also discussing the Mapping Paths study, similarly conclude that there is now a 'light but discernible' shadow of the law over mediation. Unfortunately, the inaccessibility of lawyer-led advice for many disputants after LASPO has led to a significant gap in family justice.

The purpose of this monograph is not to argue that the decline of traditional legal support within family justice is acceptable. Nor is it its purpose to suggest that this development should be accepted with no critique. However, various parts of this monograph have demonstrated that mediators can adapt, and in many ways have already adapted, to the post-LASPO landscape. Evidence from the two-stage study further suggests that mediators are doing more to ensure legal oversight in the mediation session.

Rather than rely on the application of legal norms by other practitioners or the parties themselves, much of the mediator sample would use legal norms to encourage agreement of a certain quality. Many mediators subsequently advanced the shadow of the law in such a way that meant legal oversight was still provided in mediation, even without the presence of lawyers. Legal oversight was not deferred to another third party, but conducted by mediators themselves. In other words, they were *mediating in the shadow of the law*.

This idea is demonstrated through the contrasting responses of Rosie and Judith. They both recalled a case where one party was disadvantaged by a proposal:

> I had one [case] where he had a really valuable pension and she was saying, 'That's alright, I don't really want to bother with the pensions'. Then I said, 'I think you should get legal advice at this point'. So, she then went to see a solicitor, because obviously I can't give legal advice. (*Rosie [L]*)

> It [the case] was about resigning from a company. Actually, it was not a tax problem. This was simply if you have a certain percentage of a company and you remain a director of that company when you transfer the shares, you get an entrepreneur's rate of tax which is 5, 10 per cent. As opposed to 40 per cent. It's really important that you don't resign from being a director before you transfer the shares. But they wanted to do it that way. They wanted the person to resign as director, 'You're not having control of my company! We will transfer the shares sometime'. And I was working very hard to say don't do it that way. One person, she wanted out. 'I'll sign the form now.' 'Actually, it's probably not a good idea.' I thought tax advice was quite neutral, but they got really het up about it. (*Judith [H]*)[16]

The two mediators responded differently to this scenario. Rosie referred the parties to legal advice. By comparison, Judith intervened. While both parties went beyond their helper function to encourage an agreement of a certain quality, Judith actively sought to bring the law into the negotiations. In effect, she went from helping to mediating in the shadow of the law. Judith's excerpt is a more extreme example of mediator evaluation, and only one of two instances in the interview data where a mediator claimed

[16] This excerpt also raises an interesting question about the impact of a mediator's professional background on settlement. It cannot be deduced from the data if a therapeutic mediator would be alert to the same legal issues that Judith was aware of. While the abilities of mediator sub-groups, as well as the specific legal training offered to trainee mediators, is outside the scope of this monograph, it is an extremely important line of investigation for future research.

to give advice.[17] Nonetheless, her response alludes to a form of mediator evaluation that could influence settlement and possibly even engender justice. This evaluation occurs without the involvement of any other practitioners, enabling family law's normative content to continue.

In general, the sample thought the role of the mediator was to promote an agreement that followed certain guidelines. This included general legal concepts, but also more specific provisions within family law legislation:

> I feel it's my responsibility to put forward a mediated agreement that I can feel it's fair. … Again, maybe once or twice over the 20 years, I've said, 'Look. You can put forward to go to court for whatever you want. But I can't approve this. I can't put this into a mediated agreement because you're not convincing me that there is fairness here.' I guess that's a sort of, thinking the court would not agree with it. (*Harley [T]*)

> Sometimes when you're mediating, particularly with unmarried couples, there is no income link between the adults. There is only an income link if there are children. Schedule one. … If you separated and aren't married or in a civil partnership, the woman who stayed at home can't do anything about income for themselves. They can only do it through the children. … I'm sure we all know couples … you take a job in, let's say, Berlin, and your other half will say they can get a job there but not the job they're doing now. So, they get a lesser job. … You then separate. This person has given up quite a lot of their own potential. It's nothing if you're not married. So that sort of thing is much better mediated because it's important to actually get something that's fair. Because I know the legal background, I can also explain to them in the mediation why we're doing what we're doing. (*Judith [H]*)

> [I]f I'm dealing with finance, I believe I have a professional responsibility to help the couple to find a solution which falls within section 25. So within the criteria of fairness. Both because I think that's right but also because they will want to get their financial settlement approved by the court and that will therefore need to be within the criteria. (*David [H]*)

These three mediators assumed responsibility for ensuring that a mediated outcome adhered to legal norms. Harley mentioned the importance of

[17] The second instance was mentioned by *Michael [L]*: 'I do, wherever possible, give as much general advice as I can, advice that will help move them to a position … I'm probably one of those mediators who will give more advice. There are some, I think, who will just let the clients say what they like and not really control it enough.' This approach may reflect Judith and Michael's legal backgrounds; both participants still practised as solicitors at the time of their interviews.

fairness ('you're not convincing me that there is fairness here'). Judith also referred to fairness ('it's important to actually get something that's fair') in relation to section 1 of the Children Act 1989.[18] David was one of five mediators who mentioned section 25 of the Matrimonial Causes Act 1973.[19] He felt responsible for ensuring that an agreement aligned with the law on financial provision orders ('to find a solution which falls within section 25 … because I think that's right'). While David expected parties to seek a binding court order for any financial matters, he may have been the first professional to consider the legal standing of an agreement. If the parties did not apply to court, he may have been the only practitioner to provide any evaluative support. And so, all three mediators mediated in the shadow of the law in an attempt to encourage a legally correct settlement.

Interestingly, these mediators focused on the notion of fairness. Even David, who spoke about the section 25 checklist, said this meant a good settlement was 'within the criteria of fairness'. Other lawyer mediators mentioned fairness in passing. For example, *Amy [L]* stressed the need for 'a fair way of pension sharing'. By comparison, *Rosie [L]* looked at whether an agreement was 'fair on the child'. Interestingly, *Emma [L]*, another lawyer mediator, claimed that 'your own sense of fairness' was 'equally important because it's attached to you', appearing to uphold an individualistic, rather than legal, interpretation of fairness. There was thus some evidence that family mediators from a legal background saw achieving fair outcomes, not necessarily in the sense of adhering to legal norms, as an important part of their role. Whether the agreements overseen by these flexible mediators were actually fair, however, could not be determined in this study.[20]

The sample appeared more likely to mediate in the shadow of the law when dealing with financial or property matters. This finding was to be expected following a similar conclusion by Barlow et al (2017: 188).[21] *Jessica [T]* clarified that 'the law is always involved' but had 'a heavy weighting' in financial cases as the parties tended to seek a binding consent order once mediation had completed. In a similar vein, *Jane [T]* would mention to the

---

18 Under section 1, a judge can make a financial award for children regardless of the parents' marital status.

19 The other mediators were *Charlotte [T]* and *Victoria [H]*, whose responses were cited in Chapter 5, as well as *Megan [T]* and *Rosie [L]*.

20 The risk of unfair or poor mediated agreements, particularly because of a mediator's incorrect understanding of the law, is considered in section 6.3.3 and will also be revisited in the concluding chapter.

21 This is not to say that mediators never apply legal norms to children's disputes, but rather that the shadow of the law tends to be much weaker in that context. *Rosie [L]*, for instance, emphasized: 'when I mediate, I use the criteria the court uses – the welfare checklist'.

parties: 'Your agreement in mediation is your agreement. It is something that has to be, especially financial agreements, rubberstamped by the court'. *Emma [L]* felt it would be 'wrong not to tell them [the parties] what the law says' around cohabitants. *Mary [H]* would also reality-test financial arrangements if they put one party 'under pressure'. She would ask: 'What have you actually got to pay it with? What is that going to be like?' When looking at these extracts together, it is apparent that many interviewees, comprising all three professional sub-groups, believed that they knew enough about the possible legal outcomes to, at the very least, give legal information when dealing with financial or property arrangements. They did not perceive legal oversight as a task reserved for lawyers, or even lawyer mediators. The quasi-legal role was available to all mediators, regardless of their professional background.[22] While the quality of this support cannot be deduced from these interviews, it is clear that most participants, including those from a therapeutic background, went beyond the limited mediator archetype. They were, rather, flexible mediators taking on a quasi-legal remit.

This quasi-legal role is further evidence that family mediators have expanded their responsibilities in the post-LASPO landscape. In the past, mediators were prohibited from evaluating any proposals, even if they had the legal background to know if a proposal followed the law. However, the findings from Chapter 5 indicate that mediators are evaluating much more than their traditional conceptualization allows. Additional findings from Chapter 6 show that mediators are assessing settlements against certain thresholds, guided by legal norms and expectations. A flexible mediator does not carry out the exact same role as a lawyer, but often takes on a quasi-legal or extra-legal remit.[23] She performs various techniques and functions in order to apply these legal norms to a dispute, making her better placed to support a contemporary vision of family justice. The normativity of family law in mediation subsequently prevails, albeit in a different form. Of course, this normativity may be considerably weaker than that provided by lawyers. There is also the concern that this normativity is based on incorrect understandings of family law, as discussed in section 6.3.3. While the withdrawal of legal advice through lawyers can never be completely replaced, the flexible mediator is one of many family law practitioners who seek to resolve the gap in legal support after LASPO. Openly permitting the flexible mediator

22 Barlow and Hunter (2020: 18) acknowledge that mediators from both 'legal and non-legal backgrounds' in the Mapping Paths study gave parties information about the court. It corroborates findings from this monograph, whereby the conceptualization of family mediation was widely the same across the different professional sub-groups.

23 Smith and Hitchings (2023: 670), citing Davis (1988), describe family mediation as an 'extra-legal' service.

archetype is therefore important in terms of both promoting transparency and creating a more responsive family justice system.

6.3.3 Can the quasi-legal flexible mediator support family justice?

The two-stage study suggests that mediators are screening complex cases into mediation. The data show that when mediation begins, mediators are willing to go beyond a strict interpretation of their neutrality in order to provide flexibility. They are increasingly applying legal norms to disputes and, by doing so, mediating in the shadow of the law. However, there remain serious apprehensions as to whether this extended role supports family justice or, in fact, contributes to the lack of justice within the post-LASPO family law landscape. The main concerns around the quasi-legal flexible mediator are three-fold.[24]

The development is first troublesome from a feminist perspective. The empirical two-stage study reveals a continuum of mediator functions from which the profession can begin to regulate the agreements reached in mediation. However, the influence of legal norms is not without its problems. Webley (2010: 35–36) maintains that legal norms are the 'preserve of white middle-class men'. Combined with a facilitative mediation framework, these norms can lead masculine values of 'autonomy of decision-making, detachment and rationality' to be prioritized over the feminine traits of 'emotion, dependence and subordination'. The study behind this monograph does not provide data on the quality nor the effect of the legal norms adopted by mediators. However, it is important to acknowledge that mediators' more evaluative functions, specifically assessment and even referral, could hamper justice if they are predicated on legal norms that prioritize formalistic values. Barlow et al (2017: 195) reach a similar conclusion, finding that mediated financial agreements tend to be based on formal equality which favours the male party. They also discover that within both financial and child disputes, the norms that women bring into family dispute resolution are regularly cast aside. The use of legal norms within mediation could therefore cause the structural inequalities between men and women to be massively overlooked.

Even if the law did not habitually disregard women's interests, the second concern relates to mediators' ability to apply legal norms. According to the FMC's (2022a: 20–21) professional standards, family mediators are expected to provide 'information about family law and its processes'. They must also be able to draft 'financial settlements that are capable of legal implementation and accord with current legislation'. Neither provision requires mediators

[24] This discussion is not exhaustive of all of the issues with the quasi-legal flexible mediator. For instance, the use of legal norms in mediation raises questions about the professionalism of mediators (discussed in section 7.3). It may also have further implications for mediators' professional status and indemnity insurance (Saunders 2020).

to have a comprehensive knowledge of family law. If a mediator mediates in the shadow of the law to provide legal oversight, she may incorrectly apply a number of legal norms. This risk increases with therapeutic mediators, a professional sub-group with little legal training beyond what is mandated by the FMC. Two interviewees even mentioned coming across poor-quality settlements when they worked as lawyers.[25] While these participants may have been downplaying the abilities of the other family mediator sub-group in order to promote their own skillset (Blakey 2023a), this anecdotal evidence should not be disregarded. If mediators are inaccurately applying legal norms, their mediated agreements could massively deviate from what a judge would order in the same case. The potential for mediation to ensure a justice similar to that acquired in court is thus massively reduced.

Finally, it could be claimed that the role of the quasi-legal flexible mediator, even if she applies the law correctly, is inappropriate. It was not by chance that the family mediator was originally conceptualized as a limited practitioner. Rather, restrictions were placed on her role so that she did not infringe on the work of lawyers, thereby ensuring that mediation provided a different service to legal advice and court. If mediators are increasingly evaluating and giving information in a way that potentially has the same impact as legal advice, the profession loses its distinctiveness. With this problem in mind, returning to the limited mediator archetype may be preferable. Her reintroduction is, in fact, the only way to maintain a separation of roles between lawyers and mediators.

This line of thinking needs to be considered alongside recent data on the quantity and longevity of mediated settlements. Hitchings et al's (2023) Fair Shares project, first mentioned in section 4.1.1, provides an in-depth look into the financial and property arrangements made by divorcees outside of court. Its findings raise two considerable concerns around flexible mediator practice. First, only 17 per cent of divorcees within the sample reported trying mediation (Hitchings et al 2023: 120–121). Mediation was more commonly used by respondents who had higher levels of assets: only 9 per cent of people with no assets (or only debts) upon separation had tried mediation, compared to 28 per cent of those with assets between £100,000 and £499,999. Even so, family mediation was 'a relatively unpopular avenue' for divorcing couples (Hitchings et al 2023: 360). It is unclear whether a shift towards an openly accepted quasi-legal flexible mediator would make family mediation a more attractive option to potential clients. The second, more sombre, finding from the Fair Shares project was that only 44 per cent of respondents who reached a full settlement in mediation said that the

[25] *Michael [L]* said: 'I've certainly come across some mediated agreements that are appalling'. *Rosie [L]* mentioned that she had seen arrangements drafted by therapeutic mediators 'which just don't make sense'.

agreement had worked out as expected (Hitchings et al 2023: 321–322). This suggests that if mediators are already adopting a flexible approach to their role and providing more evaluative guidance, as the current study suggests, this is not necessarily translating to viable settlements. It may be the case that mediation will never be a good fit for most family disputes, at which point there may be value in considering how to restrain the flexible mediator type. Further research on the quasi-legal flexible mediator, as well as the types of support sought by parties in mediation, is clearly needed.

Nevertheless, what if it was discovered that mediators' knowledge, understanding and application of the law were largely correct? Would this mean that mediators *do* provide something that falls under a contemporary understanding of family justice? Many family mediators originate from a legal background and even continue to practise law. The ability of these practitioners to follow legal norms and support family justice is not questioned when they act as solicitors or barristers. Notwithstanding the important question of whether this development is appropriate, a mediator applying the law correctly would be well-positioned to provide a form of legal oversight. Perhaps the problem is not whether mediators are actually capable of using legal norms, but whether they receive the proper training and guidance to do so.

The quasi-legal flexible mediator is not unfettered. Her role is met with numerous restrictions, many of which are enforced by mediators themselves. These numerous checks and balances have been discussed throughout Chapters 5 and 6. For instance, the mediator sample predicted court outcomes with caution and preferred to give legal information in the hope that it would guide parties towards a particular outcome. While the interviewees appeared to mediate in the shadow of the law, their responses suggested that they continued to refer parties to legal advice for verification.[26] Some of these mediators clarified that they would only apply legal norms when they felt able to do so. As a group, mediators appear well-experienced in knowing their limits. They are given little guidance from their regulatory bodies on how to conduct different tasks, meaning the profession is responsible for finding the appropriate balance between facilitation and evaluation. It may be the case that some mediators are already competent in applying legal norms, as well as knowing when such action is appropriate.

Time and time again, this monograph has returned to the lack of transparency within mediator practice.[27] Mediators' evaluative and quasi-legal

[26] *Victoria [H]* mentioned: 'I insist that they go to their solicitors to get legal advice. But I express what the parameters are.'

[27] A similar realization is made by Smith and Hitchings (2023: 674) about non-lawyer services, who comment that these practitioners 'operate in an under-explored wilderness, free from standards and ill-understood'.

work is often obscured in order to uphold their traditional limited image. This leads family mediators to be misunderstood in two contrasting ways. From one perspective, family mediators are said to be so limited that they cannot support anything close to justice. From another, mediator practice is regularly concealed, creating doubts about whether the role has extended too far. Regardless of the perspective taken, a more accurate understanding of the flexible mediator would be realized by first accepting her existence. This realization would allow for mediator practice to become better regulated and scrutinized, potentially supporting family justice in the process. If it was found that family mediators' quasi-legal role was unjustified and inappropriate, her practices could then be restricted. The question as to whether contemporary family mediation can support contemporary family justice is, once again, stifled not by the flexible mediator's existence, but by her concealment.

6.4 Conclusion

This chapter has continued to demonstrate the wide remit of the flexible mediator archetype. It has illustrated mediators' willingness to screen parties into mediation, even if the party dynamic rendered mediation more challenging. While mediators are traditionally understood to be strictly neutral facilitators, the interview data suggests that mediators regularly assess and intervene. Mediators appear to balance the need for flexibility with their neutrality, regardless of how strictly they interpret the latter concept.

This all has implications for contemporary family justice. Mediators do not perceive themselves as silent or backseat third parties. Rather, they attempt to obtain a settlement in light of various norms, particularly the legal. While lawyers provide legal oversight, the present study indicates that many family mediators feel they can apply legal norms themselves. There was ample evidence throughout the interviews that mediators would mediate in the shadow of the law, usually to promote an agreement of a certain quality. This strategy was evidence of a growing quasi-legal role for the flexible mediator archetype that had developed in light of the post-LASPO landscape. It thus appears that flexible mediators *can* support a contemporary vision of family justice. Whether they actually *do* support family justice in practice, however, remains a question for future research and debate.

It is clear that family mediation, like the entire English and Welsh family justice system, is in the midst of change. Research and debate must now ask: what does this mean for family mediation going forward? As a profession, what should family mediators look like? The future is an exciting time for family mediation reform, though these attempts may be hampered by extrinsic issues within the family justice landscape. The final substantive chapter of this monograph investigates this matter further.

7

The Wider Barriers to Family Mediation Reform

This monograph has revealed shifts in the way family mediation fulfils its purpose in the contemporary family justice landscape. More specifically, it has uncovered a transition in family mediator practice from the limited to the flexible archetype. This development allows mediators to adapt to the case at hand, in addition to providing more quasi-legal support, and is particularly important where more complex cases are coming to mediation after the Legal Aid, Sentencing and Punishment of Offenders Act 2012 (LASPO). Nevertheless, it is argued that the flexible mediator's full potential will not be realized without an open acknowledgement of her evaluative functions. *Rethinking Family Mediation* does not seek to change the purpose of family mediation, but rather calls for recognition that this transition has already begun to occur.

However, even if the flexible mediator type was recognized, finding the momentum to accomplish that change is a whole other challenge. Chapter 7 – the final substantive chapter – takes the monograph in a different direction by identifying some of the extrinsic and organizational obstacles to family mediation reform. It supplements the overarching arguments in *Rethinking Family Mediation*, providing a basis for forthcoming discussions on the matter.

The first section of Chapter 7 gives further justification for this investigation, revealing a concerning level of pessimism within the family mediator sample. The remainder of the chapter reflects on two problems triggered by family mediation's position within the post-LASPO family justice system. Section 2 looks at LASPO's impact on the family mediation market, providing a fresh insight into the shape of the family law landscape since 2013. Specific reference is made to the increasing commercialization of family mediation services, a need for further funding to sustain the process moving forward, and the changes in the delivery of legal advice. Section 3 explores how family mediation could be effectively regulated in the contemporary era. It outlines some recent changes implemented by the Family Mediation Council (FMC), though ultimately recognizes that further regulation is required. It is consequently asked whether family mediation should be recognized as a legal service. This discussion is not based on data from the two-stage empirical study, but on an emerging body of literature around the professionalism of unregulated legal services. After drawing on recent proposals on how to regulate the growing number of unregulated legal services, it is concluded that the legal services market is also, unsurprisingly, in a period of change.

7.1 Going beyond the intrinsic developments

Towards the end of both Chapters 5 and 6, it was reiterated that the problem with the flexible mediator archetype was not her ability to evaluate, but the ambiguity surrounding her role. This is because the tendency to equate mediator evaluation with bad mediation, as well as the association between facilitation and good mediation, has resulted in the flexible archetype's concealment. The dominant conceptualization of family mediation is subsequently incomplete, causing the circular debates around mediation reform to continue. This argument – which forms the basis of most discussions in this monograph – focuses on the intrinsic problems within family mediator practice, such as the unconditional reading of mediator neutrality.

However, attention should also be paid to the external barriers to reform. Even if the theoretical underpinnings of family mediation were redesigned to openly allow the flexible mediator type, it is unlikely that this development alone would be enough to sustain mediation in the long-term post-LASPO landscape. The decades of reform that led to the flexible mediator archetype, as examined throughout this monograph, have also impacted mediators' day-to-day work. The success of the quasi-legal family mediator, particularly in supporting justice, is determined not only by intrinsic mediation theory, but also by factors extrinsic to mediator practice.

Imagine the quasi-legal flexible mediator was a faultless practitioner. She balanced her commitment to neutrality with the demand for flexibility and always knew when it was appropriate (or inappropriate) to mediate in the shadow of the law. She had comprehensive knowledge of family law norms and correctly applied them to every single case in a way that maintained an appropriate level of party autonomy. If these tasks were performed correctly, the flexible mediator would be well-positioned to secure justice for family disputants.[1] However, whether mediation can provide justice depends on its

[1] The main concern in these instances would be whether the flexible mediator archetype itself was appropriate, as detailed in section 6.3.3.

accessibility. Similar to how lawyers can no longer ensure family justice at large if very few individuals can afford their services after LASPO, mediation is no better placed as a family justice apparatus if it cannot be accessed by the majority of disputants. Reaching a consensus on the flexible mediator type and regulating her role is one challenge; another is providing family mediation in a way that enables the flexible mediator to operate.

It quickly became apparent during the mediator interviews that many participants were pessimistic about the future of family mediation. This pessimism reflected a variety of concerns, from the lack of adequate public funding for family mediation to problems within the mediator profession. Mary was worried that mediation would become progressively inaccessible for those with limited funds:

> We're in such a state of flux. We can't say what is going to happen in any area. I have a fear that useful systems like mediation, arbitration, are going to become simply part of a private process. Like private education and state education. There will be a grossly underfunded safety net type thing for people who can't afford services. (*Mary [H]*)

Rebecca [L] thought that mediation would be overlooked in government budgets: 'It depends on spending priorities. I dare say there are a few other things they [the Ministry of Justice] are going to be spending on first. … There's a tiny budget. No one's getting excited. No one's being optimistic about it'. *Lauren [T]* cited the lack of a collective effort to foster change: 'I'm afraid I'm pessimistic, having seen decades of it. There is such a lot of half-hearted talk … it's very sad because if the whole thing was stronger and there was a more concerted effort, I think much more could be achieved and needs to be'. Finally, Michael said that he would actually discourage people from becoming a family mediator:

> I genuinely believe that if somebody was coming to me, to work for me, saying they really wanted to mediate, I'd say, 'Don't waste your money or your time on it'. As a practice, yes, but you're hardly ever going to get the experience in it. It's not going to earn you enough money. That's the reality of it. (*Michael [L]*)

Since the late 20th century, legislative reform has sought to reduce state expenditure and move mediation to the centre of the family justice system. Much of *Rethinking Family Mediation* has considered the influence of these developments on family mediator practice. However, an equally important investigation is how these changes affect the availability and accessibility of the family mediation process. This discussion is particularly important given the Ministry of Justice's (2023b; 2024a) recent interest in mandatory mediation. If there is a chance, even a slight chance, that mediation will have an increasingly prominent role in the future English and Welsh family justice system, its services must be able to keep up with demand. If not, court proceedings will be delayed even further. These reasons justify the investigation in this final substantive chapter.

7.2 The impact of LASPO on family mediation services

Before considering the impact of LASPO, it is worth mentioning that the number of practising family mediators in England and Wales has only recently become public knowledge. The FMC (2024c) originally provided a list of accredited mediators online through its 'Find your local mediator' tool. However, a high number of mediators have multiple entries under the tool, meaning the source can only be used to predict the maximum number of qualified family mediators in England and Wales. In the last few years, the FMC (2024e) has provided a full register of family mediators on its website. As of July 2024, 1,008 accredited or trainee family mediators were listed. It is unclear how quickly this register is updated when someone joins or leaves the profession. The register therefore cannot be used to accurately determine the number of individuals entering the profession in any given year, rendering much of the discussion in section 7.2 exploratory rather than conclusive.

A lot of literature has already been written about the impact of LASPO on family mediation, though most of these discussions are centred on intake. For example, the two Mediation, Information and Assessment Meeting (MIAM) studies commissioned by the Ministry of Justice (discussed in Chapter 4) found that solicitors were disincentivized from referring parties to mediation after LASPO (Bloch et al 2014: 12; Hamlyn et al 2015: 20–21). Another report by the House of Commons Justice Committee (2015: 54–55) showed that solicitors were no longer the first port of call for privately funded individuals, causing referrals to mediation to decrease.

The data from the mediator interviews in this study confirm these findings. When asked about the effect of LASPO on their mediation service, many participants spoke about the immediate fall in casework:

> Solicitors had to refer their clients into mediation before getting legal aid for their own work that's how you got loads and loads and loads of referrals. All for legal aid purposes. [Pause] As you've probably heard numerous times, it just completely fell off a cliff. It just died for a few months. ... You know all these local solicitors who I had good business relationships with ... my marketing was trying to provide a

> good, prompt, swift service etcetera. I never heard from them again, pretty much. (*Rebecca [L]*)

> We thought the referrals would increase because people had to attend a MIAM. For about two years, I think we just [pause] we dipped. So, we had to cut hours, it was really bad. There were lots of services that folded. (*Jane [T]*)

> At the peak, we were getting as many as one hundred referrals a month. There were ten mediators, and we were really busy. … I would say there was a good reputation with all these referrals. It was going well and then it suddenly crashed. Whereas before, lawyers had to refer if they wanted legal aid and then we would actually move quite a lot into mediation. Suddenly all of that stopped. (*Lauren [T]*)

In Rebecca's words, solicitor referrals 'fell off a cliff'. Jane similarly mentioned that mediation numbers 'dipped', causing many services to close. Most interviewees felt this setback was inevitable regardless of their connections with local lawyers. Lauren's service, for instance, used to receive around 100 referrals each month. Despite having a 'good reputation' with lawyers, her mediation intake immediately dropped after LASPO. Rebecca similarly mentioned that she had 'good business relationships' with local solicitors, but 'never heard from them again' once legal aid was cut. In general, most participants said they struggled in the immediate aftermath of the LASPO reforms.

This impact was particularly felt by services that offered legal aid mediation. The mediators in the interview sample who still conducted legal aid work, including Rebecca and Jane, saw a significant drop in their workload after LASPO.[2] *David [H]*, for example, estimated that his service's income from legal aid work dropped from £4,500 a month to around £1,500 after LASPO's enactment. He was optimistic that these profits had risen to roughly £4,000 a month at the time of his interview, though admitted that these earnings were 'not as high' as before.

Five interviewees, four of whom were lawyer mediators or hybrid mediators with a legal background, stopped conducting legal aid mediation after LASPO. Some of these participants spoke negatively about the bureaucracy around legal aid funding:

> The Legal Aid Agency, whatever they say about encouraging mediation, they weren't. They were heavily auditing mediation organizations in such

[2] This pattern aligns with the declining availability of legal aid work for family law solicitors over the same period (Wong and Cain 2019: 5–6).

> a way that if you hadn't got your forms exactly right, they would reject the claim. On average, you get paid a thousand pounds for mediation and they'd try and claw that back. … We were doing four to five hundred mediations a year. The combination of legal aid and the Legal Aid Agency … you wouldn't touch legal aid with a barge pole. (*Michael [L]*)

> They [the Legal Aid Agency] just claw money back, and you're not making a fortune here. If you then claw back all this money and we're spending the first sort of 35 minutes dealing with vulnerable people who may have been thrown out of their house, you say, 'Well why haven't you got your last payslip?' For goodness sake! We're not talking mega bucks. I used to get really neurotic about these forms. I hated it. I could feel my stomach going and thinking, 'I don't want to put my name to this'. The focus was all on these stupid forms and not on what you could do to help. (*Emma [L]*)

Both Michael and Emma felt that legal aid mediation had become inaccessible in recent years.[3] They were critical of the Legal Aid Agency and cited this stance as a key reason why they only worked with privately funded clients after LASPO. *Kate [H]* similarly carried out legal aid work but stopped when she became self-employed. She said that legal aid mediation carried an 'administrative burden', and was particularly worried about completing audits that were 'very easy to get wrong'.[4] *Amy [L]* also used to provide legal aid mediation at a law firm as a form of 'outreach'. However, she said this approach was no longer profitable after LASPO, and stopped providing legal aid mediation when she moved to a new service.[5] For this group of (primarily lawyer) family mediators, legal aid was simply not worth the time or effort.

While it is evident that many family mediation services struggled after LASPO, the reality is not as clear-cut as these extracts suggest. On the contrary, a small number of interviewees found the opposite and claimed that parts of their workload actually increased after LASPO. Several contextual

---

3 *Emma [L]* additionally mentioned that the scope of legal aid had been reduced: 'It was money for old rope. … And then they started making it more difficult. … The chances of you being eligible were so negligible it was unbelievable.'

4 Kate explained that privately funded mediation was easier to conduct because she did not need to spend as much time assessing the parties' eligibility for funding. She said: 'That is another reason why I wouldn't want to do legal aid. The timings. I'd like to say it would be very good for my soul, but it would stop you from doing the quality that you'd want to be doing because you'd be worried about the evidence and the payslips.'

5 *Lauren [T]* was the only therapeutic mediator who stopped providing legal aid mediation after LASPO. She first moved to a new service sometime after the reforms which 'didn't have a contract'. At the time of the interview, Lauren worked as a sole mediator and still did not provide legal aid mediation.

factors explain why some mediators felt the adverse effects of LASPO, whereas others benefited from the reforms. The following discussion is separated into three parts: the heightened focus on commercial interests, the barriers to entering the family mediator profession and the shift towards one-off legal advice. Combined, these findings provide a preliminary insight into LASPO's long-term effects on the family justice landscape.

7.2.1 The post-LASPO success stories

Some interviewees shared success stories from their services. These mediators were not necessarily making large profits; in fact, many participants spoke about the difficulties of running a family mediation service in the post-LASPO landscape. However, a noticeable trend in the interview data was a focus on the commercial elements of conducting family mediation, specifically to ensure a service's financial viability.

Before that discussion takes place, it is worth highlighting a response from Judith. Judith was a hybrid mediator who worked for a large law firm in London that did not provide legal aid. She actually saw an increase in workload after the cuts to legal aid:

> I think mediation bounced for me. We had a huge increase because we knew, we could see, that the court system was getting so bunged up. It was a sort of perfect storm because that came in and then we started shutting courts, and then we started not paying judges enough… For clients who wanted things sensibly sorted out more quickly, they wanted to come to mediation. (*Judith [H]*)

Judith identified numerous problems with the court system after LASPO, such as the rise of Litigants in Person and various administrative issues. She claimed that this led more people to attempt mediation at her service. While there was no conclusive evidence as to why Judith saw a rise in mediation numbers after LASPO, it was likely that her company's status as a privately funded law firm had some influence. Their general clientele was not eligible for legal aid before LASPO and therefore mainly impacted by the cuts to legal aid in terms of its knock-on effects, rather than the inaccessibility of legal support. With increasing delays in court, some privately funded parties turned to mediation.

Many mediators stopped providing legal aid mediation after LASPO, but two participants saw the reforms as an opportunity to monopolize their local market. Charlotte and David spoke about a rise in legal aid work:

> We got the legal aid contract subsequently [after LASPO] because the two other services had shut down. There was a gap in the market,

> and we filled it. I think we had our contract from around 2015. From then, we were really, really busy. So, for my service, it's all been fine, but that's only because the other services were no longer operating. (*Charlotte [T]*)

> We as a small mediation service survived because we weren't very dependent on legal aid. I didn't have very many salaries to pay. … I mean, we probably made a loss that year or didn't make much profit, but we survived. The five largest charitable organizations in this region closed. … Which was, in a way, good for us, because we weathered the storm and came out of it the other end. Although it took a long time. (*David [H]*)

Charlotte was based in South Wales but also worked part-time at a mediation service in the Southwest of England. She mentioned this company started accepting legal aid work after several competitors closed following LASPO. David's service had provided legal aid mediation since the mid-2000s, though most of his clients were privately funded. He explained that a number of 'charitable organizations' shut down after LASPO, causing the legal aid market to become unsaturated. David's firm could subsequently monopolize the local area. While Charlotte and David's experiences differed from the rest of the sample, their responses showed how some services actually increased their legal aid work after the 2013 reforms.

A heightened commercial mindset was further demonstrated by the prominence of sole mediators within the sample. Five interviewees worked as self-employed mediators or ran their own services. These mediators worked across all three regions selected for the study, with varying levels of experience.[6] They were not purely driven by profit; commercial drive did not equate to a lack of philanthropy. Lauren, for instance, continued to mediate children's matters because there was a lack of other mediators in her area.[7] She was worried about the cost of mediation at her previous company and left to become a sole mediator:

> I then left [law firm] and decided to just work on my own. Partly because their fees for mediation actually were so high. People couldn't

6 *Lydia [T]* and *Victoria [H]* had worked as mediators for 5–9 years and also provided legal aid work. *Kate [H]*, *Rosie [L]* and *Lauren [T]* had 15–19, 20–24 and 30+ years of experience, respectively, but did not conduct legal aid mediation at the time of their interview.

7 'I'm focusing much more on issues concerning children because there is a real shortage of mediators who are qualified and experienced in child-inclusive mediation. I'm now focusing on that area' *(Lauren [T])*.

> afford them. … I went solo. I find I'm not the only sort of sole mediator who will reduce fees or negotiate and be more flexible. There are parents who are clearly desperate for help. (*Lauren [T]*)

The other sole mediators spoke about the commercial aspects of running a mediation service, though their initial experiences differed. Kate and Rosie found it 'quick' and 'easy' to start their mediation service:

> The work came in, touch wood [laughs], without any problems at all. It happened very quickly. It was probably to do with the fact that there are few of us in this area that have been going quite a long time. I was already known anyway. I was one of the small handful who had been practising for a while in the area. (*Kate [H]*)

> Actually, it was quite easy. So, things like the insurance and other rates, I covered it in the business plan and started from there. (*Rosie [L]*)

By contrast, Lydia and Victoria recalled the difficulties in getting referrals and making a profit:

> It's been hard. Just having a website isn't enough. … I also made connections with law firms. One of the people that I trained with works at a big law firm. So, she was referring people to me for mediation. Generally, just mediation assessments because they [the parties] wanted to go to court. So, I got work through there and other law firms started referring to me. People moved to different law firms and would then refer to me. (*Lydia [T]*)

> It's probably just turning now. This is probably going to be the first year where we might not make a loss. I'm just at that point now. I think my gross income is about 50 [thousand pounds], and my expenses are 53. I've got two more weeks of this financial year. That sounds like a load of money, but I've taken just half of that for income, 25 grand. Considering my background experience and the responsibilities, that's little. (*Victoria [H]*)

Despite their varied experiences, these four mediators saw sole practice as a viable business model. While there are no published statistics on the number of self-employed mediators, it is interesting that over a quarter of the current sample had turned to sole practice after LASPO. Their prevalence suggests that mediators have adapted to the evolving family justice landscape in many ways, with a noticeable proportion viewing sole practice as more financially lucrative than working at a larger service.

This development sits in stark contrast to the prevailing trend among solicitors. In the early 2000s, Mather et al (2001: 184) identified a 'long-term decline in sole practice'. The researchers cited the rising costs of running a legal practice as the leading cause of this shift. They also warned of 'significant differences' between solicitors in firms and sole practitioners in their willingness to support parties with 'limited resources' (Mather et al 2001: 184). More recently, Mayson (2022) noted that while the number of solicitors on the roll in England and Wales increased each year from 2011 to 2021, the number of law firms dropped by approximately 10 per cent in the same period.[8] Solicitors are increasingly gravitating towards larger law firms, whereas the data from this study suggests that more family mediators are turning to self-employment.

The implications of this development are unclear. A rise in the number of self-employed mediators could make family mediation more accessible if these services were located across the country. A similar observation was made by Mayson (2022), who concluded that the falling number of law firms posed a challenge for clients who would have to travel further to see a lawyer. On the other hand, a diverse portfolio of business structures may impede efforts to unify mediators and establish standardized practices. The data derived from the mediator interviews is relatively weak on this point, underscoring the need for further discussion and research on the commercial aspects of family mediation services.

Notwithstanding the preliminary nature of these findings, it appears as if family mediation has become the survival of the fittest for its providers.[9] This development is unsurprising given the decline of state support over the last few decades; if funding is limited, there is a greater need for mediation services to become financially self-sufficient. In the late 20th century, family mediation services could usually access financial support through government funding (Parkinson 2020: 8–9). Many of the services that helped to establish family mediation, such as the Bristol Courts Family Conciliation Service,[10] also relied on the voluntary work of lawyers, therapists and court staff. Revenue was rarely sourced from private fees. By comparison, the data from this study indicates that family mediation is now primarily provided by private or commercial businesses after LASPO. It thus seems that family mediation has become more commercialized, with an increased focus on how to make profits. Further discussions around how to financially support family mediation services in this new landscape are, thus, crucial to the procedure's success.

---

[8] Mayson's findings are based on statistics published by the Law Society (2022).

[9] Likewise, Wong and Cain (2019: 10) argue that a small number of law firms continue to provide legal aid services 'by developing a niche practice'.

[10] See section 3.2.1.

7.2.2 The barriers to becoming a family mediator

Ten out of 17 interviewees had practised as a family mediator for over 20 years.[11] It was subsequently hypothesized that there was a lack of newly qualified or trainee family mediators within England and Wales. The interview data reveal some reasons for this sample bias.

A major barrier to becoming a family mediator is the cost of training in terms of both time and money. Megan started her training in 2016 and qualified two years later. She commented:

> I know it's a big expense and stuff. It's hard to be able to get into this role. I think I was really lucky because I was only four days a week [at my previous job] at the time. I had a free day that I could use to come here and work voluntarily. Just shadow and work. Whereas if I had been working full-time in a different career … I think it's so impossible to change and do this job. (*Megan [T]*)

Megan considered herself 'lucky' because she could work part-time and train as a mediator once a week. She also recognized that people would struggle to pay for the training without additional employment. Charlotte, who began her training in 2012, was dependent on financial support from her partner:

> It was terrible. Because I wasn't earning any money, it was taking a lot of time … where I did it [training], they'd say there was an appointment and that I could come, but then people wouldn't turn up. I had to arrange childcare, you know. My husband was working and earning so that was what was subsidizing the training. I don't know how anybody does it who is trying to support themselves, I don't think it's possible to do. There used to be paid placements, didn't there? They've all disappeared. No wonder there are no new mediators. (*Charlotte [T]*)

In many instances, young professionals may lack the income or capital to adequately support themselves through accreditation. They also may not receive financial support from their families. This problem was highlighted by Lydia, who also started her training in 2012:

> [N]one of us [mediators] are 18. It's very much a career for people who have gone through other bits. People fresh out of university are

[11] This sample bias was originally discussed in section 1.3.2.1.

> not going to train to be mediators, so we're an ageing population. … I got lucky in my sort of apprenticeship. Lucky in the way that I was able to afford to do that. If I was a young person, I might not have been able to afford it. (*Lydia [L]*)

The lack of placements available for trainee mediators was another barrier to entering the profession. At the time of the interviews, family mediation intake was relatively low across England and Wales. There was also no government or FMC-funded support for mediation services to take on trainee mediators. This meant there were fewer opportunities for trainee mediators to observe and mediate. As mentioned by two participants:

> It's sad that that library of experience is fast disappearing. And because there aren't enough cases around, we can't actually train others up. That's what we'd love to do. (*Michael [L]*)

> It's all fair and well training these people to become mediators, but there needs to be practice. There needs to be guidance. There needs to be more support with that. Financially because it costs a service. You've got somebody new coming in, you're taking time to give that person feedback. There is no support system financially for us. (*Jane [T]*)

Bramwell (2020: 251) reaches a similar conclusion, arguing that there is little incentive for mediation services to support trainees. This is because most trainee mediators will move to another service once they become accredited, becoming 'commercial competitors' in the process. Bramwell submits that this tension, among several other factors, renders the career route for family mediators 'notoriously difficult'.

The problem is paradoxical. There are not enough mediation services with the space to train new mediators, preventing many people from entering the profession. Yet if there are fewer accredited or trainee mediators, some services will struggle to hire enough staff. These services may have to decrease their workload, or even cease operation. There are fewer opportunities for trainee mediators as a result, continuing the cycle. Unfortunately, the number of mediators leaving the profession may be greater than those entering it: a shortage of family mediators is, at the very least, a foreseeable problem in the future if no additional funding is introduced. Altogether, these problems place family mediation in a very precarious position. Mediators have been promoted as the heart of the family justice system for decades, yet the commercial stability of the profession is, if anything, unclear.

7.2.3 The delivery of legal advice

The withdrawal of lawyers from the private family law system after LASPO has been well-documented in both policy and academic literature.[12] It was therefore expected going into the interviews that fewer mediation clients were accessing legal advice. Some data supported this hypothesis. For example, *Lauren [T]* said a 'small minority' of her clients obtained legal advice, though she mainly mediated children's matters. *Jessica [T]* worked for a private law firm and a National Family Mediation (NFM) Direct service.[13] When asked what proportion of clients accessed legal support, she responded: 'Here at [law firm], nearly all of them. At NFM, hardly any.'

However, the more common trend in the interview data was that people using family mediation still accessed legal support. Returning to *Jessica [T]*, she said that 'a very small per cent' of cases at her private law firm 'have no legal input'. *Harley [T]* similarly admitted that his clients 'almost always have access' to a lawyer. Across the sample, the majority of clients obtained legal advice, particularly when dealing with financial or property matters. Some participants gave general estimations:

> I'd say probably about 70 or 80 per cent [have legal advice]. (*Amy [L]*)

> The majority have got something. I'd say 75 to 80 per cent. (*Emma [L]*)

> 70 per cent, I'd say. (*Victoria [H]*)

> In financial cases, I'd say 70 per cent. In children only cases (pause) maybe 30, 40 per cent? It's something like that. (*Megan [T]*)

> [T]he reality is that if it's finances, they will all have legal advice. I say to them they have to. With children, they don't. (*Kate [H]*)

For the last decade, the decline of traditional legal support has been cited as the key reason for the growing demand for mediators to adapt. However, these findings suggest that the reality is not so black and white, and that many disputants continue to access some kind of legal advice.

Perhaps the way that academic commentary[14] explains the availability of legal advice has been too dichotomous. Currently, legal support is presented as being either available or unavailable. Yet legal support sits on a continuum

---

12 See section 4.1.1.

13 The latter is an outreach mediation programme, designed and funded by NFM.

14 This includes work by the monograph's author.

of activity, just like mediator facilitation and evaluation. A more nuanced analysis recognizes that while the majority of family mediation users with financial matters continue to obtain legal advice post-LASPO, the delivery of that advice has changed drastically. Rather than expecting parties to see a lawyer *throughout* their dispute, mediators now encourage them to seek legal advice *at some point* in negotiations.

This hypothesis is supported by the interview data. *David [H]* specifically recommended that parties seek legal advice 'after the second mediation' meeting.[15] *Rosie [L]* said that 'most' of her clients accessed legal advice, though they usually 'only go for one appointment'. *Lydia [T]* also emphasized that 'it is important just to get an hour of advice'. Rebecca would similarly explain to her clients that they only needed to meet with a solicitor once:

> I basically recommend everyone who is doing financial matters at some point in the process. Maybe not after the first meeting … but definitely after the second. I will always say, but I will say with a caveat. They look terrified sometimes. I say it's not that you go to a solicitor and they take on your case and there is bill, bill, bill. You can be very specific and say you just want to go to someone and literally buy an hour's worth of their time. (*Rebecca [L]*)

There was additional evidence in the interviews that disputants were accessing a variety of (mainly self-help) services. Some mediators recognized that their clients often obtained a free half-hour of advice.[16] *Amy [L]* spoke about a client who 'had been for a free appointment with somebody' and explained that 'a lot of people' did the same. *Lauren [T]* noted 'there is quite a lot of information, legal information they [the parties] can access on various websites'. *Jane [T]* spoke about 'advice services, Citizens Advice and things like that'. *Harley [T]* brought up a specific law firm where parties 'book an appointment with a solicitor who will give a sort of pro bono type thing'. *Charlotte [T]* summarized the sample's general experience: 'a lot of people have had some form of legal advice'.

15 He argued: 'The first session is going to be about the financial disclosure, the second session is going to be about looking at options and alternatives, and by the end of that you may have some ideas about what you want to do. There may be some different options on the table. Go and take some legal advice and come back for the third session and you'll be able to negotiate.'

16 *Michael [L]* mentioned that it was normal for legal advice to be 'only be a free half hour'. *Charlotte [T]* similarly said many of her clients accessed 'a free half hour or something'. Finally, *David [H]* mentioned: 'The majority probably have had a free half hour.'

Collectively, these examples allude to a change in direction for legal advice in family mediation and potentially family justice at large. Returning to Rebecca:

> When people thought, 'I need to go and get a divorce, I need to see a solicitor', they would walk to their office and the solicitor would then tell them everything. They won't have that starting point any longer. ... People need that triage but the whole way that people approach law and legal advice, and sorting out their separation, is going through a massive change, in my view. (*Rebecca [L]*)

For most disputants, legal advice has become a one-off event or a pay-as-you-go service that is topped up when required. This development undoubtedly impacts the role of the mediator and, furthermore, how family mediation is provided in the context of the whole family justice process. Family mediation is no longer a supplement to legal advice; rather, legal advice has become an add-on to mediated disputes.

This turn of events partially explains the emergence of the quasi-legal flexible mediator. Lawyers undoubtedly strengthen the shadow of the law in mediation. Yet if a client only sees their lawyer once or twice in a dispute, the level of legal oversight is reduced. Mediators are subsequently expected to provide more support. This puts increased pressure on mediators to not only evaluate, but also spend more time mediating in the shadow of the law. Yet the success of the flexible mediator heavily depends on her understanding of family law and its various norms, as discussed in Chapter 6. If mediation is going to be positioned as a process that can uphold a contemporary vision of family justice, that also depends on the quality of legal support provided by the mediator. The ability of mediators to carry out a quasi-legal role is heavily questioned, particularly where therapeutic mediators have little mandatory legal training.[17] While the rise of the quasi-legal flexible mediator is a promising start, further regulation is urgently needed. Without increased checks and balances, particularly for therapeutic mediators, the ability of mediators to provide this service and support family justice is reduced.

7.3 Regulating family mediation

It is important to recognize that a significant amount of family mediation reform has already occurred. Webley (2010: 146) previously described the UK College of Family Mediators (UKCFM) as more of a 'supervisor of its members than a gatekeeper'. She predicted that as time progressed, the organization would move towards the latter. While the UKCFM was replaced

[17] See section 6.3.3.

by the FMC in 2007, Webley's hypothesis proved to be accurate. Over the course of nearly two decades, the FMC has slowly transitioned into the gatekeeper of family mediation practice. In 2010, the FMC introduced its own Code of Practice (McEldowney 2012: para 60). In 2014, the organization published a Standards Framework which led to a register of accredited mediators. Accreditation was then streamlined through the FMC's Accredited Family Mediator status (FMC 2020). Additional work by the FMC (2016b) includes its guidance on online video mediation, which was increasingly publicized during the COVID-19 pandemic. Most of these reforms were implemented in the post-LASPO climate and are a welcome response to the challenges currently faced by mediators. However, the question remains if these developments are enough to sustain family mediation in the long-term.

The Family Mediation Standards Board (FMSB), which is part of the FMC, has conducted a Standards Review since Autumn 2018. The review covers procedures and rules in four areas: accreditation; complaints and appeals; the Standards Framework; and documenting mediation outcomes to be submitted to court (FMC and FMSB 2018). Several areas have already been reformed. For example, the rules around the case commentaries required for accreditation were adjusted in 2019 (FMC and FMSB 2019). New rules around MIAMs, comprising a Standards document, Guidance and Assurance Processes, were enforced in October 2022 (FMC 2022b). These publications are significantly more detailed than previous guidance released by the FMC. The Standards Review has continued well into the mid-2020s, with the FMSB (2023) listing accreditation and training as two areas where work was still being conducted.

The momentum for reform is increasing at some speed. In a 2022 to 2025 Vision Strategy, the FMC (2022c) described itself as the 'home of regulated family mediation' which aimed 'to generate confidence' in the process. This strategy included 'eliminat[ing] unregulated family mediation', as well as the possibility of the FMC (2022c: 3) applying for a Royal Charter to protect the title of 'family mediator'. Several months after the FMC's Vision Strategy was published, the Ministry of Justice's (2023b: 30) consultation on mandatory mediation asked whether 'more regulation is required' for family mediators, particularly in relation to the accreditation process. The government response concluded that most respondents thought 'FMC accreditation was robust, but that there was value in implementing measures to improve its effectiveness' (Ministry of Justice 2024a: 33).

Thus far, little thought has been given to what could be changed through statutory reform. McEldowney explained that legislative reform was particularly challenging to introduce:

> Statutory regulation of mediation is not a simple option or one that is likely to be introduced overnight, even if a case was made in its favour that would be accepted by the Government. Statutory regulation would

> take considerable time to plan and execute. ... Strong evidence would need to be produced to show that there are significant problems that cannot be addressed under the present, if improved, arrangements. In the meantime the FMC has a real opportunity to set its own house in order. (McEldowney 2012: para 106)

Soon after LASPO, the Family Mediation Task Force (2014: para 23) concluded that the 'onus on the FMC and its organisations to deliver reform would increase' as the regulatory body developed. While the reforms made through the Standards Review are certainly a promising start, it is questioned whether too much onus for regulation is being placed on the FMC. Many of the changes crucial to strengthening mediation's standing, including funding, go beyond the scope of the FMC and can only be introduced by competition regulators or the legislature. Reform needs to be wide-reaching and not only set out what is acceptable mediator practice, but also what mediation can achieve in light of its contemporary purpose. A coordinated effort is therefore necessary to resolve many of the issues faced by family mediation services in the contemporary climate. Pressing refresh on the mediator profession is not instantaneous and requires cultural, as well as organizational, change across various sectors.

If mediators are increasingly providing a quasi-legal service, as the two-stage study indicates, family mediation should be regulated in a way that reflects this development. Without further regulation, the legal remit of flexible mediators will remain hidden, once again causing a lack of transparency around the mediation process. The following discussion outlines a number of papers on how to regulate currently unregulated legal services, before considering their relevance to family mediation reform.

7.3.1 Regulated and unregulated legal services

The Legal Services Act 2007 outlines the regulatory framework for legal services in England and Wales. Enacted in October 2008, the legislation reduced lawyers' monopoly over the legal services market (Boon 2010; Webley 2015). Section 12(1) lists six 'reserved legal activities', including exercising the right of audience and conducting litigation, which can only be performed by authorized providers. Whether a practitioner is an authorized provider is determined by an approved regulator, such as the Law Society or Bar Council. Those regulators are then monitored by the Legal Services Board.[18] By comparison, a 'legal activity' (or non-reserved activity),[19] which includes 'legal advice and assistance' under section 12(3)(b), does not need

[18] Legal Services Act 2007 s 2, s 13 and sch 4.

[19] The term 'non-reserved activity' is adopted by Mayson (2020).

to be conducted by an authorized person. A professional conducting a non-reserved activity is only required to follow the relevant consumer laws (Bell and Rogers 2021: 116). The legislative framework consequently adopts a sharp distinction between regulated and unregulated legal services.

Calls to reform or completely replace the Legal Services Act 2007 have gathered momentum in recent years. Nearly a decade after the Legal Services Act, the Competition and Markets Authority (2016: para 6.87), the main competition regulator in the United Kingdom, argued that a new regulatory regime for legal services should be both 'targeted and proportionate'. However, they recognized that this approach may bring some unregulated providers under 'the regulatory net'. Several years later, Mayson was commissioned to review the regulatory framework for legal services. His final report summarized: 'We can no longer afford to take an "inside-out" approach to legal services regulation. Looking at regulatory issues primarily from the perspective of lawyers (from within the echo chamber of this report's subtitle) misses too many other relevant perspectives and factors' (Mayson 2020: 11).

Mayson (2020: 262) made several recommendations in his report, including the introduction of a register of services carrying out non-reserved activities. The Competition and Markets Authority (2020: paras 5.84–5.85) went on to endorse this proposal. They concluded that the current framework under the Legal Services Act unjustifiably limited competition and increased costs, all while generating a 'regulatory gap' whereby consumers unknowingly went to unregulated providers for legal advice and assistance (Competition and Markets Authority 2020: para 17). Similar conclusions were reached by the Legal Services Board (2021: 19), though they also highlighted the need for a comprehensive register of regulated providers.

These changes have become more necessary given the prominence of unregulated legal services. At the time of his report, Mayson (2020: 89) estimated that up to four-fifths of legal services in England and Wales were conducted by unregulated providers. In a later survey commissioned by the Solicitors Regulation Authority, over two-fifths of 162 unregulated services agreed that consumer demand for their work would increase in the following year (Frontier Economics 2023: 44).[20] The diversification of legal services has been particularly evident in the family law system, despite most academic discussions continuing to focus on lawyers (Smith and Hitchings 2023).

Future reform could bring unregulated providers under the scope of the Legal Services Act 2007 or a completely different legislative framework. Regardless of the approach taken, Mayson (2020: 114) emphasized that the first step towards effective reform was recognizing that unregulated services conducted *legal* work. He argued that the meaning of legal activity went well

[20] Only 4 per cent of respondents thought that demand would decrease.

beyond traditional legal support, and should be extended to cover 'advice, assistance, representation and documentation preparation'. Mayson warned that without this acknowledgement, the impact of any reform would be limited.

Regulating a wide range of unregulated legal services brings its own set of problems. It has been recognized that such reform could hinder 'innovation and affordability' (Legal Services Board 2021: 18), weakening the distinctiveness of these services in comparison to lawyer-based firms (Bell and Rogers 2021: 140). Furthermore, there is little evidence that additional regulation actually improves the quality of legal services (Webley 2015: 2359; Sandefur and Denne 2022: 33–36; Frontier Economics 2023: 74). Regulation may also place an onerous burden on unregulated services, causing some professionals or organizations to leave the market. This could lead to fewer options for consumers or, in the context of family justice, disputants. Unmet legal need could intensify as a result, rendering such reform far from perfect.

7.3.2 Regulating family mediation as a (quasi) legal service

Family mediation sits outside the scope of the Legal Services Act 2007 on two grounds. First, mediation is not included in the list of reserved legal activities under section 12(1). Second, mediation is not a non-reserved legal activity under section 12(3)(b). While legal assistance is considered to be a form of legal activity under the legislation, family mediation is said to only involve the exchange of information. Maclean and Eekelaar (2016: 127) recognize this contradiction, arguing that mediation should be regarded as a non-reserved legal activity because mediators regularly provide support that has a similar impact to giving advice. However, section 12(4) of the Legal Services Act states: 'legal activity does not include any activity of a judicial or quasi-judicial nature (including acting as a mediator)'. Section 12 thus completely excludes family mediation from the statutory framework, despite growing evidence that mediators use legal norms to encourage settlement of a certain quality. Family mediation in England and Wales is instead regulated by the FMC and its regulatory bodies, whose rules only apply to their members.[21]

Mayson (2020: 118–119) was in favour of further regulating mediation. He argued that while dispute resolution services did not provide legal advice or legal representation, they supported parties 'in relation to legal rights and duties'. Thus, it was necessary to bring these services under a regulatory framework of legal activities. Recommendation 11 of Mayson's report read:

[21] Some interviewees in the present study recognized that the 'family mediator' title was not protected. See Blakey (2023a: 151–152).

> In principle, assisting a party to a dispute for which the governing law is that of England & Wales in reaching or progressing a resolution of that dispute (other than through judicial or quasi-judicial determination or arbitration) should be regarded as a legal service. This would include mediation and conciliation, and online dispute resolution. (Mayson 2020: 118)

Mayson's issue did not stem from a complete lack of regulation: he acknowledged that mediator practice was already overseen by the Civil Mediation Council and the FMC (Mayson 2020: 117). The problem, rather, was that membership of these regulatory bodies was voluntary. If a professional referred someone to a mediator who was not accredited under either Council, the client was moved 'from a regulated environment (legal services) into an unregulated one (mediation)'. Mayson (2020: 119) consequently argued that registration for civil and family mediation services should be compulsory. His recommendation was similar to the reform proposed by the FMC in their 2022 to 2025 Vision Strategy, though it is questioned whether the regulatory body would agree that family mediation should be understood as a legal service.

The need for transparency lingers. Suppose family mediators are increasingly providing a form of legal oversight, even if only to some extent. The dominant understanding of family mediation should reflect that development. Family mediation should be regarded as a legal service, though this transition is not possible unless the quasi-legal flexible mediator is first accepted.

Interestingly, preliminary evidence suggests that this understanding of mediation already underpins the current discussions on legal services reform. In the survey commissioned by the Solicitors Regulation Authority, it was estimated that there were 3,800 unregulated legal advice services (Frontier Economics 2023: 23). Of these services, 340 were said to fall under the category of 'Mediation'.[22] The report did not explain why mediation services were legal advice providers, implying that the procedure's legal aspect was not to be questioned. If a similar understanding of mediation is not adopted in the debates around the future of family justice, the idea of the flexible mediator as a quasi-legal practitioner will only lead to limited reform.

And so, the discussion again returns to the need for a contemporary understanding of family mediation that reflects what happens in practice. The concluding chapter will recognize that the flexible mediator has emerged

---

22 Mediation was defined in the report as '[t]hird-party mediation or conciliation services to resolve legal disputes, which could relate to (non-exhaustive): employment issues; property disputes; divorce/separation'. See Frontier Economics (2023: 85).

alongside a rising hybridity within the family law system. In a similar vein, the quasi-legal family mediation service has developed alongside a plethora of other unregulated organizations that seek to respond to the decline of accessible lawyer support. The meaning of 'legal service' has massively expanded since the start of the 21st century: the term could be said to now include the use of LegalTech, as well as artificial intelligence (Bell and Rogers 2021: 131). Just like how this monograph has proposed a new, albeit unrecognized, conceptualization of family justice, perhaps a contemporary understanding of the legal services market is also coming to light.

A major task going forward is to decide how family mediation should be regulated, as well as how the dominant attitudes towards the process and family justice can be transformed to allow this change to occur. The flexible archetype has emerged in light of rising demands on mediators. Professional change must follow. The first steps are already in motion as the FMC has begun to regulate its mediators. While these developments are a promising start, the responsibility for reform should extend to legal regulators and even legislators. One way or another, what is clear is that there is a need to carefully consider and articulate the status of all legal professions, including family mediators. Recognizing the contemporary conceptualizations of these professions is important, if not crucial, to achieving this goal. The family justice system has undergone significant changes since the late 20th century, all of which necessitate a shift in the prevailing perceptions of contemporary family justice and the roles that different professionals play in ensuring such justice is achieved.

7.4 Conclusion

This monograph sought to provide a pragmatic response to the post-LASPO family justice landscape. It revealed how the conceptualization of family mediation can be altered to recognize and permit the flexible mediator archetype, in addition to a contemporary vision of family justice. However, family mediation now sits in a precarious position. The process is increasingly promoted, yet it is unclear whether family mediators can meet rising demand. The lack of comprehensive regulation around family mediation, an increasingly quasi-legal service that appears to support the obtainment of justice for many of its users, does little to alleviate these problems.

More must be done to recognize not only the quasi-legal flexible mediator, but also the legal elements of the family mediation process. The FMC has taken many positive steps towards reform, though the impact of these developments is limited without further change. Whether unregulated legal services, including family mediation, should come under a new regulatory regime must be revisited throughout the next decade. While such reform would result in a very different legal services market, change should not be abandoned simply on the basis that it would weaken or destroy lawyers' centrality in family justice. To quote the Legal Services Board (2021: 9): 'What shape the market takes in future is much less important than that the market delivers legal services that better meet society's needs.' Now more than ever before, thorough and pragmatic change is needed. The contemporary family justice system – and the legal market regulation framework as a whole – must reflect what happens in reality, not what *would* work if lawyers were both available and accessible to the majority.

8

Conclusion

The aim of *Rethinking Family Mediation* was to uncover the purpose of family mediation in the contemporary family justice system. It showed that the role of the family mediator has undergone significant changes since family mediation was first introduced in England and Wales during the late 20th century. These developments are unaccounted for in the general debates around reform, despite their tacit acceptance by family mediation's regulatory bodies and, to some extent, their mediators. Many concepts fundamental to the traditional conceptualization of the family mediator, including neutrality and facilitation, remain at the core of the profession's ethos. However, these ideals are now upheld alongside other contrasting values, notably flexibility and evaluation. The premise behind *Rethinking Family Mediation* was not to criticize these practices, but rather to highlight their concealment.

Thus, this monograph offered a fresh and original perspective on family mediation's position in the current and future family justice systems. By adopting a theoretical lens, it uncovered a disconnect between orthodox theory and family mediation's modern purpose. Concurrent to this investigation was a two-stage empirical project that provided a fresh insight into regulatory bodies' and family mediators' understanding of the mediation process. The findings from both parts of the study have significant implications for the contemporary understanding of mediator practice, and, if accepted, could reinvigorate the discussions around family mediation.

The project underpinning this monograph sought to provide fresh data on family mediation after the cuts to legal aid under the Legal Aid, Sentencing and Punishment of Offenders Act 2012 (LASPO). Chapter 2 tracked the development of family mediation, demonstrating how decades of reform moved the process to the centre of the family justice system. Despite attempts to encourage more parties into family mediation, LASPO caused a sharp increase in the number of self-representing litigants, known as Litigants in Person (LiPs). The bulk of the contemporary family justice literature has subsequently concentrated on the needs of LiPs inside court. However, research on the equivalent of LiPs in mediation is less frequent. While mediation is nowhere close to a universal solution for private family matters, it is crucial to explore how the process has evolved, and will continue to evolve, in response to its changing clientele, as well as the potential effects of these developments on the future of family justice. This study thus makes a critical contribution to the family justice literature by examining family mediator practice at a time when fewer disputants access a lawyer throughout their dispute.

Across eight chapters, *Rethinking Family Mediation* has shown that the contemporary understanding of family mediation and its mediators is highly nuanced. For decades, mediators have been conceptualized as limited third parties. The *limited mediator archetype*, identified and explained in Chapter 3, is confined to neutral facilitation and dependent on lawyers to provide more partisan evaluation. Yet it was evident – even in the early days of family mediation – that mediators were under pressure to evaluate. This predicament led to the evolution of the *flexible mediator archetype*, as covered in Chapter 4. To summarize, flexible mediators are still facilitative third parties but also employ more evaluative strategies. They balance their neutrality with the rising need for flexibility, though these practices are currently hidden in order to promote mediators' traditional conceptualization. Some evidence suggested that the flexible mediator type had become more prominent after LASPO as mediators were seeing an increasingly diverse and complex client base with limited legal support, bolstering the demand for evaluation.

Chapters 5 and 6 proved the existence of the flexible mediator type through a small-scale empirical project, comprising a content analysis of six family mediation Codes of Practice and semi-structured interviews with 17 family mediators. The former chapter proposed a new theoretical framework premised on four functions of mediator practice. These functions, plotted across the continuum of facilitative to evaluative strategies, demonstrate how mediators are still understood (by themselves and by their regulatory bodies) to be helpers. They are allowed to be referrers, though changes to Codes of Practice indicate that this function has become more evaluative over time as mediators are now expected to only refer parties to legal advice when desirable. The third and fourth functions, assessor and intervenor, are more explicitly evaluative and appear to be increasingly used by flexible mediators to adapt to the case at hand. Chapter 6 expanded on this theoretical framework by considering how the flexible mediator archetype could support contemporary family justice. It outlined various findings from the mediator interviews, revealing a consensus throughout the sample that they could react to difficult party dynamics and evaluate regardless of the interpretation of mediator neutrality they followed. There was ample evidence that these mediators not only thought they could evaluate but did so in light of various legal norms. Altogether, these findings alluded to a quasi-legal role for flexible mediators in the post-LASPO landscape.

This monograph has often advanced the flexible mediator archetype as a welcome, albeit fallible, development. Two particular challenges remain. The first concerns the lack of transparency around the flexible mediator. The two-stage empirical project proves that the archetype has existed for some time. However, their actions are often disguised as neutral and limited forms of information. This concealment has implications beyond the mediation setting, rendering the debate around family mediation reform circular and stagnant. While there is a growing recognition that mediators need to update their practices, the profession is forced to conceal their new strategies in light of the widely held and harsh understanding of their neutrality. In order to effectively study, scrutinize and regulate contemporary mediator practice, it must first be recognized that mediators now balance their neutrality alongside an increasingly important ethos: flexibility. Unfortunately, the orthodox conceptualization of family mediation, whereby limited mediators do not evaluate, continues to persist in the discussions around family mediation reform.

The second problem relates to the structural issues surrounding family mediation. Even if a contemporary conceptualization of family mediators is realised, changes to the family justice system have left the procedure in a precarious position. This issue was the focus of Chapter 7. Concerns related to how family mediation services were funded, as well as whether there were enough family mediators to sustain the profession. Later parts of the chapter questioned whether family mediation should be regarded as a legal service, linking this possibility to a broader discussion around the emergence of unregulated legal services. Reform must address these extrinsic issues to ensure that family mediation remains accessible, though many of the necessary changes cannot be enacted by the Family Mediation Council (FMC) alone.

Throughout each chapter, this monograph has outlined the various implications of its findings. For example, it was advanced in Chapter 4 that mediator neutrality must be re-envisioned to permit flexibility or, more specifically, mediator evaluation. This reconceptualization is only possible if neutrality is understood in a way that no longer renders the concept sacrosanct or absolute. However, following the interview data outlined in Chapter 6, it may be preferable to replace 'neutrality' with the concept of 'impartiality'. Similarly, whether mediators should be included in the broader reforms around non-legal services, as mentioned in Chapter 7, has significant implications regarding the type of reform sought and which bodies are responsible for enacting that change. As *Rethinking Family Mediation* draws to an end, the author wishes to highlight three broad implications of her work. It is hoped that by briefly examining these points, conversations on how to reform family mediation will evolve well beyond the arguments advanced across these eight chapters.

8.1 What does the flexible family mediator mean for contemporary family justice?

The developments around family mediation allude to a shift in the delivery of family justice. It appears that over several decades, family justice has transformed into a category. The concept is no longer solely associated with legal representation in court, though that premise does, and *should*, remain at the heart of contemporary family justice. However, the source of justice in contemporary times is not necessarily through access to a particular service. It is instead by 'realising substantively just solutions' to legal problems (Sandefur 2020: 285). A growing body of work, including *Rethinking Family Mediation*, seeks to move beyond a 'lawyer-centric' view of family justice (Smith and Hitchings 2023: 675). Such literature investigates a plethora of services beyond lawyers that provide support, and thus possibly justice, to many family law disputants in the contemporary landscape.

There are, of course, valid reasons why some scholars reject this idea. The court is a pivotal forum for justice, yet it has become increasingly reserved for a small and narrowly construed group of cases. The use of lawyers to ensure legal oversight throughout a dispute is also becoming more and more inaccessible. Access to these systems is a constitutional right and any limitations placed upon them must be critiqued. Nonetheless, whether a justice that aligns with legal norms and expectations can be achieved through other procedures still merits consideration. Suppose, as the two-stage study suggests, that decisions analogous to those made in court can be reached in family dispute resolution (or other extra-legal services) through the use of legal norms to engender settlement of a particular quality. If done correctly, these resolutions may not be that far from the justice long associated with court (Sandefur and Denne 2022: 31). While most professionals in the broader family justice system cannot determine or lay down a specific outcome, there was evidence within the interview data that family mediators could be direct – blunt, even – when they thought a proposed agreement was unjust or unfair. In the contemporary family justice landscape, it is unrealistic to claim that judges and lawyers are the only practitioners capable of providing legal oversight and thus engendering justice (Smith and Hitchings 2023). The argument that lawyers, and lawyers only, are effective at legal support is also unsubstantiated, with few studies actually assessing the quality of their work (Sandefur 2020: 298). This development should be welcomed, rather than immediately cast aside as poor practice. Only through such 'radical thinking', as envisaged by Hitchings and Miles (2016: 192), can mediators and other family justice professionals be seen as more than mere conduits of legal information.

This investigation is even more crucial where the separation of roles among different family justice professionals has eroded over time. Davis and Pearce

(1999) originally identified a 'degree of merging, or hybridity' across the work of solicitors, welfare officers (often acting as in-court conciliators) and district judges. This hybridity has expanded in the last two decades, as evidenced by the quasi-legal space for legal and non-legal professionals in the post-LASPO era. The space is occupied by solicitors and court workers, in line with Davis and Pearce's argument, but now includes McKenzie Friends (Smith et al 2017: 5), advice agencies (Maclean and Eekelaar 2019: 171) and, as advanced by this monograph, family mediators. Non-professionals also inhabit this space as many individuals seek the support of their friends, families and colleagues upon relationship breakdown (Davis 1988: 35). The exact size of the quasi-legal space is unclear, but it appears to have grown exponentially since the late 20th century. Nonetheless, the work of most family justice professionals within the quasi-legal sphere remains understudied, with Smith and Hitchings (2023: 660) arguing that the high levels of legal need not met by lawyers is 'only one half of a bigger picture'.

The hybridity within contemporary family justice is not a one-sided invasion of lawyers' territory. In fact, lawyers have significantly developed their domain over the last few decades. While solicitors are portrayed as partisan and adversarial advisers, many adopt a consensus-based and facilitative approach to their work. Through observations and meetings with family solicitors and their clients, Wright (2007: 490) discovered that most solicitors were 'conciliatory' and 'neutral', two concepts traditionally associated with mediation. This led Wright to question if there was 'a new hybrid profession emerging, influenced both by the tenets of mediation and by the principles of legal representation'. More recently, the 'one-lawyer-two-clients' model of legal advice, whereby both parties are advised and assisted by the same lawyer, has gained particular interest. Bowden (2022: 1283) acknowledges the procedure's similarities to family dispute resolution, arguing that the model 'only has a chance of working if it looks like mediation'. Despite concerns that the one-lawyer-two-clients model is unregulated and inappropriate for high-conflict disputes, the format is set to be increasingly used in the mid to late 2020s. In a 2021 Family Justice Briefing by Resolution, Lake-Carroll (2021: 14) declared: 'If the government's intent is to reduce conflict within families, they may come to consider that not being able to receive services jointly from a single legal adviser may of itself fuel conflicts.' Resolution (2022) introduced its one-lawyer-two-clients model, Resolution Together, the following year, though the service has yet to be scrutinized.

The current study builds on this growing evidence base to reveal a quasi-legal space in which the roles of mediators and solicitors have become increasingly distorted. It suggests that mediators (many of whom have a legal background) are portrayed as facilitative helpers yet regularly evaluate and seek settlement of a certain quality. At the same time, lawyers, who for centuries have been presented as harsh partisans, often take a more conciliatory and facilitative approach to family matters. Mediators and lawyers have blended their practices, contributing to the rising hybridity within contemporary family justice following LASPO. Maclean and Eekelaar (2016: 122) reach the same conclusion, acknowledging that 'family mediation appears to be becoming increasingly integrated into legal practice'.

It is easily forgotten that family mediators are a relatively new profession, whereas family solicitors have operated for several centuries. Even in the quasi-legal space, lawyers' monopoly over legal advice and their rights of audience provide them with a unique selling point from which to preserve their professional identity. The profession is also subjected to an extensive and legally enshrined regulatory framework. By contrast, family mediators have struggled to create a distinct identity from the very beginning. While a growing body of literature has called for a major overhaul of lawyers' professionalism and ethics (Pleasence et al 2012; Moorhead 2014; Susskind and Susskind 2015), comparable literature on family mediation is in its infancy. Family mediation is often explained by what it does *not* provide, such as the opportunity for legal advice or a legally binding outcome. Because of these comparisons, mediation has had little opportunity to prove itself as a possible family justice apparatus. Mediation certainly cannot cure the issues within contemporary family justice, but the same statement rings true of other procedures, such as adversarialism and solicitor negotiation, that are increasingly inaccessible yet still accepted as fundamental parts of the family justice discourse.

The interview data covered in this monograph suggest that family mediators are increasingly using family law norms to inform their practices. Family mediators continue to refer parties to legal advice, particularly in financial matters. Yet there appear to be many instances where mediators feel well-equipped to provide a form of legal oversight. They mediate in the shadow of the law, an action which enables family law's normative content to prevail. While the mediator sample did not explicitly associate mediation with access to justice, they appeared to make judgements about the quality of settlement. References to potential court outcomes, as well as various other evaluative actions, were also prevalent across the interview data. Combined, the two-stage study indicates that contemporary family mediation has the potential to be about justice.

8.2 Is the flexible mediator archetype the only way to understand contemporary family mediator practice?

Chapters 1 and 2 recognized that a return to the traditional family justice system, premised on access to the courts and legal support, is highly unlikely. Reform must be pragmatic and respond to the contemporary, not the orthodox, family justice landscape. Mant (2022: 164) explains that this response necessitates new empirical work coupled with theoretical critique, followed by a 'reflection on the kinds of assumptions that underpin' the English and Welsh family justice system. The concept of the quasi-legal flexible mediator archetype, a professional who undertakes several different functions, is founded on all three elements. However, it is worth considering two alternative proposals to the flexible mediator archetype.

Maclean and Eekelaar (2016: 125–126) conclude that the distinction between the two professions is 'unrealistic'. Despite the prohibition on giving advice, the researchers discover that mediators regularly use information 'in the interests of the participants or a child'. Maclean and Eekelaar submit that this action is not dissimilar to how and why a solicitor advises. In light of this revelation, they propose that lawyers should be able to see two parties at once. Maclean and Eekelaar argue that lawyers would need to be trained to conduct family mediation (or undergo similar training) in order to prove that they can facilitate agreement. They emphasize that lawyers should not be the only professionals capable of this role and advance a model of 'legally assisted family mediation'. Under the model, mediators would be permitted to give legal advice. They could conduct this model regardless of their professional background, though therapeutic mediators (referred to by Maclean and Eekelaar as 'non-lawyer mediators') would require additional legal training. To the two commentators, the legally assisted model removes the 'artificial distinction between acting as a mediator and acting as a lawyer' (Maclean and Eekelaar 2016: 134).

There are some similarities between legally assisted family mediation and the flexible mediator archetype. Maclean and Eekelaar (2016: 136) describe the model as 'a form of one-stop mediation with legal uplift'. Similarly, Chapter 6 revealed that flexible mediators mediate in the shadow of the law by using legal norms to encourage settlement of a certain quality. Both proposals also have significant implications for the concept of mediator neutrality. Maclean and Eekelaar (2016: 135) recognize that a mediator performing legally assisted family mediation would no longer be neutral in regard to the mediated outcome, though she would remain 'impartial as between the participants'. The flexible mediator archetype is, by contrast, allowed to depart from a moderate interpretation of neutrality (or impartiality) when such action is justified.

A different approach is sought by Skinner (2019: 271) who, in collaboration with Resolution, piloted the Family Matters Service. The professionals working for the Family Matters Service, called Guides, were family mediators who could not give legal advice. They worked with the parties together to reach an agreement, gave legal information and, ultimately, responded to problems in a 'holistic way' (Skinner and Foster 2016: 8). All six Guides in the study were lawyers, most of whom only trained as mediators for the project (Skinner and Foster 2016: 20). Following the pilot, the Guides praised Family Matters as a 'flexible service' took parties' needs into account (Skinner 2019: 272). The Guides felt they provided a different – perhaps more enhanced – service to family mediation, largely because they could 'challenge' parties' different perceptions and proposals (Skinner and Foster 2016: 26–27).

Both legally assisted family mediation and the Family Matters Service have merit, particularly when considering the concerns surrounding the quasi-legal flexible mediator (discussed towards the end of Chapter 6). The two proposals seek to strengthen the shadow of the law. Mediators conducting legally assisted family mediation would undergo more legal training if they originated from a therapeutic background. All the Guides in Skinner's study were practising lawyers, suggesting that this profession, if implemented more widely, would largely consist of lawyer mediators. These mediators (or Guides) may therefore be better equipped to apply legal norms than the flexible mediator. Furthermore, their role may also be more appropriate as mediator evaluation would be ring-fenced into a niche model or service. Direct legal assistance would be reserved for a specific type of mediation, or a different profession altogether, thereby protecting the facilitative framework that underpins the orthodox family mediation model. Family mediators could subsequently return to their limited archetype, only taking on a more active and quasi-legal role when their clients explicitly agreed to it.

However, there are weaknesses to either approach. Under Maclean and Eekelaar's model of legally assisted family mediation, mediators would be allowed to advise on the basis that information is not inherently facilitative. This approach ensures transparency. Maclean and Eekelaar's proposal holds strength in this regard, though it may not be widely accepted as a result. This is because the distinction between information and advice has massively limited the conceptualization of the family mediator since the late 20th century, distinguishing the profession from other family law practitioners. Most, if not all, mediators and their regulatory bodies regard the word 'advice' as an indicator of improper practice. Seven years have passed since Maclean and Eekelaar's monograph was published, yet legally assisted family mediation has not been trialled or piloted. Similar to how family justice reform needs to be pragmatic, proposals to alter family mediation should also be designed in a way that is more likely to be accepted by the majority of practitioners. By comparison, the flexible mediator archetype mediates in the shadow of the law: she reality-tests, predicts court outcomes and so on. She is, however, barred from giving advice.

Furthermore, the findings from this monograph suggest that the Guides are simply flexible mediators in all but name. The interview data covered in Chapters 5 to 7 shows that family mediators conceptualize their role to comprise a variety of strategies that enable them to challenge unfair agreements. This directness is frequently permitted by mediation's regulatory bodies, though it remains concealed by a facilitative guise. A Guide is not necessarily a distinct entity from mediators; rather, her title appears to signal a linguistical choice to make the practitioner's evaluative work more obvious to the parties.

Each chapter in *Rethinking Family Mediation* has advocated for the explicit recognition of family mediators' evaluative work. Introducing a new mediation model or a hybrid profession does not necessarily achieve this goal (or do so in a way that is affordable to most disputants). Intriguingly, both legally assisted family mediation and the Family Matters service are premised on a one-lawyer-two-clients model of legal support in which a solicitor advises both parties. The researchers primarily focus on the work of lawyers, arguing that their findings have implications for mediator practice. The responsibility for navigating these new and flexible rules is subsequently placed on mediators themselves. By comparison, a conceptualization that starts with family mediators, which then has implications for lawyers, is more alert to the profession's position after LASPO. In the 2020s, there exists a clear demand for mediators to be flexible and evaluate. The notion of the flexible mediator, reflecting the nuances and subtleties of mediator practice, seeks to give the profession explicit guidance on this matter. This approach, combined with the four-function framework, understands mediators in light of their own actions, not those of the practitioners around them.

The correct way forward cannot be decided by this monograph alone. It is something the entire family justice community must address as a collective. What is clear, however, is that the debate on family mediation reform has focused on the negative. It has focused on what mediators do badly and what they cannot perform under a traditional understanding of family justice. Concern about the flexible mediator type is understandable, but her evolution appears to have numerous benefits.

8.3 How can the flexible mediator be better understood?

This monograph has repeatedly returned to the need for pragmatic reform. Its author has advanced her own views and, in particular, suggested that the flexible mediator could do more in the contemporary family justice landscape if the archetype was openly recognized. However, *Rethinking Family Mediation* is more concerned with reinvigorating the debate on family mediation and family justice than pushing a particular agenda. Some may read all eight chapters and conclude that the role of the mediator has gone too far. This reading is to be welcomed, so long as it is focused on today's mediators and not the practices of mediators from long ago.

The advancements in mediator practice have not been properly recognized because of, once again, a lack of transparency. Throughout each chapter that considered the flexible mediator archetype, the issues around her concealment have resurfaced. Further research on the flexible mediator, as well as other practitioners within the quasi-legal space, will be invaluable in determining whether these professionals can support contemporary family justice. Of course, subsequent research may reveal that family mediators cannot ensure justice. Access to legal oversight is not necessarily the same as access to justice: the quality of that legal oversight also hinges on the skills of the practitioner providing support. The author is, once again, not against this view if it is reached in light of thorough evidence.

The two-stage study indicates that the flexible mediator type could provide a high level of support in some instances. The data suggests that flexible mediators are responsive and often well-positioned to respond to power imbalances. While the mediator sample did not seem to grasp how their evaluative actions implicated their neutrality, their responses nonetheless suggested that they felt capable of taking action to engender settlement of a certain quality. However, this study only reveals what regulatory bodies and family mediators *believed* the profession could achieve, rather than how they acted in practice. While these findings indicate that the flexible mediator archetype has promise, they also uncover various risks if her practices are poorly and inconsistently conducted. For these reasons, future research must determine exactly how mediators respond in different situations. As is true with any kind of reform, realizing the flexible mediator's full potential requires a coordinated effort among researchers, practitioners, regulatory bodies and policy makers. The FMC has already taken significant strides towards this goal: it is imperative that this momentum continues.

Some commentators have already recognized the need to reform family mediation. Chapter 4 referred to the concluding paragraph of Barlow et al's (2017: 211) *Mapping Paths to Family Justice*, which identified 'an urgent need to consider how mediation can be redesigned to operate more effectively'. *Rethinking Family Mediation* has considered how to redesign – or rethink – family mediation. However, its findings are derived from a small study that would benefit from additional corroboration. Forthcoming research would massively aid in confirming the flexible mediator's existence, as well as identifying her shortcomings. For instance, research could be conducted on whether mediators are prepared to act as family justice providers. In what instances do mediators support or hinder justice? Furthermore, what can be done to improve the family mediator accreditation process? The effectiveness of the flexible mediator greatly depends on her skillset, yet the current process means she undergoes very little training. Certain mediator sub-groups may be more effective at the legal or therapeutic elements of family mediation depending on their professional background, though the present study cannot confirm this hypothesis. These discussions would be massively aided by observational data on the work of family mediators both in and out of mediation sessions.

Unfortunately, a crucial perspective is missing from this book: the disputant. Time and time again, family mediation has been pushed by successive governments. The views and feelings of those involved in the mediation process have rarely been taken into account beyond quantitative satisfaction rates. These statistics must be understood in the broader context of what a party thought mediation was intended to provide, how they thought the mediator acted and their perception of the mediated outcome. There is a pressing need to speak to family mediation users, especially those without lawyers, in the post-LASPO climate. This work is essential to understanding how family mediation, in addition to the flexible mediator, is perceived by its ever-diversifying clientele.

Family mediation now sits at a crossroads. One road returns to the traditional conceptualization of family mediation and the limited mediator, continuing a strict and certain, but perhaps idealistic, vision of the profession. It is a well-trodden path with familiarity for family mediators. However, remaining on this path will only support family justice if other professionals and their procedures become more accessible to disputing families. The other road leads to explicit acknowledgement and development of the flexible mediator archetype, recognizing that she conducts more evaluative practices alongside her facilitative remit. This path ensures flexibility to cater to an increasingly diverse client base and has been increasingly used over time, though it is not currently considered the official or proper way for mediators to act. While the latter route is a more apt response to the LASPO reforms, it is reasonable for discussion and debate to be cynical of the flexible mediator. This scepticism should not lead family mediation to be instantly dismissed, but instead prompt further conversation on the types of support that various family justice professionals can, and should, provide going forward. The future of family justice is uncertain, but part of the solution may have been right in front of us all along.

References

Albiston, C.R. and Sandefur, R.L. (2013) 'Expanding the empirical study of access to justice'. *Wisconsin Law Review*, 1, 101–120.

Astor, H. (2007) 'Mediator neutrality: making sense of theory and practice'. *Social & Legal Studies*, 16(2), 221–239.

Auerbach, J. (1983) *Justice without Law? Resolving Disputes without Lawyers*. Oxford: Oxford University Press.

Banakar, R. and Travers, M. (2005a) 'Introduction' in Banakar, R. and Travers, M. (eds), *Theory and Method in Socio-Legal Research*. Oxford: Hart Publishing, pp 10–15.

Banakar, R. and Travers, M. (2005b) 'Introduction to section six' in Banakar, R. and Travers, M. (eds), *Theory and Method in Socio-Legal Research*. Oxford: Hart Publishing, pp 248–251.

Barlow, A. and Hunter, R. (2020) 'Reconstruction of family mediation in a post-justice world' in Roberts, M. and Moscati, M.F. (eds), *Family Mediation: Contemporary Issues*. London: Bloomsbury Professional, pp 11–32.

Barlow, A., Hunter, R., Smithson, J. and Ewing, J. (2014) *Mapping Paths to Family Justice: Briefing Paper and Report on Key Findings*. Exeter: University of Exeter.

Barlow, A., Hunter, R., Smithson, J. and Ewing, J. (2017) *Mapping Paths to Family Justice: Resolving Family Justice in Neoliberal Times*. London: Palgrave Macmillan.

Batagol, B. and Brown, T. (2011) *Bargaining in the Shadow of the Law? The Case of Family Mediation*. Annandale: Themis Press.

Becker, D. (2013) *The Controversy over Mediator Neutrality: Input from New Zealand Mediators* (LLM). Dunedin: University of Otago.

Bell, F. and Rogers, J. (2021) '"Fit and proper" codes? How might legal service delivery by non-lawyers be regulated?'. *Legal Ethics*, 24(2), 111–140.

Bhatt, N. (2009) 'Evolution and legislative history of mediation'. *GNLU Journal of Law, Development and Politics*, 1(2), 83–95.

Blakey, R. (2020) 'Cracking the code: the role of mediators and flexibility post-LASPO'. *Child and Family Law Quarterly*, 32(1), 53–74.

Blakey, R. (2023a) '"Mediators mediating themselves": tensions within the family mediator profession'. *Legal Studies*, 43(1), 139–158.

Blakey, R. (2023b) 'Studying family mediators in a changing justice system' in Newman, D. (ed), *Leading Works on the Legal Profession*. Abingdon: Routledge, pp 227–240.

Blakey, R. (2024) 'Assessing the availability of legal support through the "Help with Family Mediation" legal aid scheme'. *Journal of Social Welfare and Family Law*, 46(1), 82–103.

Bloch, A., McLeod, R. and Toombs, B. (2014) *Mediation Information and Assessment Meetings (MIAMs) and Mediation in Private Family Law Disputes: Qualitative Research Findings*. London: Ministry of Justice.

Bogdanoski, T. (2009) 'The "neutral" mediator's perennial dilemma: to intervene or not to intervene?'. *Queensland University of Technology Law and Justice Journal*, 9(1), 26–43.

Boon, A. (2010) 'Professionalism under the Legal Services Act 2007'. *International Journal of the Legal Profession*, 17(3), 195–232.

Boulle, L. (2005) *Mediation: Principles, Process, Practice* (2nd edn). Chatswood: LexisNexis.

Bowden, C. (2022) 'Two into one: does it go?'. *Family Law*, 52(10), 1278–1284.

Braithwaite, A. (2016) 'Mediators drafting consent orders'. *Family Law*, 46(11), 1362–1365.

Bramwell, L. (2008) 'The UK College of Family Mediators'. *Family Law*, 38(2), 172–172.

Bramwell, L. (2020) 'Creative paths to practice: helping new mediators to navigate the route to artistry' in Roberts, M. and Moscati, M.F. (eds), *Family Mediation: Contemporary Issues*. London: Bloomsbury Professional, pp 251–272.

Brooke, H. (2017) 'The history of legal aid 1945–2010', *Fabian Society*, [online] September. Available from: https://fabians.org.uk/wp-content/uploads/2017/09/Bach-Commission-Appendix-6-F-1-1.pdf [accessed 9 July 2024].

Brown, W. (2015) *Undoing the Demos: Neoliberalism's Stealth Revolution*. New York: Zone Books.

Burnett, M. and Sandefur, R.L. (2022) 'Designing just solutions at scale: lawyerless legal services and evidence-based regulation'. *Direito Público*, 19(102), 104–119.

Bush, R.A.B. and Folger, J.P. (1994) *The Promise of Mediation*. San Francisco: Jossey-Bass.

Byrom, N. (2017) 'Cuts to civil legal aid and the identity crisis in lawyering: lessons from the experience of England and Wales' in Flynn, A. and Hodgson, J. (eds), *Access to Justice and Legal Aid: Comparative Perspectives on Unmet Legal Need*. Oxford: Hart Publishing, pp 221–238.

Cantwell, B. (2006) 'CAFCASS: in-court conciliation and out-of-court mediation'. *Family Law*, 36(5), 389–392.

Cameron, G. (2015) 'Family justice reforms: how are they working in practice?'. *Family Law*, 45(9), 1025–1027.

Choudhry, S. and Herring, J. (2017) 'A human right to legal aid? The implications of changes to the legal aid scheme for victims of domestic abuse'. *Journal of Social Welfare and Family Law*, 39(2), 152–167.

Civil Justice Review (1988) *The Report of the Review Body on Civil Justice* (Cmd 394).

Clarke, J. (2004) 'Dissolving the public realm? The logics and limits of neo-liberalism'. *Journal of Social Policy*, 33(1), 27–48.

Cohen, O., Dattner, N. and Luxenburg, A. (1999) 'The limits of the mediator's neutrality'. *Mediation Quarterly*, 16(4), 341–348.

College of Mediators (2019) *Code of Practice for Mediators*, [online]. Available from: www.collegeofmediators.co.uk/wp-content/uploads/2021/05/CoM-Code-of-Practice-V2-1.pdf [accessed 9 July 2024].

Committee on One-Parent Families (1974) *Report of the Committee on One-Parent Families: Volume 1* (Cmd 5619).

Competition and Markets Authority (2016) *Legal Services Market Study: Final Report*. London: Crown.

Competition and Markets Authority (2020) *Review of the Legal Services Study in England and Wales*. London: Crown.

Cooks, L.M. and Hale, C.L. (1994) 'The construction of ethics in mediation'. *Mediation Quarterly*, 12(1), 55–76.

Cookson, G. (2011) *Unintended Consequences: The Cost of the Government's Legal Aid Reforms*. London: King's College London.

Cowan, D. and Wincott, D. (eds) (2016) *Exploring the 'Legal' in Socio-Legal Studies*. London: Palgrave Macmillan.

Cretney, S. (1998) *Law, Law Reform and the Family*. Oxford: Oxford University Press.

Crowe, J. and Field, R. (2019) 'The empty idea of mediator impartiality'. *Australasian Dispute Resolution Journal*, 29(4), 273–280.

Davis, G. (1980) *Report of a Research to Monitor the Work of the Bristol Courts Family Conciliation Service in its First Year of Operation*. Bristol: University of Bristol.

Davis, G. (1983) 'Mediation in divorce: A theoretical perspective'. *Journal of Social Welfare and Family Law*, 5(3), 131–140.

Davis, G. (1988) *Partisans and Mediators: The Resolution of Divorce Disputes*. Oxford: Clarendon Press.

Davis, G. (2004) 'A research perspective' in Westcott, J. (ed), *Family Mediation: Past, Present and Future*. Bristol: Jordan Publishing, pp 59–69.

Davis, G. and Bader, K. (1985a) 'In court mediation: the consumer view I'. *Family Law*, 15(2), 42–49.

Davis, G. and Bader, K. (1985b) 'In court mediation: the consumer view II'. *Family Law*, 15(3), 82–86.

Davis, G. and Roberts, M. (1988) *Access to Agreement*. Milton Keynes: Open University Press.

Davis, G. and Pearce, J. (1999) 'The hybrid practitioner'. *Family Law*, 29(8), 547–555.

Davis, G., Cretney, S. and Collins, J. (1994) *Simple Quarrels: Negotiating Money and Property Disputes on Divorce*. Oxford: Clarendon Press.

Davis, G. et al (2000) *Monitoring Publicly Funded Family Mediation: Summary Report to the Legal Services Commission*. London: Legal Services Commission.

Delgado, R. et al (1985) 'Fairness and formality: minimizing the risk of prejudice in alternative dispute resolution'. *Wisconsin Law Review*, 6, 1359–1404.

Devlin, P. (1979) *The Judge*. Oxford: Oxford University Press.

Dewar, J. (1998) 'The normal chaos of family law'. *Modern Law Review*, 61(4), 467–485.

Dick, A.H. (2020) 'Family mediation: the Scottish perspective' in Roberts, M. and Moscati, M.F. (eds), *Family Mediation: Contemporary Issues*. London: Bloomsbury Professional, pp 75–96.

Diduck, A. (2013) 'Autonomy and vulnerability in family law: the missing link' in Wallbank, J. and Herring, J. (eds), *Vulnerabilities, Care and Family Law*. London: Routledge, pp 95–114.

Diduck, A. (2016) 'Autonomy and family justice'. *Child and Family Law Quarterly*, 28(2), 133–149.

Dingwall, R. (1986) 'Some observations on divorce mediation in Britain and the United States'. *Mediation Quarterly*, 11, 5–23.

Donovan, C., Hester, M., Holmes, J. and McCarry, M. (2006) *Comparing Domestic Abuse in Same Sex and Heterosexual Relationships*. University of Sunderland and University of Bristol, [online] November. Available from: https://argyllwomensaid.org.uk/wp-content/uploads/2017/08/Comparing-Domestic-Abuse-in-Same-Sex-Heterosexual-Relationships.pdf [accessed 9 July 2024].

Doughty, J. and Murch, M. (2012) 'Judicial independence and the restructuring of family courts and their support services'. *Child and Family Law Quarterly*, 24(3), 333–354.

Douglas, S. (2009) *Mediator Neutrality: A Model for Understanding Practice* (DPhil). Queensland: University of the Sunshine Coast.

Edwards, J. (2016) 'Closer collaboration between the judicial and mediation communities part 1: mediation/MIAMs – how they work in practice'. *Family Law*, 46(9), 1168–1171.

Eekelaar, J. (2011) 'The Arbitration and Mediation Services (Equality) Bill 2011'. *Family Law*, 41(11), 1209–1215.

Eekelaar, J. and Dingwall, R. (1988) 'The development of conciliation in England' in Dingwall, R. and Eekelaar, J. (eds), *Divorce Mediation and the Legal Process*. Oxford: Clarendon Press, pp 3–22.

Eekelaar, J., Maclean, M. and Beinart, S. (2000) *Family Lawyers: The Divorce Work of Solicitors*. Oxford: Hart Publishing.

Eisenberg, M.A. (1976) 'Private ordering through negotiation: dispute-settlement and rulemaking'. *Harvard Law Review*, 89(4), 637–681.

Elson, A. (1946) 'The Rushcliffe report'. *University of Chicago Law Review*, 13(2), 131–144.

Engler, R. (2012) 'Opportunities and challenges: non-lawyer forms of assistance in providing access to justice for middle-income earners' in Trebilcock, M., Duggan, A. and Sossin, L. (eds), *Middle Income Access to Justice*. Toronto: University of Toronto Press, 145–172.

Exon, S.N. (2006) 'How can a mediator be both impartial and fair: why ethical standards of conduct create chaos for mediators'. *Journal of Dispute Resolution*, 2, 387–434.

Family Justice Review (2011a) *Family Justice Review: Interim Report*. London: Crown.

Family Justice Review (2011b) *Family Justice Review: Final Report*. London: Crown.

Family Mediation Task Force (2014) *Report of the Family Mediation Task Force*. London: Ministry of Justice.

Family Solutions Group (2020) *"What about me?" Reframing Support for Families following Parental Separation. Family Solutions Group* [online]. Available from: https://www.familysolutionsgroup.co.uk/ [accessed 19 September 2024.

Feenan, D. (ed) (2013) *Exploring the 'Socio' of Socio-Legal Studies*. London: Palgrave Macmillan.

Felstiner, W.L.F., Abel, R.L. and Sarat, A. (1980) 'The emergence and transformation of disputes: naming, blaming, claiming …'. *Law & Society Review*, 15(3/4), 631–654.

Field, R. (2000) 'Neutrality and power: myths and reality'. *The ADR Bulletin*, 3(1), 16–20.

Fineman, M.A. (2004) *The Autonomy Myth: A Theory of Dependency*. New York: New Press.

FMC (2016a) 'Consultation: family mediators drafting consent orders'. *FMC*, [online] 30 November. Available from: www.familymediationcouncil.org.uk/wp-content/uploads/2016/11/Consultation-Family-Mediators-Drafting-Consent-Orders-30.11.16.pdf [accessed 9 July 2024].

FMC (2016b) 'Guidance for online video mediation'. *FMC*, [online] September. Available from: www.familymediationcouncil.org.uk/wp-content/uploads/2016/09/FMC-Guidance-for-Online-Video-Mediation-September-2016.pdf [accessed 9 July 2024].

FMC (2017) 'Overview of consultation responses: family mediators drafting consent orders'. *FMC*, [online] 12 May. Available from: www.familymediationcouncil.org.uk/wp-content/uploads/2017/05/FMC-Overview-consultation-responses-family-mediators-drafting-consent-orders.pdf [accessed 9 July 2024].

FMC (2018a) *Code of Practice for Family Mediators*, [online] November. Available from: www.familymediationcouncil.org.uk/wp-content/uploads/2018/11/FMC-Code-of-Practice-v1.3-November-2018.pdf [accessed 9 July 2024].

FMC (2018b) 'FMC newsletter: September 2018'. *FMC*, [online] 28 September. Available from: www.familymediationcouncil.org.uk/wp-content/uploads/2018/09/FMC-Newsletter-September-2018.pdf [accessed 9 July 2024].

FMC (2018c) 'Safeguarding policies and procedures for family mediators'. *FMC*, [online] September. Available from: www.familymediationcouncil.org.uk/safeguarding-policies-and-procedures-for-family-mediators [accessed 9 July 2024].

FMC (2020) 'Family mediation survey 2019 – results'. *FMC*, [online] 20 January. Available from: www.familymediationcouncil.org.uk/wp-content/uploads/2020/01/Family-Mediation-Survey-Autumn-2019-Results.pdf [accessed 9 July 2024].

FMC (2022a) *FMC Manual of Professional Standards and Self-Regulatory Framework*. *FMC*, [online] 1 March. Available from: www.familymediationcouncil.org.uk/wp-content/uploads/2022/05/FMC-Manual-of-Professonal-Standards-Regulatory-Framework-v1.4.1-Updated-1-March-2022.pdf [accessed 9 July 2024].

FMC (2022b) 'MIAM standards'. *FMC*, [online] 1 October. Available from: www.familymediationcouncil.org.uk/miam-standards/ [accessed 9 July 2024].

FMC (2022c) 'The home of regulated family mediation'. *FMC*, [online] October. Available from: www.familymediationcouncil.org.uk/wp-content/uploads/2022/10/FMC-Vision-Strategy-2022-2025.pdf [accessed 9 July 2024].

FMC (2024a) 'What is family mediation?'. *FMC*, [online]. Available from: www.familymediationcouncil.org.uk/family-mediation [accessed 9 July 2024].

FMC (2024b) *Code of Practice for Family Mediators*, [online] September. Available from: www.familymediationcouncil.org.uk/wp-content/uploads/2024/09/FMC-Code-of-Practice-v1.4-September-2024.pdf [accessed 19 September 2024].

FMC (2024c) 'Find your local mediator'. *FMC*, [online]. Available from: www.familymediationcouncil.org.uk/find-local-mediator [accessed 9 July 2024].

FMC (2024d) *FMC Manual of Professional Standards and Self-Regulatory Framework. FMC*, [online] September. Available from: www.familymediationcouncil.org.uk/wp-content/uploads/2024/09/FMC-Manual-of-Professonal-Standards-Regulatory-Framework-v1.5-September-2024.pdf [accessed 19 September 2024].

FMC (2024e) 'FMC full register'. *FMC*, [online]. Available from: www.familymediationcouncil.org.uk/fmc-full-register [accessed 9 July 2024].

FMC and FMSB (2018) 'Summary of context and the work streams in FMC Standards Review'. *FMC*, [online] November. Available from: www.familymediationcouncil.org.uk/wp-content/uploads/2018/11/FMC-FMSB-Standards-Review-Summary.pdf [accessed 9 July 2024].

FMC and FMSB (2019) 'Changes to the FMC Standards Framework agreed by the FMC Board 12.6.19'. *FMC*, [online] June. Available from: www.familymediationcouncil.org.uk/wp-content/uploads/2019/06/Changes-to-Standards-Framework-Agreed-12.6.19.pdf [accessed 9 July 2024].

FMC and Family Justice Council (2021) 'Family mediation in England and Wales: a guide for judges, magistrates and legal advisors'. *Judiciary.UK*, [online] November. Available from: www.judiciary.uk/wp-content/uploads/2021/12/mediation-guide-for-judges-may2014.-updated-Nov-21.pdf [accessed 9 July 2024].

FMSB (2023) 'Review of 2022 workplan'. *FMC*, [online] April. Available from: www.familymediationcouncil.org.uk/wp-content/uploads/2023/04/FMSB-2022-Workplan-Review-FMC-Newsletter.pdf [accessed 9 July 2024].

Folberg, J. (1983) 'A mediation overview: history and dimensions of practice'. *Mediation Quarterly*, 1, 3–13.

Franklyn, R., Budd, T., Verrill, R. and Willoughby, M. (2017) *Findings from the Legal Problem and Resolution Survey, 2014–15*. London: Ministry of Justice.

Freeman, M. (1984) 'Questioning the delegalization movement in family law: do we really want a family court?' in Eekelaar, J. and Katz, S. (eds), *The Resolution of Family Conflict: Comparative Legal Perspectives*. Toronto: Butterworth & Co, pp 7–25.

Freeman, M. (1996) 'Divorce: contemporary problems and future prospects' in Freeman, M. (ed), *Divorce: Where Next?* Aldershot: Dartmouth Publishing Company, pp 1–8.

Frontier Economics (2023) 'Understanding the unreserved market: a report for the solicitors regulation authority'. *SRA*, [online] 13 June. Available from: www.sra.org.uk/sra/research-publications/understanding-unreserved-market [accessed 9 July 2024].

Galanter, M. (1981) 'Justice in many rooms: courts, private ordering, and indigenous law'. *Journal of Legal Pluralism*, 13(19), 1–47.

Genn, H. (1999) *Paths to Justice: What People Do and Think about Going to Law*. Oxford: Hart Publishing.

Genn, H. (2010) *Judging Civil Justice*. Cambridge: Cambridge University Press.

Genn, H. (2012) 'What is civil justice for – reform, ADR, and access to justice'. *Yale Journal of Law and the Humanities*, 24(1), 397–417.

George, A.L. (1959) 'Quantitative and qualitative approaches to content analysis' in Pool, I.S. (ed), *Trends in Content Analysis*. Urbana: University of Illinois Press, pp 7–32.

Giddings, J. and Robertson, M. (2002) '"Lay people, for God's sake! Surely I should be dealing with lawyers?" Towards an assessment of self-help legal services in Australia'. *Griffith Law Review*, 11(2), 436–464.

Girdner, L. (1988) 'How people process disputes' in Folberg, J. and Milne, A. (eds), *Divorce Mediation: Theory and Practice*. New York: Guildford Press, pp 45–57.

Goriely, T. (1994) 'Rushcliffe fifty years on: the changing role of civil legal aid within the welfare state'. *Journal of Law and Society*, 21(4), 545–566.

Greatbatch, D. and Dingwall, R. (1989) 'Selective facilitation: some preliminary observations on a strategy used by divorce mediators'. *Law & Society Review*, 24(4), 613–642.

Guggenheimer, L. (1996) 'A modest proposal: the feminomics of drafting premarital agreements'. *Women's Rights Law Reporter*, 17(2), 147–208.

Gulliver, P.H. (1979) *Disputes and Negotiations: A Cross-Cultural Perspective*. New York: Academic Press.

Hale, B. (2011) 'Equal access to justice in the big society'. *Supreme Court*, [online] 27 June. Available from: www.supremecourt.uk/docs/speech_110627.pdf [accessed 9 July 2024].

Hamlyn, B., Coleman, E. and Sefton, M. (2015) *Mediation Information and Assessment Meetings (MIAMs) and Mediation in Private Family Law Disputes: Quantitative Research Findings*. London: Ministry of Justice.

Harvey, D. (2005) *A Brief History of Neoliberalism*. Oxford: Oxford University Press.

Hester, M., Pearson, C.D. and Radford, L. (1997) *Domestic Violence: A National Survey of Court Welfare and Voluntary Sector Mediation Practice*. Bristol: Policy Press.

Hitchings, E. (2017) 'Official, operative and outsider justice: the ties that (may not) bind in family financial disputes'. *Child and Family Law Quarterly*, 29(4), 359–378.

Hitchings, E. and Miles, J. (2016) 'Mediation, financial remedies, information provision and legal advice: the post-LASPO conundrum'. *Journal of Social Welfare and Family Law*, 38(2), 175–195.

Hitchings, E., Miles, J. and Woodward, H. (2013) *Assembling the Jigsaw Puzzle: Understanding Financial Settlement on Divorce*. Bristol: University of Bristol.

Hitchings, E., Bryson, C., Douglas, G., Purdon, S. and Birchall, J. (2023) *Fair Shares? Sorting Out Money and Property on Divorce. Final Report*. Bristol: University of Bristol.

HM Treasury (2010) *Spending Review 2010* (Cm 7942).

Home Office (1979) *Marriage Matters: A Consultative Document by the Working Party on Marriage Guidance*. London: HMSO.

House of Commons Justice Committee (2011a) *Government's Proposed Reform of Legal Aid: Volume II* (HC 681-II).

House of Commons Justice Committee (2011b) *Government's Proposed Reform of Legal Aid: Volume III* (HC 681-III).

House of Commons Justice Committee (2015) *Impact of Changes to Civil Legal Aid Under Part 1 of the Legal Aid, Sentencing and Punishment of Offenders Act 2012* (HC 311).

House of Lords (2023) 'Constitution committee: oral evidence Wednesday 1 March 2023'. *Parliament.UK*, [online] 1 March. Available from: https://committees.parliament.uk/oralevidence/12754/pdf [accessed 9 July 2024].

Hughes, P. (2008) 'Law commissions and access to justice: what justice should we be talking about?'. *Osgoode Hall Law Journal*, 46(4), 773–806.

Hunter, R. (2003) 'Adversarial mythologies: policy assumptions and research evidence in family law'. *Journal of Law and Society*, 30(1), 156–176.

Hunter, R. (2017) 'Inducing demand for family mediation – before and after LASPO'. *Journal of Social Welfare and Family Law*, 39(2), 189–202.

Hunter, R., Barlow, A., Smithson, J. and Ewing, J. (2014) 'Mapping paths to family justice: matching parties, cases and processes'. *Family Law*, 44(10), 1404–1411.

Hunter, R., Barlow, A., Smithson, J. and Ewing, J. (2017) 'Access to what? LASPO and mediation' in Flynn, A. and Hodgson, J. (eds), *Access to Justice and Legal Aid: Comparative Perspectives on Unmet Legal Need*. Oxford: Hart Publishing, pp 239–254.

Hunter, R., Olesen, A. and Sandefur, R.L. (2022) 'Lawyers and access to justice' in Schultz, U., Hammerslev, O. and Sommerlad, H. (eds), *Lawyers in 21st-century Societies: Volume 2*. London: Hart Publishing, pp 303–325.

Hynes, S. (2012) *Austerity Justice*. Hampshire: Legal Action Group.

Hynes, S. and Robins, J. (2009) *The Justice Gap*. Hampshire: Legal Action Group.

Izumi, C. (2010) 'Implicit bias and the illusion of mediator neutrality'. *Washington University Journal of Law & Policy*, 34, 71–155.

James, A.L. and Hay, W. (1993) *Court Welfare in Action: Practice and Theory*. Hertfordshire: Harvester Wheatsheaf.

Jeffs, H. (1996) *Family Law Bill [HL] [Bill 82 of 1995/96] Divorce Law Reform* (Research Paper 96/42).

Joint Committee of Human Rights (2018) *Enforcing Human Rights* (HC 669, HL 171).

Kaganas, F. (2017) 'Justifying the LASPO Act: authenticity, necessity, suitability, responsibility and autonomy'. *Journal of Social Welfare and Family Law*, 39(2), 168–188.

Kelly, J. (2004) 'Family mediation research: is there empirical support for the field?'. *Conflict Resolution Quarterly*, 22(1–2), 3–35.

King, M., Freiberg, A., Batagol, B. and Hyams, R. (2014) *Non-Adversarial Justice*. Sydney: The Federation Press.

Kirwan, S., Clarke, J., McDermont, M. and Kite, A. (2017) 'Introduction' in Kirwan, S. (ed), *Advising in Austerity: Reflections on Challenging Times for Advice Agencies*. Bristol: Policy Press, pp 1–14.

Kishore, S. (2006) 'The evolving concepts of neutrality and impartiality in mediation'. *Commonwealth Law Bulletin*, 32(2), 221–225.

Kovach, K.K. and Love, L.P. (1996) '"Evaluative" mediation is an oxymoron'. *CPR Institute for Dispute Resolution*, 14(3), 31–32.

Krippendorff, K. (2003) *Content Analysis: An Introduction to its Methodology* (2nd edn). London: SAGE.

Lacey, N. (1995) 'Feminist legal theory beyond neutrality'. *Current Legal Problems*, 48(2), 1–38.

Lake-Carroll, A. (2021) 'Family justice briefing 2021'. *Resolution*, [online] November. Available from: https://resolution.org.uk/resolution-family-justice-briefing-2021 [accessed 9 July 2024].

Law Centres Network (2024) 'List of law centres'. *Law Centres Network*, [online]. Available from: www.lawcentres.org.uk/list-of-law-centres [accessed 9 July 2024].

Law Commission (1966) *Reform of the Grounds of Divorce: The Field of Choice* (Cmnd 3123).

Law Commission (1981) *The Financial Consequences of Divorce: The Response to the Law Commission's Discussion Paper, and Recommendations on the Policy of the Law* (Law Com No 112).

Law Commission (1988) *Facing the Future: A Discussion Paper on the Ground for Divorce* (Law Com No 170).

Law Commission (1990) *Family Law: The Ground for Divorce* (Law Com No 192).

Law Society (2017) 'Law Society response to Family Mediation Council consultation on family mediators drafting consent orders'. *Law Society*, [online] 3 February. Available from: https://web.archive.org/web/20170622002138/http://www.lawsociety.org.uk/policy-campaigns/consultation-responses/family-mediation-council-consultation-on-family-mediators-drafting-consent-orders---law-society-response [accessed 9 July 2024].

Law Society (2022) 'Trends in the solicitors' profession: Annual Statistics Report 2021'. *Law Society*, [online] 21 September. Available from: www.lawsociety.org.uk/topics/research/annual-statistics-report-2021 [accessed 9 July 2024].

Law Society and Resolution (2019) 'Guidance for mediators in incorporating standard consent order precedents'. *Law Society*, [online] 20 November. Available from: www.lawsociety.org.uk/topics/family-and-children/guidance-for-mediators-in-incorporating-standard-consent-order-precedents [accessed 9 July 2024].

Legal Aid Agency (2023) 'Lord Chancellor's guidance to determining financial eligibility for controlled work and family mediation (September 2023)'. *GOV.UK*, [online] 28 July. Available from: www.gov.uk/guidance/civil-legal-aid-means-testing [accessed 9 July 2024].

Legal Services Board (2021) 'Reshaping legal services: a sector-wide strategy'. *LSB*, [online] March. Available from: https://legalservicesboard.org.uk/wp-content/uploads/2021/03/Strategy_FINAL-For-Web2.pdf [accessed 9 July 2024].

Legal Services Commission (2007) *Legal Aid and Mediation for People Involved in Family Breakdown* (HC 256).

Lewis, P. (2000) *Assumptions about Lawyers in Policy Statements: A Survey of Relevant Research*. London: Lord Chancellor's Department.

Lord Chancellor (1948) *Summary of the Proposed New Service* (Cmnd 7563).

Lord Chancellor's Department (1993) *Looking to the Future: Mediation and the Ground for Divorce a Consultation Paper* (Cm 2424).

Lord Chancellor's Department (1995a) *Looking to the Future: Mediation and the Ground for Divorce* (Cm 2799).

Lord Chancellor's Department (1995b) *Legal Aid – Targeting Need* (Cm 2854).

Lord Chancellor's Department (1996) *Striking the Balance: The Future of Legal Aid in England and Wales* (Cm 3305).

Lord Chancellor's Department (1998) *Modernising Justice* (Cm 4155).

Low Commission (2015) 'Getting it right in social welfare law: the Low Commission's follow-up report'. *Legal Action Group*, [online] March. Available from: www.lag.org.uk/about-us/policy/the-low-commission-200551 [accessed 9 July 2024].

Maclean, M. and Eekelaar, J. (2016) *Lawyers and Mediators: The Brave New World of Services for Separating Families*. Oxford: Hart Publishing.

Maclean, M. and Eekelaar, J. (2019) *After the Act: Access to Family Justice after LASPO*. Oxford: Hart Publishing.

Main, T.O. (2005) 'ADR: the new equity'. *University of Cincinnati Law Review*, 74, 329–404.

Mant, J. (2017) 'Neoliberalism, family law and the cost of access to justice'. *Journal of Social Welfare and Family Law*, 39(2), 246–258.

Mant, J. (2020) 'Placing litigants in person at the centre of the post-LASPO family court process'. *Child and Family Law Quarterly*, 32(4), 421–440.

Mant, J. (2022) *Litigants in Person and the Family Justice System*. Oxford: Hart Publishing.

Marshall, T.F. (1990) 'The power of mediation'. *Mediation Quarterly*, 8(2), 115–124.

Marshall, T.H. (1950) *Citizenship and Social Class*. Cambridge: Cambridge University Press.

Mather, L., McEwen, C.A. and Maiman, R.J. (2001) *Divorce Lawyers at Work: Varieties of Professionalism in Practice*. Oxford: Oxford University Press.

Matrimonial Causes Procedure Committee (1985) *Report of the Matrimonial Causes Procedure Committee*. London: Stationery Office.

Mayer, B. (2012) 'What we talk about when we talk about neutrality: a commentary on the Susskind-Stulberg debate, 2011 edition'. *Marquette Law Review*, 95(3), 859–872.

Mayson, S. (2020) *Reforming Legal Services: Regulation Beyond the Echo Chambers (Final Report of the Independent Review of Legal Services Regulation)*. London: Centre for Ethics & Law, UCL.

Mayson, S. (2022) 'Market structure: continuing growth in the solicitors' profession'. *Stephen Mayson*, [online] 27 September. Available from: www.stephenmayson.com/2022/09/27/market-structure-continuing-growth-in-the-solicitors-profession [accessed 9 July 2024].

McEldowney, J. (2012) 'Family mediation in a time of change: FMC review final report'. *FMC*, [online] February. Available from: www.familymediationcouncil.org.uk/wp-content/uploads/2014/02/fmc_review_mceldowney_report.pdf [accessed 9 July 2024].

McKeever, G., Royal-Dawson, L., Kirk, E. and McCord, J. (2022) 'The snakes and ladders of legal participation: litigants in person and the right to a fair trial under Article 6 of the European Convention on Human Rights'. *Journal of Law and Society*, 49(1), 71–92.

Meyers, N.I. (1996) 'Power (im)balance and the failure of impartiality in attorney-mediated divorce'. *University of Toledo Law Review*, 27, 853–884.

Meyerson, D. and Mackenzie, C. (2018) 'Procedural justice and the law'. *Philosophy Compass*, 13(12) [online]. Available from: https://doi.org/10.1111/phc3.12548 [accessed 9 July 2024].

Ministry of Justice (2010) *Proposals for the Reform of Legal Aid in England and Wales* (Cm 7967).

Ministry of Justice (2011a) *Reform of Legal Aid in England and Wales: The Government Response* (Cm 8072).

Ministry of Justice (2011b) *Government Response to Justice Committee's Third Report of Session 2010–11: The Government's Proposed Reform of Legal Aid* (Cm 8111).

Ministry of Justice (2011c) *Solving Disputes in the County Courts: Creating a Simpler, Quicker and More Proportionate System* (Cm 8045).

Ministry of Justice (2014) 'Written evidence from the Ministry of Justice (LAS 73): impact of changes to civil legal aid under the Legal Aid, Sentencing and Punishment of Offenders Act 2012'. *Parliament.UK*, [online] May. Available from: http://data.parliament.uk/writtenevidence/committeeevidence.svc/evidencedocument/justice-committee/impact-of-changes-to-civil-legal-aid-under-laspo/written/8982.pdf [accessed 9 July 2024].

Ministry of Justice (2019) *Post-Implementation Review of Part 1 of the Legal Aid, Sentencing and Punishment of Offenders Act 2012 (LASPO)* (CP 37).

Ministry of Justice (2021a) '£1 million voucher scheme to help families resolve disputes outside of court'. *Gov.UK*, [online] 26 March. Available from: www.gov.uk/government/news/1-million-voucher-scheme-to-help-families-resolve-disputes-outside-of-court [accessed 9 July 2024].

Ministry of Justice (2021b) 'Voucher scheme boost to help thousands more families resolve disputes away from court'. *Gov.UK*, [online] 28 August. Available from: www.gov.uk/government/news/voucher-scheme-boost-to-help-thousands-more-families-resolve-disputes-away-from-court [accessed 9 July 2024].

Ministry of Justice (2021c) 'Dispute resolution in England and Wales: call for evidence'. *Gov.UK*, [online] 3 August. Available from: www.gov.uk/government/calls-for-evidence/dispute-resolution-in-england-and-wales-call-for-evidence [accessed 9 July 2024].

Ministry of Justice (2022a) *Legal Aid Means Test Review* (CP 646).

Ministry of Justice (2022b) 'Family mediation scheme to help thousands more parents'. *Gov.UK*, [online] 16 January. Available from: www.gov.uk/government/news/family-mediation-scheme-to-help-thousands-more-parents [accessed 9 July 2024].

Ministry of Justice (2022c) 'Mediation to help thousands more families avoid costly legal battles'. *Gov.UK*, [online] 3 June. Available from: www.gov.uk/government/news/mediation-to-help-thousands-more-families-avoid-costly-legal-battles [accessed 9 July 2024].

Ministry of Justice (2022d) *Increasing the Use of Mediation in the Civil Justice System* (CP 721).

Ministry of Justice (2022e) 'Call for evidence on dispute resolution in England and Wales: summary of responses'. *Gov.UK*, [online] 29 March. Available from: www.gov.uk/government/calls-for-evidence/dispute-resolution-in-england-and-wales-call-for-evidence [accessed 9 July 2024].

Ministry of Justice (2023a) *Government Response to Legal Aid Means Test Review* (CP 842).

Ministry of Justice (2023b) 'Plans to protect children under new mediation reforms'. *Gov.UK*, [online] 23 March. Available from: www.gov.uk/government/news/plans-to-protect-children-under-new-mediation-reforms [accessed 9 July 2024].

Ministry of Justice (2023c) *Supporting Earlier Resolution of Private Family Law Arrangements: A Consultation on Resolving Private Family Disputes Earlier through Family Mediation* (CP 824).

Ministry of Justice (2024a) 'Supporting earlier resolution of private family law arrangements: government response'. *Gov.UK*, [online] 26 January. Available from: www.gov.uk/government/consultations/supporting-earlier-resolution-of-private-family-law-arrangements [accessed 9 July 2024].

Ministry of Justice (2024b) 'Legal aid statistics England and Wales tables January to March 2024. *Gov.UK*, [online] 27 June. Available from: www.gov.uk/government/statistics/legal-aid-statistics-quarterly-january-to-march-2024 [accessed 9 July 2024].

Ministry of Justice (2024c) 'Family court tables: January to March 2024'. *Gov.UK*, [online] 27 June. Available from: www.gov.uk/government/statistics/family-court-statistics-quarterly-january-to-march-2024 [accessed 9 July 2024].

Ministry of Justice and Legal Aid Agency (2014) *Implementing Reforms to Civil Legal Aid* (HC 784).

Mnookin, R. and Kornhauser, L. (1979) 'Bargaining in the shadow of the law: the case of divorce'. *The Yale Law Journal*, 88(5), 950–997.

Moberly, R.B. (1997) 'Mediator gag rules: is it ethical for mediators to evaluate or advise?'. *South Texas Law Review*, 38, 669–679.

Moore, S. and Newbury, A. (2017) *Legal Aid in Crisis: Assessing the Impact of Reform*. Bristol: Policy Press.

Moorhead, R. (2007) 'The passive arbiter: litigants in person and the challenge to neutrality'. *Social & Legal Studies*, 16(3), 405–424.

Moorhead, R. (2014) 'Precarious professionalism: some empirical and behavioural perspectives of lawyers'. *Current Legal Problems*, 67(1), 447–481.

Morris, P. (2013) 'Mediation, the Legal Aid, Sentencing and Punishment of Offenders Act of 2012 and the Mediation Information Assessment Meeting'. *Journal of Social Welfare and Family Law*, 35(4), 445–457.

Moscati, M.F. (2020) 'We have the method but still there is so much to do: mediation for gender and sexually diverse relationships' in Roberts, M. and Moscati, M.F. (eds), *Family Mediation: Contemporary Issues*. London: Bloomsbury Professional, pp 227–250.

Mulcahy, L. (2001) 'The possibilities and desirability of mediator neutrality: towards an ethic of partiality?'. *Social & Legal Studies*, 10(4), 505–527.

Murch, M. and Hooper, D. (1992) *The Family Justice System*. Bristol: Family Law.

Neuberger, D. (2015) 'Keynote address: a view from on high'. *Civil Mediation Conference*, [online] 12 May. Available from: www.supremecourt.uk/docs/speech-150512-civil-mediation-conference-2015.pdf [accessed 9 July 2024].

NFCC (1984) 'The code of practice for conciliation services'. *Family Law*, 14, 107–109.
NFCC (1985) 'Extended code of practice for family conciliation services'. *Family Law*, 15, 274–276.
Noce, D.J.N. (2009) 'Evaluative mediation: in search of practice competencies'. *Conflict Resolution Quarterly*, 27(2), 193–214.
Nolan-Haley, H. (1998) 'Informed consent in mediation: a guiding principle for truly educated decisionmaking'. *Notre Dame Law Review*, 74(3), 775–840.
Noone, M.A. and Ojelabi, L.A. (2020) 'Alternative dispute resolution and access to justice in Australia'. *International Journal of Law in Context*, 16(2), 108–127.
Office for National Statistics (2024) 'Divorces in England and Wales: 2022'. *ONS*, [online] 22 February. Available from: www.ons.gov.uk/peoplepopulationandcommunity/birthsdeathsandmarriages/divorce/bulletins/divorcesinenglandandwales/2022 [accessed 9 July 2024].
Ogus, A., Walker, J. and Jones-Lee, M. (1989) *The Costs and Effectiveness of Conciliation in England and Wales*. Newcastle: University of Newcastle.
Ojelabi, L.A. and Gutman, J. (2020) 'Family dispute resolution and access to justice in Australia'. *International Journal of Law in Context*, 16, 197–215.
Okin, S.M. (2016) 'Justice, gender, and the family' in Engster, D. and Metz, T. (eds), *Justice, Politics and the Family*. Oxfordshire: Routledge, pp 63–87.
Parkinson, L. (1986) *Conciliation in Separation and Divorce*. London: Routledge.
Parkinson, L. (2013) 'The place of mediation in the family justice system'. *Child and Family Quarterly*, 25(2), 200–214.
Parkinson, L. (2016) 'Expanding the model without breaking the mould: developing practice and theory in family mediation'. *Family Law*, 46(1), 110–115.
Parkinson, L. (2020) *Family Mediation* (4th edn). Hampshire: LexisNexis.
Partington, M. (2005) 'The relationship between law reform and access to justice: a case study – the Renting Homes Project'. *Windsor Yearbook of Access to Justice*, 23(2), 375–392.
Peacey, V. and Hunt, J. (2009) *I'm Not Saying It was Easy … Contact Problems in Separated Families*. London: Gingerbread.
Piper, C. (1993) *The Responsible Parent: A Study in Divorce Mediation*. London: Harvester Wheatsheaf.
Pleasence, P. (2004) *Causes of Action: Civil Law and Social Justice*. London: Stationery Office.
Pleasence, P., Balmer, N.J. and Moorhead, R. (2012) *A Time of Change: Solicitors' Firms in England and Wales*. London: Law Society.
Prior, L. (2003) *Using Documents in Social Research*. London: SAGE.

Puppis, M. (2019) 'Analyzing talk and text I: qualitative content analysis' in Bulck, H.V.B., Puppis, M., Donders, K. and Audenhove, L.V. (eds), *The Palgrave Handbook of Methods for Media Policy Research*. Cham: Palgrave Macmillan, pp 367–384.

Reece, H. (2003) *Divorcing Responsibly*. Oxford: Hart Publishing.

Regina, W.F. (2011) *Applying Family Systems Theory to Mediation: A Practitioner's Guide*. Plymouth: University Press of America.

Resolution (2007) 'New group will be "voice of mediation" in UK'. *Resolution*, [online] 5 October. Available from: https://web.archive.org/web/20160913051128/http://www.resolution.org.uk/news-list.asp?page_id=228&page=1&n_id=21&n_year=2007&n_month=10 [accessed 9 July 2024].

Resolution (2017) 'Family mediators drafting consent orders: Resolution's response to the Family Mediation Council'. *Resolution*, [online]. Available from: www.resolution.org.uk/site_content_files/files/resolution_response_to_fmc mediators_drafting_consent_orders_january_2017.pdf [accessed 11 July 2017].

Resolution (2018) *Guide to Good Practice on Mediation*. London: Resolution.

Resolution (2022) 'Resolution reveals innovative new model to help couples divorce amicably with just one lawyer'. *Resolution* [online] 1 August. Available from: https://resolution.org.uk/news/resolution-reveals-innovative-new-model-to-help-couples-divorce-amicably-with-just-one-lawyer [accessed 9 July 2024].

Richardson, K.L. and Speed, A.K. (2019) 'Restrictions on legal aid in family law cases in England and Wales: creating a necessary barrier to public funding or simply increasing the burden on the family courts?'. *Journal of Social Welfare and Family Law*, 41(2), 135–152.

Rickman, N., Fenn, P. and Gray, A. (1999) 'The reform of legal aid in England and Wales'. *Fiscal Studies*, 20(3), 261–286.

Rifkin, J., Millen, J. and Cobb, S. (1991) 'Toward a new discourse for mediation: a critique of neutrality'. *Mediation Quarterly*, 9(2), 151–164.

Riskin, L. (1996) 'Understanding mediators' orientations, strategies, and techniques: a grid for the perplexed'. *Harvard Negotiation Law Review*, 1, 7–51.

Riskin, L. (2003) 'Decisionmaking in mediation: the new old grid and the new grid system'. *Notre Dame Law Review*, 79(1), 1–54.

Roberts, M. (2014a) *Mediation in Family Disputes: Principles of Practice* (4th edn). Farnham: Ashgate.

Roberts, M. (2014b) 'A view from the coal face: interdisciplinary influences on family mediation in the United Kingdom'. *Journal of Comparative Law*, 9(2), 108–118.

Roberts, S. (1983) 'Mediation in family disputes'. *Modern Law Review*, 46(5), 537–557.

Roberts, S. (2002) 'Institutionalized settlement in England: a contemporary panorama'. *Willamette Journal of International Law and Dispute Resolution*, 10(1), 17–35.

Roberts, S. (2013) *Order and Dispute: An Introduction to Legal Anthropology* (2nd edn). New Orleans: Quid Pro Books.

Rushcliffe Committee (1945) *Report of the Committee on Legal Aid and Legal Advice in England and Wales* (Cmd 6641).

Sandefur, R.L. (2019) 'Access to what?'. *Daedalus: The Journal of the American Academy of Arts and Sciences*, 148(1), 49–55.

Sandefur, R.L. (2020) 'Legal advice from nonlawyers: consumer demand, provider quality, and public harms'. *Stanford Journal of Civil Rights & Civil Liberties*, 16(2), 283–314.

Sandefur, R.L. and Denne, E. (2022) 'Access to justice and legal services regulatory reform'. *Annual Review of Law and Social*, 18, 27–42.

Sarat, A. and Felstiner, W.L.F. (1995) *Divorce Lawyers and Their Clients: Power & Meaning in the Legal Process*. Oxford: Oxford University Press.

Saunders, L. (2020) 'Development of the regulatory framework for the practice of family mediation in the UK.' in Roberts, M. and Moscati, M.F. (eds), *Family Mediation: Contemporary Issues*. London: Bloomsbury Professional, pp 33–54.

Semple, N. (2012) 'Mandatory family mediation and the settlement mission: a feminist critique'. *Canadian Journal of Women and the Law*, 24(1), 207–239.

Simpson, B. (1989) 'Giving children a voice in divorce: the role of family conciliation'. *Children & Society*, 3(3), 261–274.

Sims, A. (2020) 'Exploring the scope of family mediation in England and Wales' in Roberts, M. and Moscati, M.F. (eds), *Family Mediation: Contemporary Issues*. London: Bloomsbury Professional, pp 295–318.

Sixsmith, A. (2023) 'Mediators' perspectives on the Family Mediation Voucher Scheme'. *Child and Family Law Quarterly*, 35(1), 9–26.

Skinner, C. (2019) 'One lawyer acting for two clients: implications arising from an experimental practice model "Family Matters"'. *Journal of Social Welfare and Family Law*, 41(3), 265–279.

Skinner, C. and Foster, I. (2016) *Guiding Parents Through Separation: Family Matters – An Innovative Support Service from Resolution*. York: University of York.

Smith, I. (1997) 'Explaining the growth of divorce in Great Britain'. *Scottish Journal of Political Economy*, 44(5), 519–543.

Smith, L. and Hitchings, E. (2023) 'Where the wild things are: the challenges and opportunities of the unregulated legal services landscape in family law'. *Legal Studies*, 43(4), 658–675.

Smith, L., Hitchings, E. and Sefton, M. (2017) *A Study of Fee-Charging McKenzie Friends and Their Work in Private Family Law Cases*. Cardiff: Cardiff University.

Smithson, J., Barlow, A., Hunter, R. and Ewing, J. (2015) 'The "child's best interests" as an argumentative resource in family mediation sessions'. *Discourse Studies*, 17(5), 609–623.

Smoron, K. (1998) 'Conflicting roles in child custody mediation: impartiality/neutrality and the best interests of the child'. *Family and Conciliation Courts Review*, 36(2), 258–280.

Solicitors Regulation Authority (2015) 'Question of ethics: August 2015'. *SRA*, [online] August. Available from: https://web.archive.org/web/20170709174548/www.sra.org.uk/solicitors/code-of-conduct/guidance/questionofethics/August-2015.page [accessed 9 July 2024].

Sommerlad, H. (2004) 'Some reflections on the relationship between access to justice and the reform of legal aid'. *Journal of Law & Society*, 31(3), 345–368.

Sommerlad, H. (2008) 'Reflections on the reconfiguration of access to justice'. *International Journal of the Legal Profession*, 15(3), 179–194.

Sorabji, J. (2014) *English Civil Justice after the Woolf and Jackson Reforms: A Critical Analysis*. Cambridge: Cambridge University Press.

Stylianou, K. (2020) 'Teaching family mediation in higher education: what an academic family mediation course could look like' in Roberts, M. and Moscati, M.F. (eds), *Family Mediation: Contemporary Issues*. London: Bloomsbury Professional, pp 273–294.

Susskind, R. and Susskind, D. (2015) *The Future of the Professions*. Oxford: Oxford University Press.

Thompson, S. and Sandberg, R. (2017) 'Common defects of the Divorce Bill and Arbitration and Mediation Services (Equality) Bill 2016–2017'. *Family Law*, 47(4), 447–451.

Tjosvold, D. and van de Vliert, E. (1994) 'Applying cooperative and competitive conflict theory to mediation', *Mediation Quarterly*, 11(4), 303–311.

Travers, M. (2005) 'Evaluation research and legal services' in Banakar, R. and Travers, M. (eds), *Theory and Method in Socio-Legal Research*. Oxford: Hart Publishing, pp 290–305.

Trebilcock, M., Duggan, A. and Sossin, L. (2012) 'Introduction' in Trebilcock, M., Duggan, A. and Sossin, L. (eds), *Middle Income Access to Justice*. Toronto: University of Toronto Press, pp 3–23.

Trinder, L. (2008) 'Conciliation, the Private Law Programme and children's well-being: two steps forward, one step back?'. *Family Law*, 36(4), 338–342.

Trinder, L., Connolly, J., Kellett, J., Notley, C. and Swift, L. (2006) *Making Contact Happen or Making Contact Work? The Process and Outcomes of In-court Conciliation*. London: Department for Constitutional Affairs.

Trinder, L., Hunt, J. Macleod, A., Pearce, J., Woodward, H. et al (2013) *Enforcing Contact Orders: Problem-solving or Punishment?* Exeter: University of Exeter.

Trinder, L., Hunter, R., Hitchings, E., Miles, J., Moorhead, R., Smith, L. et al (2014) *Litigants in Person in Private Family Law Cases*. London: Ministry of Justice.

UKCFM (1997) *UK College of Family Mediators: Directory & Handbook 1997/98*. London: Sweet & Maxwell.

UKCFM (1998) *UK College of Family Mediators: Directory & Handbook 1998/99*. London: Sweet & Maxwell.

Walker, J. (1992) 'Conciliation research' in Fisher, T. (ed), *Family Conciliation within the UK: Policy and Practice* (2nd edn). Bristol: Family Law, pp 155–162.

Walker, J. (1996) 'Is there a future for lawyers in divorce?'. *International Journal of Law, Policy and the Family*, 10, 52–73.

Walker, J., McCarthy, P. and Timms, N. (1994) *Mediation: The Making and Remaking of Co-operative Relationships: An Evaluation of the Effectiveness of Comprehensive Mediation*. Newcastle upon Tyne: Relate Centre for Family Studies.

Webley, L.C. (2010) *Adversarialism and Consensus? The Professions' Construction of Solicitor and Family Mediator Identity and Role*. New Orleans: Quid Pro Books.

Webley, L.C. (2015) 'Legal professional de(re)regulation, equality, and inclusion, and the contested space of professionalism within the legal market in England and Wales'. *Fordham Law Review*, 83(5), 2349–2367.

Welsh, N.A. (2001) 'The thinning vision of self-determination in court-connected mediation: the inevitable price of institutionalisation?'. *Harvard Negotiation Law Review*, 6, 1–96.

Wiggan, J. (2012) 'Telling stories of 21st century welfare: the UK coalition government and the neo-liberal discourse of worklessness and dependency'. *Critical Social Policy*, 32(3), 383–405.

Wong, S. and Cain, R. (2019) 'The impact of cuts in legal aid funding of private family law cases'. *Journal of Social Welfare and Family Law*, 41(1), 3–14.

Woolf, H. (1995) *Access to Justice: Interim Report to the Lord Chancellor on the Civil Justice System in England and Wales*. London: Stationery Office.

Woolf, H. (1996) *Access to Justice: Final Report to the Lord Chancellor on the Civil Justice System in England and Wales*. London: Stationery Office.

Wright, K. (2007) 'The role of solicitors in divorce: a note of caution'. *Child and Family Law Quarterly*, 19(4), 481–495.

Xianyi, Z. (2009) 'Mediation in China – past and present'. *Asia Pacific Law Review*, 17(1), 1–29.

YouGov (2020) 'Legal needs of individuals in England and Wales: technical report 2019/20'. *YouGov*, [online] 27 January. Available from: https://legalservicesboard.org.uk/wp-content/uploads/2020/01/Legal-Needs-of-Individuals-Technical-Report-Final-January-2020.pdf [accessed 9 July 2024].

Index